PRAISE for *Times They Were A-Changing*

"We lived in the Haight-Ashbury and on Bourbon Street and the high plains of Oklahoma. We wore hip-huggers, tie-dyes, military uniforms, and fringed ponchos embroidered with peace signs. We danced and marched and organized and loved and broke all the rules. We were changing, and we changed the world. I love this book because it is written by women who were on the scene—and such a scene it was! If you were there, it will remind you of those remarkable years. If you weren't, you'll be amazed and delighted and proud of the brave women who have written these stories and poems. Thank you, lovely women, for telling us about it!"

—**Susan Wittig Albert**
author of *A Wilder Rose*
and founder of Story Circle Network

"This intriguing anthology delves into the personal lives of women who challenged social norms during a time when self-empowerment and freedom of expression became the vehicle for unprecedented social change."

—**Joanne S. Bodin, Ph.D.**
author of International Book Awards and
New Mexico Book Awards winner
Walking Fish: A Novel and New Mexico Book
Awards finalist *Piggybacked: Poetry*

"Whether you managed to grab hold of the '60s and '70s the first time around or not, be sure to grab a copy of *Times They Were A-Changing*. The stories will make you laugh out loud and sob until your tears run dry. They recall the trails blazed during those momentous decades by the women who walked them. They will have you remembering women's rights, gay rights, Woodstock, Berkeley, activist politics, changing work environments, no-fault divorce, illegal abortion, sexual revolution, drugs, the Vietnam War, and so much more."

— **Matilda Butler**
award-winning co-author of the collective memoir *Rosie's Daughters: The "First Woman To" Generation Tells Its Story* and *Writing Alchemy: How to Write Fast and Deep*, and co-founder of WomensMemoirs.com

"*Times They Were A-Changing* is the book long missing from the packed second-wave feminism shelf. Finally, the women you never heard from are speaking in their own powerful voices about how each in her own way and in places you might never imagine pushed America toward greater equality and justice. If you are a woman over a certain age, you will find yourself in this book's stories. If you are a woman of any other age, you will find your own story informed and enriched by these beautifully written, honest, and evocative essays."

— **Gloria Feldt,**
co-founder and president of Take the Lead, author of *No Excuses: 9 Ways Women Can Change How We Think About Power*, and former president of Planned Parenthood Federation of America

"This marvelous anthology shows the vital role outrider women played in changing our world—often overlooked, they were the heart of the '60s revolution."

—**Brenda Knight**
author of *Women of the Beat Generation:
The Writers, Artists and Muses at the Heart
of a Revolution*

"These stories highlight the prices that some women paid in a domestic war that was never declared or overtly acknowledged. Forty-eight authentic voices join in a rousing chorus to convey the passionate essence of an era from a focused female perspective. If you were part of the crusade, they will take you back. If you were distracted by diapers and dishes back then, or born earlier, later, or male, these stories give a powerful view of eruptions of anger, angst, and insights of the time."

—**Sharon Lippincott**
author of the *Heart and Craft of Writing* book
and blog

"*Times They Were A-Changing* challenges us to see past the clichés of the '60s and '70s to see the unique experiences of young people who were rebelling against their parents' teachings to reinvent not just themselves but the whole world. The pieces in this anthology open a window into a fascinating, important time, seen through the eyes of those who lived it. This collection lets us look back and see the era with wisdom, humor, power, and grace."

—**Jerry Waxler**
author of *The Memoir Revolution* and founder
of the blog Memory Writers Network.

Times They Were A-
CHANGING

Times They Were A-CHANGING

Women Remember the '60s & '70s

**Edited by Kate Farrell,
Linda Joy Myers, & Amber Lea Starfire**

SHE WRITES PRESS

Published 2013
Printed in the United States of America
ISBN: 978-1-938314-04-9
Library of Congress Control Number: 2013948094

For information, address:
She Writes Press
1563 Solano Ave #546
Berkeley, CA 94707

The portrait, "Rachel," in front cover design used with
permission of the artist, Bryan Collins

To the women who were there, and remember.
To the women who were not, and wish they were.

Contents

Part III: Long Time Passing

* *Prize Winner*

Foreword

During the '60s and '70s, in every part of our country, women were waking up to their power, intelligence, right to succeed in life, and opportunities to contribute their gifts without inhibition. The road ahead was not a smooth one. It was fraught with conflict between offspring and their parents, between students and teachers, and between those questioning the status quo and traditionally civic-minded people. Many women felt conflict between who they were raised and trained to believe they would be and who they wanted to become.

As a college student at the University of Wisconsin, Madison from 1966 to 1970, I was involved in anti-war demonstrations that got students beaten and arrested—that called into question the attitudes of the police and state (and are now commemorated with bronze plaques around the campus). As a mother of two children born in 1973 and 1975, I was part of the Lamaze movement and the idea that women could be seen in public, of all things, nursing their babies (how uncomfortable people were when we began doing this, even with our baggy sweaters for privacy). In the tide of energy that followed the events of the anti-war movement in the '60s, women turned toward liberating themselves from second-class citizenship, and by then institutions were listening. Universities that were formerly all-male with separate women's colleges united their campuses into one institution; girls who had been led to believe a college education was only for their brothers insisted on attending schools, and they studied for jobs that were outside of their parents' comfort zone (women had most usually been encouraged to become teachers or nurses since those were jobs to "fall back on" if one didn't find a husband or if something happened to him).

The birth control pill was approved by the FDA in 1960 and eventually led to higher numbers of women graduating from college (though even today, since birth control medication and devices require prescriptions, access is limited). We read and shared the beloved book *Our Bodies, Ourselves*, published in 1971, and started women's clinics as we learned to love and understand our bodies. *MS* magazine began publishing in 1972, making headlines with a story that included the names of women who spoke of having abortions when they were still illegal in this country. A year later, the *Roe v. Wade* decision legalized abortion the same year Betty Friedan's *The Feminist Mystique* was published, articulating an image for women much different than the one many had grown up with in the '50s. Daughters raised in the '50s and '60s formed consciousness-raising groups; women introduced women's studies and feminist literature into university curricula, helped their mothers stand up for their rights as individuals inside marriages and in the work force, and raised their own daughters and sons to respect women's rights.

We are now well beyond the years the UN dubbed "the decade of women." We are working at jobs that have clout nationally and internationally, whether as heads of high tech companies or US Cabinet members. We are doctors and lawyers and newscasters. We win literary prizes and hold professorships in greater numbers than in the past. We are awarded grants to continue our research. We have flown in space. I believe there is no going back to the time when women accepted a double standard and lived under the ceiling men lowered upon them. Even so, state governments are currently passing laws to abolish women's rights to choose and the US Congress accuses the Supreme Court of ruling the country when its role is to try cases to determine the constitutionality of new laws.

There are those in government who will fight before they'll finally accept the changes women gained in the '60s and '70s. And so it is important to read what women lived with, lived through, felt, and did when they began this rise to today's more powerful standing. It is important that this part of our history not be forgotten or understated or ignored. Anthologies such as *Times They Were A-Changing* are good reading; they are also reading of the utmost importance. For a woman to know herself, she must know whose shoulders she stands upon.

I thank the editors and the authors in *Times They Were A-Changing* for sharing so much with us, so honestly, and for bringing these two important decades of their lives to the page so readers can experience (and, in so many cases, re-experience) those years—decades not always lived with clarity, but fully lived nonetheless; decades that are crucial to our times now. I thank the writers and editors for keeping in our national memory women's engagement in celebrating a more open, accepting, and complex world.

Sheila Bender, Poet and Author
www.writingitreal.com

Part I
Crack in Time

The Novelty Wears Off

Elizabeth Kerlikowske

Plates the cobalt blue of Evening in Paris perfume
spin on *The Ed Sullivan Show* in 1962, an audience
of pink rosettes smiling in their seats, their applause
like water spattered onto heat as a man in gray pants
the audience hopes are red (the plates scream "gypsy!"
"Hungarian!") runs from one slow, dangerously wobbling
plate to the next, each galaxy unwinding in its own way,
oceans of concentration pool in his mouth. Swallow.

Don't swallow. He is not the kind of man that Ed talks up
afterwards. To sweat so openly is un-American. A band-aid
of hair flaps as he boosts the plates' velocity. Ed's jaw rests
in his hand, wishing they were both in the Catskills instead
of onstage with another ethnic madman, the Italian glass singer
who rubs his wetted finger around each crystal lip, whose caterpillar
eyebrows rear back to urge the pitch up, higher, waiting for Bill
Dana to kill Jose Jimenez's career by insulting their host.
Topo Gigio's little voice makes women cry.

It's Cuban Missile Crisis eve. Even in the fallout
shelters the TV whispers songs about Tom Dooley and the Great
Russian Bear, hard to take seriously as the Kirov black bears
wearing party hats we wish are orange and green ride trikes in

the make-believe ring. What does a Bay of Pigs have to do with dancing
dogs in perhaps pink tutus or a man pounding on a UN table with his shoe?
Under the tables (therefore safe from fallout) we draw pictures of smoking
Castro and our president rocking under a shock of Catholic hair.
Ed welcomes Vaughn Meader, whose career will die too in '63.

"And here's young Lew Alcindor" unfurling from his chair like the black
National Anthem. Once in a while a plate crashes to the floor but
the really big shoe goes on. "Schmuck" is all Bill Dana says,
but one word changes everything. The glasses spit water at the kliegs,
the dancing bears forget their steppes, and all those plate spinners,
glass singers, spoon togglers, cup balancers, and lizard jugglers
retire to places we can never find again, restaurants where acrobats
serve tea with their toes, every third guy is a prestidigitator, and clowns
explode from foreign cars but bystanders never die.

Proud Spinster

Patricia A. Vestal

Childhood in North Carolina, late 1940s–early 1950s: Big family gatherings. Women cook. Everyone eats. Men retreat to backyard, porch, or living room to smoke and relax. Women clear tables, wash dishes, clean up. As a child, I am exempt and free to play with the other kids, boys and girls. At some point, I am ushered into the kitchen and given dish towels. I listen to the talk dominated by *female problems*. Why is being female a problem? As I advance into adulthood and the experience of womanhood during the 1960s and 1970s, myriad answers to this question pop up, but mostly not what my relatives discussed in hushed tones.

I am always vaguely aware of gender double standards, but the journey to full awareness and consequent action is tumultuous, distressing, and exhilarating.

Fast forward to mid-late 1950s: I'm a Florida teenager, nothing like the stories my parents tell of the wacky exploits of their innocent teen years or those in the Archie comic books I devoured in childhood. I am an unpopular, introverted oddball, burying myself in books. We are a working-class family living on the edge of an upper-middle-class area whose kids dominate my small high school. My parents advise me to take a business course, so that I can get a job after high school until Prince Charming arrives. They will struggle to send my brother to college, because, after all, he will have to support a family.

3

The 1960s remain firmly attached by umbilical cord to the conservative '50s. Now it's Time to be a Lady. In the South *ladies* still wear hats and gloves and judge each other by the cleanliness and decor of their homes, to which they are officially married. Hence the identification: housewife. I am supposed to find a suitable husband, but I am feeling like the cliché fish out of water. Girls have few career options. Having an education means being a teacher, or maybe a nurse. No education equals sales clerk, office worker, or, if you're lucky, secretary, which moves you into more contact with eligible young businessmen. On the brink of Old Maidhood, I plod along, living at home, moving from one dismal office job to another until I find a niche at an insurance company.

But an alternate persona lurks within. Always a bookworm, living in my imagination, I become intrigued by beatniks and their rejection of convention. I think that maybe I am supposed to be a writer. When I start working and can afford it, I take a correspondence course and the "famous writers" who critique my work announce that I have potential. I will drudge at my day job and write in my spare time. I will become even more of an oddball. An eccentric old maid.

Then I am yanked from my doom by an extraordinary phenomenon. Four guys called "mop heads," who write, sing, and play original music, have invaded from Britain. Then another bunch arrives on the scene, looking a bit like "the other side of the tracks," but with glamorous flourishes. All these British Invaders are my age—give or take a year or so. My age! If the Beatles and the Rolling Stones were girls, would they be tolerated? Wouldn't they be labeled tramps? Worse, grown women acting like teenagers. Their *destiny* isn't to marry houses and procreate. They are males.

I have an "ah-ha" moment. My lifelong observation of the double standard has always influenced my attitudes and behavior. Now my vision is expanding. Small rifts are erupting in the cultural tectonics. The guys are leading and the chicks and birds follow in their wake, the musical and sexual revolution falling into the timeworn ruts of sexism.

I have always yearned to visit New York City and I get the chance with a trip to the 1963–1964 New York World's Fair with a group from work. To me Greenwich Village is almost a mythical place, the epicenter of bohemian culture akin to Paris's Left Bank. A group member's local relative takes us there on a tour. We visit an authentic coffeehouse and see the home of Bob Dylan. A sense of certainty pervades me. I *am* a fish out of water. I belong here.

Back home, I subscribe to the weekly newspaper *The Village Voice* and am delighted to read about the unique cafes, coffeehouses, and unconventional spaces that house a renaissance in music and theater. I am especially intrigued by what has been dubbed "off-off-Broadway" and the experimental theater it nourishes.

I hatch a plan to break out of my prison. I will keep working and save money. I will even sell my beloved ivory and teal '63 Chevy Impala hardtop to stake a move to Greenwich Village to be a writer. Not just any kind of writer, but a playwright.

Spring 1966: I do it. It all seems like a dream. Things have never gone the way I wanted them to. Usually, they have gone the opposite, as if I were the butt of some *cosmic joke*. Now, things fall into place almost like magic. I take the train to New York City and stay in a little room in a hotel near Times Square. Look for a job. Within a couple of days I get a clerical job with New York University. Even more amazing, it is with the department that oversees campus buildings and I get a large studio apartment a block from Washington Square. It is rent-controlled and affordable, even with a doorman and elevator, which I am quickly learning are Manhattan luxuries. I am living in Greenwich Village! My family is amazed. They expected me home by now.

Despite living alone for the first time in this drastically new lifestyle, I feel content and secure. My job and family of co-workers, along with the security of my apartment, form a sort of cocoon. Unlike other New York neighborhoods that often exude a strong ethnic identity, the Village is eclectic and egalitarian. If there is an overriding culture it is simply the culture of *hip*.

Old, shabby walk-up apartments with kitchen bathtubs rub shoulders with quaint but often pricey townhouses, lofts, and apartments. Street floors offer shops, bars, coffeehouses, intimate music clubs, restaurants, and theaters. Tourists and day-trippers from New Jersey and the outer boroughs flock to Washington Square Park on weekends. A festive atmosphere prevails, as musicians claim space on the fountain and strangers bond.

Dominated by New York University, this heart of the Village is where I live. All the necessities are within walking distance. I even walk to work. I feel that I truly do live in a village.

After settling into my new job and home, I immediately enroll in evening courses in playwriting and screenwriting at NYU. I write plays. I join theater groups. I get workshop and off-off-Broadway productions. I am a playwright.

Of course, this is all noncommercial, meaning no profit, meaning if I don't keep my day job I am the veritable starving artist. A writing instructor has warned me not to do for a living what I do for art. It will destroy my unique creative voice. Of course, didn't the beatniks disdain commercialism? So I reject suggestions that I look into writing for soap operas or advertising. Somehow publishing seems nobler, so I set my sights in that direction.

The people I work with at NYU are like family, but I still check the employment ads in every Sunday's *Times*. One day I know I must answer one of those ads. The job is with *The Village Voice*. They are looking for an assistant in the Display Advertising Department. Soon every day I am trudging in heat, rain, and snow through Washington Square, across Sixth Avenue, to the quaint, Paris-esque Sheridan Square. I work at the coolest publisher in the city. I also learn the true meaning of the word "deadline." If you cross that time line, you are dead. Deadline is absolute. Deadlines define the rest of my working life, albeit without the high-end perks I might earn if I had the savvy, confidence, and assertiveness to pursue the peak of my abilities. The sheltered Southern lady will not entirely disappear. She is too entrenched.

So I delve into the counterculture. I am naive, a semi-flower child, a semi-bohemian, unable to turn my back on family, decency, and work ethic. I want safety and a modicum of comfort. I don't want to live in squalor with no privacy. I am embarrassed to let acquaintances who are real hippies know where I live. I am even ashamed to have a steady job. But that is my lifeline to independence.

I don't want to be some guy's "ole lady" and I don't want an "ole man." I don't want to be defined by a man. I don't want to give up my name and take on a man's name. I don't want to immerse myself in the lives of children. I want to learn. I want to live my own life. Perhaps I am immature and selfish. But I am willing to work and support myself. I'm willing to spend my free time getting an education.

Nevertheless, I harbor romantic fantasies of a charming soul mate, an equal partner who can do his own laundry and cook his own breakfast. I stumble through several relationships that leave me wistful, but wiser. Everything in our culture is in upheaval except sexism. The sexual revolution just gives men a chance to frolic among the chicks. The women now have freedom to frolic too, but many of us can't shake the yoke of emotional attachment and desire for monogamy and commitment that the guys want no part of.

Why is this? How far back does it go? How much of it is biology and how much is cultural? I integrate the search for answers into my college curriculum at SUNY's wonderful new university-without-walls concept, Empire State College, which enables me to earn my Bachelor degree and move on to a Masters in Drama at NYU. I examine the presentation of women and relationships in literature, media, and movies. My horizons expand back to the Stone Age and through human history, mythology, and art. Other women are doing the same. Brilliant minds express eloquent revolutionary ideas. Feminism becomes an entity, a word revered and reviled. Our lives are our laboratories. We shove hapless boyfriends through the proverbial ringer. They are remarkably resilient, but continue to demonstrate our theories. From somewhere comes the gauge: "Is your life better with him or without him?" For perhaps the first time in history, women are in a position to say "without."

I march toward middle age, knowing that each passing year takes me further from the probability of marriage and motherhood. It's fine. Okay. That romantic, sympathetic soul mate might still appear. Maybe not. I don't really think about it. I am occupied with too many other things. When I finally return to Florida, I decide to dive into the waters of single home ownership. It is 1985. I have a stable professional job and salary with an established publishing company. (Although I learn later that the department head position I should have immediately moved into was denied me because the hiring director didn't think women should be managers.) My credit rating is excellent. I have a wad of saved cash for a down payment. I can't get approved for a mortgage. Because I am a single woman, I can only buy a home by finding an existing mortgage to assume. I feel as if the angst and effort of the prior decades were for nothing. Times they are a-changing, but in some areas, way too slowly.

Finally now, in the new millennia, it is common for single women even in their twenties to buy homes. This is largely because their educational and career options have far fewer limits now. Other barriers have fallen. If a woman wants a child today, she has one. Marriage is no longer a prerequisite. I worry that they take all this for granted, unaware and unappreciative of the prices paid for this freedom and opportunity. Yet prices are still being paid. We still witness and experience rampant instances of old-style sexism, rampant abuse, and outright discrimination.

I witnessed and participated in all the upheaval, the turmoil, the grief, and the joys: the changes of the 1960s and 1970s. Even now, when people learn I lived in New York in the late '60s their inevitable question is if I went to Woodstock. Yes, I did. That event exemplifies the cultural character of the time. Moral barriers fell, anti-war and civil rights victories were won, but the defining change for me was feminism. Looking back, I see myself in a wave of women, tumbling onto the shoreline and changing it forever. We were the first generation of totally self-reliant, self-supporting women.

Up to the very recent past, a woman not only was expected to marry, marriage was vital for her survival. Not marrying was not a choice; it was a catastrophe. In rare cases when she came from money or had family to take her in, a woman might be able to remain a respectable spinster. If not, she did what she had to for survival, a grim, often horrifying prospect. Single women were pitiful oddities or spawns of the devil.

Now I enjoy the tranquility of retirement in my beloved Blue Ridge Mountains in North Carolina, sponsored by my decades of work and single determination. I can devote my time and attention to the creative writing that was eclipsed by the priorities of self-support. I meet interesting, talented, good women—some married, some divorced, too many widowed, but seldom single. They have stories equally resonant, some more tragic, some brighter.

Once I listened to a woman speaking of her life, a good one with fond memories—marriage, children, work, family, church, a Southern Lady's life—and I was struck with the thought: You are the woman I ran away from becoming. No better. No worse. Just different. But possible.

The Magician

Laura Singh

Living in the heart of the Haight-Ashbury, I was a freshman at San Francisco State studying art and costume design. It was a time of "you are what you wear," so I knew I had to make myself a costume. I poured over my costume history book until I found something that looked medieval, a knave's costume from the fourteenth century. I made a short red cape with a form-fitting hood and a long tail that dangled from the back of my head to my waist and swung from side to side when I walked. I wore the cape over a tight, thigh-high, blue velour tunic on which I stitched a red Maltese cross to the center of the chest. I wore the tunic and cape over a red turtleneck and green tights. I finished off the look by buying two pairs of pointy-toed suede ankle boots, ones that I'm sure Robin Hood himself would have been proud to wear. I bought one pair in apple red and one in emerald green and I just wore one shoe of each. When I walked down the streets of San Francisco, people turned their heads to look at me: exactly the effect I wanted.

Every Friday night I went to the Avalon Ballroom, the vortex of hippie culture at the time. This was in 1966, before the Summer of Love or the rise of the Fillmore. Driving by, the only way you'd know something was going on there was seeing the crowds of hippies in their outlandish finery huddled together smoking outside. The entrance was a simple doorway on a side street off Van Ness. Once inside you descended into the underworld, down a rickety wooden staircase that opened into a Victorian-era dancehall, a windowless room with a wood floor and a stage in one corner. The walls were covered in red-flocked wallpaper and punctuated with gilded mirrors. Well-worn, red velvet, overstuffed couches ringed the room and were crammed with hippies in ruffled granny dresses, miniskirts, top hats, tie-dyed T-shirts, twelve-inch-wide bell-bottoms, leather sandals, and cowboy boots.

A white bedsheet was pinned to the ceiling above the dance floor. On it were floating projected images of Hindu gods and American Indians passing peace pipes. Film loops of topless girls, long blonde hair blowing in the wind, running through tall grass, flickered across the folds of the fabric. Color bubbles swished and swirled, spinning around the room from ceiling to walls to floor.

Once the bands started to play, the music would hit you with a roar.

The only light was a gigantic ultraviolet strobe light hanging in the middle of the room, flashing on and off to the music, freezing the distorted poses of the dancers like a flash of lightning every second and then plunging them again into darkness. It was hot and womb-like with everything pulsating and beating to the rhythm of the music. Joints could be seen passing freely between friends and strangers. I wasn't there for the drugs; I was there for the dancing, the costumes, and the music.

A commune called the Family Dog ran the dancehall. Chet Helms, the manager of Janis Joplin's band, Big Brother and the Holding Company, was the leader. He presided over the music scene like the grand wizard, mixing the psychedelic bands like Quicksilver Messenger Service with up-and-coming bands like the Doors and traditional blues like John Hammond.

I went to the dances by myself, which was fine because everyone danced alone but together. I used the whole floor to dance, weaving through the throng, waving my arms and shimmying my shoulders to the beat of the drummer. If I caught someone's eye, for a few minutes I'd have a partner. We'd hook into each other's dance rhythm.

If it was a bluesy song like Janis wailing "Ball and Chain," we would wind our arms around each other like two octopuses in a mating ritual, one leaning forward while the other leaned back, all without ever touching, in perfect unison. After a while, this temporary union would dissolve; we would drift apart and disappear into the mass of dancers, each of us caught by another's glance. There was no commitment. At the end of the evening the dancers would all join together in one giant snake dance, hands on each other's hips, winding their way in and out of each other, covering the whole dance floor, reaching out to grab the stragglers until they had included everyone who was there.

Of course, the Avalon Ballroom was also a great place to pick up guys.

I was too shy to be a groupie for the bands. Like all the other girls, I was attracted by the intensity of the rock musicians, but I knew there was no way I could smoke enough dope to keep up with them, and I had no idea how to get their attention. And like all the other unattached girls, I came to the dance hoping to be noticed and chosen by someone.

One night, while I was leaning against the wall, resting from dancing, a guy came up and leaned right next to me without saying anything. I knew this meant he was making a move. He was tall and thin in the way that hippie men were, because they didn't eat right, took too many drugs, and didn't exercise. His wavy jet-black hair hung past his shoulders making his skin look pasty white. I could tell he never saw the sun. He was handsome, with angular features, dark eyes, long eyelashes, and a handlebar mustache. But what attracted me were his clothes.

Everything he had on looked handmade. He wore a long fringed leather vest made of jagged patches over tight leather pants slit from knee to the hem. A wedge of flower print fabric was stitched into the slit, making the hems flare into bell-bottoms. He had on high-heeled cowboy boots and a collarless, gauze peasant shirt with long, flowing sleeves that fluttered when he walked. Slung low on his hips was a braided belt with a large silver belt buckle. He'd tied a red bandanna around his neck and wore layers of amulets, silver charms, and bits of real bone wrapped in multicolored thread hanging down his chest. His wrists were wrapped in tooled leather bands interlaced with beads, decorated in the signs of the zodiac. On every finger he had a different silver ring. I imagined that everything he had on must have a personal symbolic meaning for him.

He seemed shy, almost vulnerable, in contrast to the drama of his outfit. We leaned there against the wall for a while together, getting comfortable with each other, exchanging only a few words. He was older than I was, maybe twenty-seven or even thirty.

"You want to come see my pad at the Family Dog House?" He tossed his hair out of his eyes.

"Sure." I said. *Wow, he's from the Family Dog.* Then he softly slipped his hand in mine and led me firmly and silently through the dancers into the street.

While we were walking, he told me he was a founding member of the commune. I knew that meant he was part of the inner sanctum, living in the center of the rock scene. To me, if he was a member of the Family Dog it meant he must be one of the hypercreative ones from whom all the new ideas churning around us were emanating. And he'd picked *me* out of the crowd. I was thrilled.

"What's your name?" I asked as we entered the large Victorian mansion on Fell Street they called the Dog House.

"They call me Maroon the Magician."

We passed through a hallway painted in florescent psychedelic swirls, and he slid back the double doors to what must have once been the large dining room. Maroon didn't turn on any lights; instead he walked around and lit the votive candles and incense that were on every surface. The windows were covered with black fabric. As the glow of candlelight illuminated the room, I could see the plaster ceiling was painted in Van Gogh-like swirls in shades of midnight blue, white stars dotting the firmament, with all the signs of the zodiac around the edge of the sky.

I stood in the doorway, amazed. As my eyes adjusted to the light, I saw that in the center of the room was an enormous dead tree with a trunk that was at least two feet in diameter. Branches wound out from the top of the trunk in every direction. There was not a single leaf on it. It stood over ten feet tall. It filled the room, almost touching the ceiling. I wondered how he got it in there without breaking any of the branches—like a ship in a bottle.

Every branch had small objects dangling down from leather thongs like a Christmas tree. There were pictures in miniature frames, perfume bottles filled with colored liquids, fetish dolls, even bits of dried animal bone wrapped in colored thread. The room was crammed with funky antique furniture. At one end of the room was an altar made from a bureau covered in an old brocade with small antique boxes made of tarnished silver, brass bowls filled with dried plants, and small painted figurines tucked in between candles and incense holders laid carefully on its surface. On the top of the altar was an image of some angry-looking Eastern god. At the front of the altar was a real human skull. When I saw the skull, I looked around the room and saw that he had other dried animal bones lying around. As the shadow of the tree flickered against the wall and up to the ceiling, the room was filled with a kind of eerie beauty.

"What is all this stuff for?" I asked, walking slowly around the room and looking at everything, trying to take it all in.

"I am a magician, a practitioner of white magic. Good magic." He took me to another corner where he had a glass cabinet that looked like it should have been in an old apothecary shop. In front of it was a table with scales and beakers and odd-shaped bottles filled with strange liquids.

"Lately I've been getting into alchemy." I wondered what he meant by that, but I was too shy to ask. He picked up a beaker half filled with yellow liquid and held it up so it glowed in the candle light. "I also make money as an astrologer, doing people's charts."

"What sign are you?" I asked. If I knew his sign, I could get a sense of him.

"Scorpio. What are you?" He put the beaker down and turned and looked at me.

"Gemini." He nodded, noncommittal.

On one wall were some scary, frenetic paintings of stylized, jagged figures made out of sharp angles all in dark reds, blues, and purples.

He saw me looking at the paintings and said, "I'm an artist, too."

As I listened to him talk in a voice that was barely louder than a whisper, telling me about his art and his magic, I felt that by stepping into his room I had entered his mind. I was spellbound by the level of detail and effort that had gone into making that tree and the altar and all the little handmade artifacts hanging from it. As an art student, I knew how many hours he must have spent alone in that room creating all those exquisite, intricate talismans.

In the far corner of the room was a giant wooden loft built out of logs. We climbed up a narrow hand-built ladder to get to his bed on top, which was right near the ceiling. From the bed, which felt warm and cozy, I had a panoramic view of the rich, dark world he had created for himself inside this old mansion.

We slept together, but it wasn't important—it was so incidental to the otherworldly experience of being in that room. We didn't talk much either. I figured my medieval costume told everyone my story; likewise, he figured his room said it all for him.

When I told him how I had made my outfit, I could tell he was impressed. He showed me some gifts a few of the other girls living in the commune had made for him, pieces of handmade jewelry and a sequined box to hold his dope.

The next morning, lying under the quilts high up in the loft near the ceiling painted with crooked stars, he said, "Hey baby, you're cool, man. I dig you. Move in with me. You can live with me in my room here in the Dog House and be my old lady."

"I don't know. Actually, I'm still in college. At San Francisco State." It seemed prissy when I said it.

"College is bullshit. You're wasting your time," he insisted. "You don't need college, you can really do your thing here. I'm sure you'll dig it. Live with me here at the Family Dog."

I was flattered. Someone who had so carefully created such a richly layered, unique world saw me as a kindred spirit. But I was scared. I wasn't sure I was ready to abandon the straight world completely like the musicians and the Family Dog. And I knew I couldn't take the amounts and types of drugs that would be required for admission to this exclusive club.

When it came down to it, I didn't know if I could live inside someone else's world, no matter how creative, if it meant I'd have to give up my own. So I declined. It was a crossroads for me. At the time a lot of people around me in school and in the Haight-Ashbury dropped out and severed all ties with conventional life, saying they wanted to create a new society with their own rules.

After that night, I never saw him again around the dancehall. A year later I saw one of his friends.

"Hey, you know Maroon, don't you? I haven't seen him around. What's he doing now?"

"Oh man, didn't you hear? He moved to the country a while ago, but I just heard he's dead, man—it's too sad. He OD'd on methamphetamine."

Then I understood why his world was fleshed out with such an intensity of detail; why he covered the windows in black fabric; why the figures in his paintings looked frenetic, and what he really meant when he told me he practiced alchemy. Most of all I was glad I hadn't made the mistake of joining Maroon in his dark world. Who knows where I would have ended up?

Better to live in the sunlight.

When the Haight descended into drug-filled chaos, I flew off into the unknown with my backpack and some money saved from sorting mail at the post office to begin my own search for the creative, adventurous life. It led me across Europe, overland to India, back to school in textiles, out again to work in Korea, to Hong Kong, and back to India once again where I found my mate and my calling.

I met my husband, Kiran, in India. Our first date lasted thirty-six hours. Auspiciously it was on the full moon of the color festival of Holi, when people run wild throwing powdered color on each other in the streets. At sunset we took a magical boat ride on a lake in a bird sanctuary. Surrounded by flocks of birds shadowed against a glowing sky of oranges, pinks, and purples, floating along in an old faded gray wooden rowboat, we discovered our mutual love of Indian textiles and shared our dreams of living a creative life. On that first date we sketched out the lines of the business we are still doing today, thirty years later: Laura & Kiran. People use our hand-crafted fabrics to create their own richly layered worlds.

Before the Summer of Love

Merimee Moffett

Sometime in '66, desperation foggy and not unfun
sex a sometimes commodity, we
met at the laundromat on Haight
our pads on parallel streets just up the hill
"Wanna come up to the house?"

I'd given him the eye, eyeing
his greasy dark, abundant locks
those electric-blue blue eyes
burly arms, blemished white musician's skin—
his tubby in plain-white-undershirt yearning look

We humped our laundry up the sidewalk
eye to eye
to their communal home
tension on low double low—easy pace
my fate could turn on his or not
—it wasn't pressing

Their drawing room held a bevy of
girls in perfunctory circle
the Oriental rug, their manager
politely passing a joint—
behind me Pigpen retreated,
vacating the burgundy-velvet settee
and my aura
he so liking booze and heavy heavy
a teasing, macho man, I demurred

No career moves that summer day—
I went home one block over
to my bass-playing blond Adonis
who gave me leash, our ethereal tether
long enough for the city
each other's skin and curves
his Nordic jaw and famously sweet lips
always a warm curving fit
my job not to wander too far
but to keep the spell on him
turn him again and again
in our dizzying search for God

Two Sisters

Marcia Gaye

1964—Prayer

Katherine and I gather on our big double bed after our brothers have been tucked into their own beds. The boys got stories from C. S. Lewis and Lewis Carroll. Now the two of us will read from the storybook that is all true. Straight backs and crossed legs, we settle into quiet attention. The Bible on her knees, Katherine reads aloud.

We have been through creation and the flood. I've marveled at the perfect pronunciation Katherine gives to all the strange names. She shows me the divided kingdoms on the map as we travel alongside the kings. While she reads I twirl my fingers over the chenille and embroidery of the quilt. I trace the patterns of just the white flowers, and then just the pink ones.

After a chapter we face each other, knees touching, and we pray. *Thank you, Lord, for your words. Thank you for our family. Please bless us and those who seek you. Goodnight, Lord.*

After nights of plagues and battles, we decide to skip ahead to the New Testament and read about Jesus. There we begin the begats: Hezron, Amminadab, Asaph, Jehoshaphat, Zerubbabel. What a joy it is to finally read about happy miracles and parables—about birds of the air, five fishes that multiply to feed thousands, and mustard seeds and fig trees. Our prayers become longer and more sincere in detail, in recognition of the miracles in our lives, simple and huge.

We rotate by chapter; Katherine reads, then I read. But I'm too slow and not dramatic enough. She begs to take my turns as well as her own.

1966—Meditation

Ethereal wisps of incense curl into the room like ribbons. A lone window hints of streetlamps behind a red paisley scarf tacked over the pane. We again sit cross-legged facing each other, a brass bowl of smoky sandalwood between us. Katherine holds my rapt attention as she sways.

"Om" she hums. "Om." The syllable reverberates from wall to wall. Her eyes are closed; her hands are on her knees, palms open upward to welcome passing auras. I watch and wait; I do not hum Om. I focus only on the sitar music, on the fate of people who lose themselves in self-centered futile desire, who cannot see the world, the universe, as a symbiotic wholeness. George explains it in song. Life is within you and without you, all around you, and will go on. George provides my sanctuary.

Katherine tilts her head back, face to the ceiling and beyond. A bright eye appears in the center of her outstretched neck. It looks at me, winking as it sways, searching for a like-minded soul. The eye is blue and white, outlined in thick hideous black. There sounds a sharp crack as the oil lamp beside the incense bowl breaks from the heat of its own flame.

Frantically, I pat out the sparks then jump to snatch the scarf from the window. Katherine pauses in mid-hum. Slowly returning, slowly opening her eyes, she blinks. "Why did you do that?" So carefully had we prepared our scene. Our bed pushed aside. Her small tasseled rug, in greens and ivory, placed in the center of the floor. The window covered. The Beatles cued to the flat needle space between vinyl grooves. Our collection of psychedelic tokens assembled: incense and bowl, matches, decorative oil lamp from a souvenir shop in Chinatown, peace symbol medallion, paper daisies.

Seed and puka shell necklaces draped over our heads and around our ankles, and hung from bedpost and windowsill. Love beads. We braided sections of our hair entwined with lengths of mohair yarn and strips of rawhide. Then Katherine had brought forth makeup pencils and powders, eyeliner with which she drew hearts and happy words on our arms and cheeks and foreheads. She'd lowered a mirror and drew herself an extra eye just above that little notch between collarbones.

"A third eye," she'd explained, with which one "might see what is unseen, what is beyond the physical."

She hopes there is more to be revealed beyond our little room, beyond psychedelic music and neon Peter Max posters. She hopes there is more to her life than high school, where she understands at a level beyond what she is taught. She hopes love can still be possible without Paul, whose engagement ring shines from Jane Asher's hand.

※

1968—Decision

I know who she is, this hippie chick who is sitting on our front porch rail. She feels her given name is superfluous, a non-identifying restriction. She is the sister who mentors, the one who dwells on a higher plane.

She smells good, depending on which way the breeze comes by. Her smell is sandalwood, honeysuckle, body odor, pheromones, skin warmed by the sun.

She is all light, her face pale, her hands luminous, her eyes pale too, with the sun shining on them like on blue glacier ice.

She is all color, colors floating, hovering around her: gauzy stripes and paisley, beads around her neck, wrists, and ankles. Shells, seeds of every hue, glistening abalone shards, jade on her finger, silver and turquoise. Red hair cascades down her back, over her arms, forming a veil across her face when she leans forward. Tiny honeysuckle flowers from our own yard entwine through it.

She sits in colors, breathes in colors.

She holds court with her feet swung over the porch rail. I'm not listening; except now she is saying, "…the Vietnamese don't want to be a miniature America…" I watch her eyes widen and dilate. Her bare feet are white under a fine coat of dirt, with nails trimmed and filed.

Her voice is soft but clear and precise. She is saying something about Russian gymnasts. I see her mouth, her lips making shapes into words: "…everybody has a purpose, and each is needed as part of the whole; you be a farmer, I'll be a teacher, and she'll be a gymnast…"

As she speaks her hand gently lifts a spider from her lap to place it on a vine across the railing. I vaguely hear other voices, sporadic and hesitant; some of them cause her to smile. Like Mona Lisa, she suffers fools indulgently.

"…Jesus."

I hear His name and I am tuned in. "Jesus lived pure love," she is saying. "He didn't have running water or aftershave or two coats." I want to know what more she might say about Jesus, and I feel the mood on the porch shift. A cat stirs from a patch of sun to jump onto her lap and she strokes it while it undulates in her hands. No one pursues the life of Jesus, and I lean back again.

I wish the cat would come to me. It stretches and curls up and languidly blinks its eyes. Her eyes blink in the same way, closing in slow motion, opening as if they'd rather not.

The conversation moves, and I try to listen while the voices lull me and the warm afternoon wraps me; and then I am startled by a strident punctuation.

"Do you believe in free love, then?" someone asks.

She is Mona Lisa again. "Well, I certainly don't believe in paying for it."

❧

1970—Conviction

I am articulate, well informed, poised and polite; in short, brilliant. The man in the doorway, standing just beyond his threshold, the handle of a glass storm door in hand, isn't convinced.

"So, how old is she?" He tilts his head toward Katherine, on the sidewalk with her baby in the stroller. I don't understand what that has to do with declaring war in Vietnam.

"She's nineteen. All we are asking is that the government stops pretending that the war is a 'police action' and just admits it's a war. There are legal steps, actions that should be in place if the government wants to keep boys in Vietnam. We just want the government to follow its own rules. That's what this petition states. Will you sign here, sir?"

"How old are you, Miss? Why are you out here bothering people with things you don't understand? That girl there, she's too young to have a baby. You kids need to be home getting ready for school. Go take care of that baby."

"You won't sign this, telling the president that if we're at war, we need to be honest and say 'war' instead of 'police action'?"

"No, little girl. Get on home and study some more. Knocking around on doors isn't safe. That baby needs to be raised right." He takes one step backward and the glass closes between us.

The next house is a lovely old brick, just like most all others in this Cleveland family neighborhood. Stone steps lead to a broad porch with hanging baskets of flowers. The elderly couple smiles warmly as I explain about the semantics of terms and wars, and they tell me they have a nephew who is in the army and that they worry for him and all in his platoon. They talk about the honor of serving in the military. The American flag hangs listlessly in the lack of breeze, but they point out it has decorated their home since 1942. We are agreed that we love America, and I say that is why we have to force the government to follow the law. If they will sign the petition we'll be on our way to righting the wrongs that the United States has inflicted on the world—on itself.

We talk and share and yet they decline to sign. They smile as I thank them for their time.

Skipping off the wide-swept porch, I cover the distance to where Katherine stands waiting on the sidewalk. I can't wait for the praise she will offer for my well-reasoned discourse with the couple in the brick house.

"Don't ever do that again! You've wasted so much time with that guy. He was never going to sign the petition; you could see that. When they are so close-minded, it's useless to go on and on. Look at the baby. She's hot and hungry, and now we don't have time to finish this street." Katherine jerks the stroller around and I see little Jade's tear-streaked face under her sunbonnet. "Come on, this day is finished. We only got twenty signatures in five blocks. We're not ever going to fill up this page."

I follow her home, wondering what I could have said to that nice, ignorant man that might have persuaded him to admit that the illegal, unconstitutional killing of our boys is not helping Vietnam one bit.

I watch Katherine's back as she trots along. Her hair swings straight, brushing her shoulder blades. We are barefoot, she and I, her heels and toes peeking through the frays of her jeans as she maneuvers the cracks and curbs. She is so together, completely composed. She thinks I am a fool.

"Dirty hippies!" somebody yells as we pass by. Katherine looks at me and I look at her and we laugh.

1972—Revolution
Katherine comes to my high school graduation. I take her around to everyone I know, and it is to say: *See! She is real as I told you.*

We have little Jade in tow. As an infant she drooled incessantly; as a child she is sweaty, her red curls stuck to her forehead. She is aware that her mother is somehow special and she basks in the reflected attention, as do I.

In the heat of Cleveland's summer nights we escape to the front stoop again, imagining we can see the stars that we know are above the streetlamps that practically scream with crackly light. Along comes a man, a boy, I am unsure which to decide he is. He wobbles and stops. Katherine offers him a beer and rushes inside to retrieve it. I watch them flirt as he swallows and then he resumes his trek down the sidewalk. Katherine tells me he couldn't take his eyes off me. I can't tell if this makes her angry or pleased. She is smiling that half-smile.

Next it is a whole group of men-boys stumbling along after the one o'clock last call at the Red Dog Saloon on our corner. Katherine retrieves Boones Farm Strawberry Hill wine, the green bottle with a screw top. I drink neither beer nor wine, but she sends me inside for glasses. I bring out a stack of plastic disposable cups because I know you are never supposed to serve wine in plastic. I am angry that she chides me for this without realizing that I am doing it on purpose. My rebellion is lost on her.

The nauseating smell of lighter fluid hits my sinuses, worse than wine or pot or even beer. There is a flash, a momentary whiff of flint and then the scent of damp night earth. This collection of stoop strangers has come up with a novel way to alleviate boredom. They are squirting their initials in the grass, letting fire tattoo the tiny square of yard.

Harmless idiots, I think to myself as I watch miniature flames play staccato harmony. Flare, flash, flash. Flare, flash, flash.

I consider all the other things that are burning or have been burned. Draft cards, flags, books, bras, Detroit to the north, Watts to the west, napalm in the East, churches in the South, crosses on front lawns. Free-falling ash is covering America, searing our wounds, purging, cleansing, covering raw, sensitive scars.

Our yard burns with initials of a little band of revolutionaries—my sister and some drunken guys, passersby from the Red Dog Saloon—who make their mark on the world, as deep as a blade of grass.

This Girl Who Is Me

Jeanne Northrup

The girl leaves the run-down boarding house on Bourbon Street and in a few blocks reaches Jackson Square. She feels that she has finally arrived—somewhere. It is 1966. Artists all around the Square are painting and drawing under gaily-colored beach umbrellas. An old black man surrounded by young white people soulfully plays a metal dobro. Further into the Square, a lanky young man with wind-wild hair plays a harmonica, accompanied by another strange man dressed like a gypsy who plays guitar, his tongue hanging out and his head tipped to the side, appearing at once both innocent and maniacal. He maintains a continual mesmerizing beat, rocking back and forth as the music possesses him. The entire Square is filled with young people—an impromptu festival—no adults need apply.

She smooths out her bell-bottom hip huggers, tucks in her pale yellow, lace-trimmed blouse, and sets her tan cord cap at a jaunty angle, very Mary Quant-ish, then walks through the black iron gates. The music is familiar, the sound of people singing along alluring, and the lack of authority figures exhilarating. This is where she belongs. She sits back on one of the park benches a little distant from the crowd, pulls a sketchpad out of a bag made from a Mexican serape, and begins to draw the group seated around the guitar and harmonica players. People pass around a bottle of wine and throw bread to the pigeons. Others dance singly or together, each to her or

29

his own beat. Some unabashedly neck with one another, rolling in the vibrant green grass like puppies.

It's a warm and sensuous fall day. The air smells faintly of coffee with a hint of the redolence of the river. Overpowering, however, is the scent of an as yet unidentified flowering bush that perfumes the breezes with a fragrance that will forever identify the French Quarter. The entire atmosphere tingles with anticipation, rainbow-colored like the young people's psychedelic clothing. Today is a Southern version of Haight-Ashbury, and she feels at home.

The afternoon passes languidly. People come and go. Musicians change places. Entranced, though detached, she draws the tableau before her. She is the plain sparrow amid a garden filled with exotic feathered creatures. Like Dorothy, she's not in Kansas anymore, but she still visualizes herself in sepia.

Eventually, the bells of the cathedral ring the end of the workday. Perhaps somewhere adults leave mundane jobs, going home to a regular life of meals and chores and family. But not her—she left that behind. This place is new. This place is where she belongs, and she is never going to be a part of a boring adult world that doesn't know how to have fun.

Daylight lessens and she begins to put her drawing supplies away. One of the guys from a group around the musicians comes over to her. He is tall and handsome, with blond hair, blue eyes, and a cleft chin, like a very young Kirk Douglas. Unlike most of his colorfully dressed companions, he is conservatively attired in tan cords with a neat white shirt and a jacket sporting leather elbow patches.

"Let's see what you are drawing." he says, passing her a half-full bottle of Chianti as he sits down beside her. He seriously considers her drawings of the day and nods without comment.

"You an artist?" she asks.

"No, I'm a writer."

"Wow, what do you write?"

"Poetry, mostly."

"Wow." She takes a swallow of wine.

"Do you stay around here?" he asks.

"I've got a room over on Bourbon, but I'm moving in with a friend soon." She lives someplace off the streetcar line. She gives him back the bottle.

He takes a swallow and hands the bottle back to her. "Well, we're having a party over at my pad on Decatur if you want to come along."

"Sure, maybe I could read some of your poetry."

"Yeah, and you can draw me a picture."

⁂

The flat occupies an entire top floor of what was once a warehouse on the lower end of Decatur Street. Michael is his name, not Mike, and he hasn't paid the electricity bill so the huge flat is dimly lit by candles sticking out of Chianti bottles that provide a romantic, though somewhat unsteady, light. A bare mattress, on which are sprawled several people of indeterminate age and sex, is placed before the balcony doors so that anyone needing a breath of fresh air must first navigate around it. A beat-up refrigerator right out of the 1940s hums asthmatically in one dark corner powered by an extension cord that disappears mysteriously out the balcony doors. Two walls are covered with cluttered bookshelves made of concrete blocks and rough lumber. There are no chairs.

Michael leads her to a makeshift table, made of an old door held nearly level with the help of several large books stacked irregularly at each corner. The table is cluttered with books, ashtrays, bottles, cigarette papers, and baggies full of weed. In the center is a huge colorful hookah, currently not in use. Several other young people sit on pillows on the floor around the table passing bottles and, what she assumes from her reading, are marijuana cigarettes. One person reads aloud from Baudelaire's *Flowers of Evil*.

Wow, she thinks, hugging her art bag, this is what Kerouac was writing about. To Michael she says, "Neat place."

"Certainly not tidily neat," Michael replies, smiling. "Put your bag here on the table and let me introduce you around."

He takes a deep drag from a proffered joint and offers it to her. She shakes her head.

"I don't smoke."

"Nothing?" Michael laughs. "You will."

Who Wrote the Book of Love?

Dianalee Velie

In The Still of The Night,
Under the Boardwalk
Little Bitty Pretty One,
Runaround Sue,
Sittin' In Ya Ya
Uh-Uh:

Cryin'
Goodnite, Sweetheart, Goodnite:
Satisfaction
In the Midnight Hour,
Poor Little Fool.

It's All in the Game,
Little Darlin'.
Don't Be Cruel,
Let Your Love Flow,
Earth Angel.

The Birds and the Bees
Can't Help Falling in Love.
All I Have To Do Is Dream,

Gloria.
Gimme Some Lovin'!

Honky Tonk Woman,
I Wanna Do It!
Let's Dance
At the Hop,
Barefootin'.

Hello, Mary Lou.
This Magic Moment,
You Are My Special Angel,
Help Me Make It through the Night.
It's Only Make Believe!

Oh, Pretty Woman,
Lucille,
Love Me
One Night,
Party Doll!

Hanky Panky?
Louie, Louie,
Keep Your Hands to Yourself!
Get Back,
Wild Thing!

Johnny B. Goode,
Daddy's Home.
Great Balls of Fire
Bad Moon Rising:
Folsom Prison Blues.

Jail House Rock
Night Life:
Owee Baby!

Right or Wrong,
I Like It Like That.

Rip It Up,
Rock Around the Clock,
Rock This Town,
Rave On!
My Guy:

Bad, Bad Leroy Brown.
He's So Fine,
I Will Follow Him.
Stupid Cupid,
Love Hurts.

Good Lovin'
When A Man Loves a Woman.
You Cheated, You Lied?
Heartbreak Hotel?
Blame It On The Bossa Nova.

The Twist:
Last Kiss,
The Letter,
All Shook Up.
Only Love Can Break Your Heart.

My Prayer:
Sing, Sing A Song,
That's My Desire:
Poetry In Motion.

*Author's Note: Each line is a song title from the '60s.

Fast-Forwarding Evolution

Linda J. Nordquist

Summer 1961

A heat wave smothered the city of Detroit the summer I turned eighteen. Temperatures topped 100 degrees, and air-conditioning was rare. Nothing moved in the stagnant air.

I was struggling to shed my "tomboyish" ways, something my mother deemed essential if I was ever to "catch a husband." Her turn of phrase brought to mind a bug-eyed catfish flopping on a wharf, a hook piercing his lip. This did not endear me to the marriage concept. Nor did her warning that, under no circumstances, should I ever compete with the opposite sex. Worse, if I found myself besting a man, especially intellectually (impossible as that might seem), I should retreat.

"Let him think he's winning," she said, dispensing her sapient advice confidently. "You don't want to humiliate him, do you? You'll never get a husband that way."

Objections gurgled in my stomach. Don't misunderstand. The resistance I felt to her advice was not cognitive. It was a feeling state, as if I teetered on the precipice of a great loss. Is it possible to grieve an unknown in advance?

Disarmed with her influence, I sat in my new boyfriend's shady backyard sipping iced tea and, despite my best efforts at imitating

Grace Kelly, feeling every strand of hair kinking in the humidity. Dick was an art teacher and six years older than I. It was imperative that I appear sophisticated and coy. I flipped the pages of *Vogue* while Dick poured over the newspaper.

"Says here," he snickered, "that some women plan to defy the Amateur Athletic Union's ban on women running in men's road races. Why do they have to do that? They ought to leave it be."

My pulse sped up. Before I could stifle my impulsivity, I blurted, "Why shouldn't they run if they want to?"

A raised eyebrow projected a look of mild tolerance. "The officials say that if women run more than half a mile their uteruses might fall out. Imagine that."

How was I to remain poised while the word "uterus" was being bandied about? More, how could I argue against science?

Ignoring the blotches popping out on my cheeks, I plunged ahead. "I think that women, if they have the talent, should do anything they want to do."

"Fine," Dick snapped. "But they can't win, so why compete against men?"

"They're not competing *against* men"—my voice raised an octave—"they are—"

"Then why demand to run a man's race? What are they trying to prove? As I said, they should stick to themselves. Besides, in all of history, what have women ever accomplished?" He snapped the newspaper open and raised it like a drawbridge, ending the discussion.

I yearned to make a list, even a short list—a lousy name or two—of the accomplishments of my sex. Anyone besides Joan of Arc. Nothing came to mind.

It was I, not him, awash in humiliation.

Fall 1965

The bar was thick with cigarette smoke. Chas and I, newly married, sat at a small table drinking beer with our friends, Bill and Carol. Rock 'n' roll blared from the jukebox, while men whooped and backslapped at the pool table. It was Saturday night, and the place was jammed.

Carol, an art student, was the polar opposite of me: she was petite and delicate and moved with the grace of a geisha—all of which belied her provocative nature. I, on the other hand, took big strides with my shoe-box-sized feet and, like the bull, barely managed to leave the china intact. Where Carol enjoyed controversy, I preferred the peace that came with acquiescence. Despite our differences, we were close friends.

"Did you read that Betty Friedan's book, *The Feminine Mystique?*" Carol shouted over the din.

"You mean the feminine mistake, don't you?" Bill laughed and gave Carol a proprietary hug.

"Parts of it," I said, frowning as I recalled Friedan's unsettling message. I didn't know any upper-middle-class, suburban housewives, so it was difficult for me to relate to their mysterious angst. Even Friedan couldn't pinpoint the problem with exactitude. She called it "the problem that had no name."

"What's it about?" Chas asked.

"Women who have everything wanting more."

"Bill, that's not it," Carol admonished, slapping his bulging bicep. "It's about the message society gives women: that our only purpose in life is to take care of the family. That's it! No professions, no careers, no outside life. Locked away in suburban boxes with our brain cells rotting. Second-class—"

"Whoa, Carol." Chas chuckled. "Isn't that a bit dramatic? Cells rotting?"

"It's not dramatic," Carol shot back, swiping a fallen curl from her forehead. "Being surrounded by kids all day is hardly mental stimulation. Face it: there are millions of women out there who would love to have lunch with someone not wearing a bib."

Chas leaned forward as though readying to pounce. "Next, they'll want to wear the pants in the family. Then what? Two generals and no troops?"

I grabbed his arm, hoping to slow his momentum, but Carol, no doubt thinking I had her back, hurled the challenge in my direction. "Do you believe the family is a military unit? Is Chas your general?"

Suddenly the cacophony in the bar stopped and all heads turned in my direction, a spotlight lit up my face—or so it seemed. Time stood still.

Chas's head pivoted slowly in my direction. "Well?"

Bill sat ramrod straight, his eyes boring holes into Carol's head.

The grin on Carol's face sagged while an expression of disbelief crept into her eyes.

No matter what I said, someone I loved was going to taste the bitterness of betrayal.

The issue of egalitarian marital relationships had never been put to me before. My reaction was to agree with Carol. It seemed fair, but it was butting heads with years of accepted dogma. A growing unease began to surface. Was I harboring a subversive thought?

This was no longer a conversation amongst friends. A line had been drawn: men on one side, Carol on the other, and me teetering in the middle.

Chas, his face reddening, seemed to be holding his breath. I felt his tension and wanted desperately to help him. My mother's warning rang in my ears: *Don't humiliate him.* At the same time, I wanted to reassure that place in my being where dignity dwelled. I couldn't dispel the feeling that I was a guppy in a tank of piranhas.

Focusing on my glass of beer, I mumbled, "If Chas and I ever had a serious disagreement, I would accept his opinion. After all, he is the man in the family."

A look of satisfaction spread across Chas's face. He patted my hand—the same gesture he used to pat our dog. "That's my girl," he said.

Bill displayed an all-knowing smirk.

Carol groaned softly.

A wad of shame lodged in my throat.

❧

Winter 1968

A tsunami of political and cultural change rolled over the land. The quietude of the 1950s ended with the birth of social movements that challenged national laws (racial discrimination), policies of war (even forcing one president into early retirement during wartime), and long accepted beliefs about the inferiority of women. It was not a time for fence sitting.

My coat flapped open as a howling wind blew up Woodward Avenue. I grabbed the edges and trudged through the snow toward the bus stop. The bitter temperature hurt my teeth, but I couldn't close my mouth. I giggled and guffawed, and occasionally pumped my fist in the air. I wanted to hug someone—anyone—but the somber faces of passersby changed my mind. Instead, I gulped frigid air into my lungs and shouted, "I'm free. Free!"

I was an hour into my new status and loving every minute. The judge agreed. Chas and I were incompatible, the way diminished oxygen is incompatible with life. Outside the lawyer's office Chas called me a selfish, ungrateful bitch, an unrecognizable life form. And he was right, except for the "bitch" part, unless that meant I was no longer his shadow. If "selfish" meant equal, I was guilty. If "ungrateful" meant no longer thankful for his very existence, guilty again. And if "unrecognizable life form" meant independence in thought and deed—Eureka! Guilty!

The next day I strolled among the stacks of the cavernous main library, a woman on a mission. I had heard a radio station play famous quotes commemorating the life of Malcolm X. His voice, ringing with conviction, urged his people to rise up off their knees. He said that history was a people's memory, and if people didn't have that memory, they were nothing.

It was an "ah-ha" moment.

The bespectacled librarian frowned. "Elizabeth Cady Stanton? Wasn't she a close associate of Susan something-or-other? I think they tried to vote."

It irked me that he knew more than I did. "Yes, that's her," I bluffed. Chagrined, I added, "You have a long shelf of books about her husband, but nothing about her."

I had come across her name while reading a book about Henry Stanton. A footnote described her as an abolitionist and a tireless defender of women's rights. Really? I had never heard of her and, given the abundance of books about her husband and the lack thereof about her, there seemed little likelihood that I ever would.

He walked to the stacks and began thumbing his way along the books. "Well, I'll be. Guess you're right. Something may be in the basement. That's where we store old books. Wait here." He strode off.

I was about to give up waiting when he finally appeared, his chin resting on top of a stack of books in his arms. "This is all I could find," he said. "You can check them out, just be careful with some of the spines; they're cracking from age."

Certainly not from overuse, I thought, running my fingers along the embossed authors' names: Mary Wollstonecraft, Carrie Chapman Catt, Alice Paul, Lucretia Mott, Susan B. Anthony, and Elizabeth Cady Stanton. Who were these women? Why were they consigned to oblivion?

Little did I know I had uncovered rare jewels—or that I would never be the same.

In an instant, history became destiny.

Spring 1973

Crooner, my golden retriever, raced across the soggy field, leaped, and snatched the Frisbee in his jaws. We were enjoying a rare sunny day after a week of thunderstorms when I heard a familiar voice.

"Is it really you?"

I turned and faced Carol standing on the sidewalk behind a baby carriage, two small children clinging to her dress.

"My God, I don't believe it. How long has it been?" I leaned over her children and hugged her. It was like hugging a hanger.

We had grown apart since my divorce. Changing circumstances brought different interests and goals, consigning our friendship to the past.

"Years," she said, shushing a whining toddler.

As she introduced me to her children, I noticed a slight tremor in her fingers. "It's nothing." She stuffed her hands in her pockets.

"How is Bill?"

"Oh, you know," she said with a nervous giggle. "Bill is Bill."

We moved to a nearby bench. She loosed the kids from their safety leashes and sat with a tired sigh. "I've kept track of you," she said. "I saw you on TV a lot. Remember when you debated in favor of a woman's right to choose? You said that what the other side wanted was a form of religious tyranny where we would all live under their beliefs." Her eyes lit up and she grabbed my arm. "Oh, I loved that."

"Yes, I remember…"

"And twice I snuck off to Wayne State's campus to hear you speak. One time you were urging people to go to DC for one of those big anti-war demonstrations."

It all seemed so far away, yet only four months had passed since the Supreme Court decided Roe v. Wade and the US government signed the Paris Peace Accords—two huge victories in less than a week. They had occupied my life for five years. Now I felt adrift.

Carol chatted on. "And the other time you talked about women's history—*herstory*, you called it. I even have a scrapbook of newspaper clippings. It's pretty thick. Oh, I'm so proud of you."

Her hand rose to wipe away a tear from under her sunglasses. That's when I saw the greenish-yellow bruising under her eye.

"Carol, what the hell—"

She cut me off.

"I know what you're thinking but you're wrong. It's not Bill. It's me, okay? I fell." She looked up and down the sidewalk as though scouting out an escape, her face twisted in anguish. "I drink. I drink a lot. And right now I need a drink bad." She pulled a small flask from under the baby's blanket, put it to her mouth and gulped.

With a self-deprecating mien, she spoke of the guilt she felt over her unhappiness. "I have a perfect life—a good husband, three children that I would sacrifice my life for, a beautiful home. I'm busy all the time with the kids, the house, cooking. Bill helps sometimes, but his job is demanding." A short hysterical cackle escaped. "My art supplies are in the attic gathering dust. There's no time." She stopped and stared at the flask in her hand. "Sometimes I feel like someone I once knew is following me—a ghost from the past." She hesitated. A sob clutched her bony chest. "I...I think the ghost is me."

I held her until she stopped crying. "The ghost is you, Carol. Feisty you. Remember when Betty Friedan wrote about the problem that has no name? It had no name because it was the aspirations of young women that were bargained away in exchange for a husband and motherhood. That can be satisfying, but it is not the sum total of a woman. The ghost *is* you, Carol. She's still there. Reclaim her."

I hugged her tight when we parted and promised to take her to lunch the following week, no bibs allowed.

In the Family Way

Carol Derfner

Over a lunch of chicken salad, melon balls, and cigarettes, my mother
and her sister beamed with satisfaction as they gestured toward the
delicate blue envelope placed on the table between us. Inside were
the one hundred and fifty dollars Linda needed and a little more for
gas money. As I sat speechless, they rattled off stipulations:

"No one must know we are giving you this money, especially our
husbands."

"The money is a gift, not a loan. Neither Linda or you should feel
responsible to pay us back."

"You are not to drive Linda to Tijuana alone."

"You must never get yourself into the situation your friend is in."

Several weeks before, Linda Simmons, a gentle, shy college girl
who wanted desperately to be a kindergarten teacher, found herself
three months pregnant. She came to me, a sorority sister, because I
was studying to be a nurse and, as she put it, I could keep a secret.

In 1964, unwanted pregnancies were only whispered about. "In
trouble," "knocked up," and "PG" were code to describe teenaged
girls and unmarried women who were expecting a baby, and the
word *abortion* was never uttered. America's women had few choices,
often gruesome: a fast marriage, an illegal and unsafe abortion, or
a dreary home for unwed mothers. Frightened and ashamed, most
women in this situation quickly gave up their babies for adoption.
Other mothers found institutions to raise the children they could

not take care of. Lacking other options, some newborns were left to die.

Abortion was still criminalized in California at the time. Hospitals and clinics were prohibited from terminating a pregnancy except for the direst of medical conditions, and only with the State's prior approval. The legal risks for doctors and other trained medical personnel were so high that doctors would not perform an abortion even when a woman's health was in danger. Any woman who had an abortion, or even sought one, could be imprisoned, as could anyone who assisted. It would be three years before California's governor would sign a quixotic "therapeutic abortion" bill into law. Roe v. Wade was seven years away.

Nevertheless, Linda decided to get an abortion, and I decided to help her. I found an American-run clinic in Tijuana known to be reasonably safe and hygienic. The fee was five hundred dollars paid up front, in cash, and they would not take a patient who was more than four months along.

Five hundred dollars proved to be an insurmountable amount of money for two cash-strapped students. After twisting the arm of the frat-boy father, pooling our savings, and pleading for advances on our meager afterschool salaries, we still came up one hundred and fifty dollars short. Linda's clock continued to tick. Desperate for ideas, I asked my mother if she knew of any other ways to help a girl who was pregnant. Mom suggested bringing her older sister into the conversation.

❦

The sisters could not have been more different. Alene was my Auntie Mame. Tall, dark-haired, and dramatic, she was unconventional, adventuresome, and fun loving. My mother, Mildred, was blonde, more traditional, and reserved. Mom liked to say she was the June Allyson to Alene's Rosalind Russell, or the less glamorous Ethel Mertz to madcap Lucy Ricardo. But even with such fundamental differences between them, the sisters were remarkably close and spoke to each other several times a week.

Alene had given birth to a boy in San Diego during World War II when she was only sixteen. Rushed into a marriage with the baby's teenaged father, she was divorced by the time she was nineteen. Within the family it was rumored my cousin Pat was "retarded" and needed special care, so Alene and her two small sons lived with my grandparents until she married again some years later.

Mom married a handsome sailor she met while he was on shore leave, and I was born several months later.

At the time of our lunch, neither of the women worked outside the home so I knew they must have cobbled the money together somehow. When I asked why they had such compassion and generosity toward a girl they had never met, the sisters glanced at each other tenderly. First one, then the other, responded, with my aunt speaking first.

"Because it's just plain wrong to have a baby when a girl's too young and silly to take care of it." She took a drag on her cigarette and blew the white smoke upward. "She'll just resent it." Aunt Alene stubbed the cigarette butt out in the half-filled ashtray without looking at us. "And that's not a good thing for a kid. They can feel that, you know."

I wasn't sure what Mom would say. She had a habit of retreating into a well-hewn reticence whenever a conversation verged on something emotional. I half expected her to jump up and begin clearing away the dishes, so I was very surprised when she reached over the maple table and entwined her fingers with those of her older sister. Her voice was hesitant, thin and quiet.

"I think a woman should be able to live a life she really wants. Babies coming too soon and too often make that almost impossible." She paused for a moment. "I wouldn't want that for your friend."

Mom had given birth to seven children by the time she was forty. The hint of dreams long gone from her own life hung in the air for what seemed forever before she twisted in her seat and looked at me with saddened eyes. "And *no* child should bear the burden of having been born an accident," she said.

Abruptly Mom turned back to her sister, a flash of anger on her face. There was no mistaking the conviction in her voice as she declared, "Because no one, not a man *or* a woman—and certainly not a child—should be *forced* to get married. Or worse yet, have to *stay* married for years and years to the wrong person." Mom was on fire!" All because of a tiny moment of wrong timing," she snorted with derision. "That's the *real* crime in my book!"

With that, Aunt Alene slapped the table hard with an open hand. "Damned right, little sister!" she cried out triumphantly. "Damned right!"

The women's words sent a current of loving kinship through me with stunning force. In one split second, I understood that because believing motherhood and marriage were the forces that dominated *their* lives, my mother and her sister wanted Linda and me to have something more in ours. In their oblique way, as they handed over the tissue-thin envelope, they were empowering us to be our truest selves.

I can still picture how fierce and proud my mother and her sister looked. Never did I love these two women more than in that moment.

$$\clubsuit\xi$$

Later in the week, I drove Linda to Tijuana and she was able to have a safe abortion with no complications. It was the first of numerous trips I would make to the clinic in Mexico before moving to Alaska in 1970. It didn't take long to meet up with like-minded feminist women in the Last Frontier. Together we battled sexism and racism in bold and risky ways. Eventually, I became a politician and a lobbyist. Along the way, I became skilled at raising money for causes that go a long way toward making the world more welcoming and safe for women and their children.

The Sherman sisters were my first anonymous donors.

Dispatches from the Heartland

Dorothy Alexander

Prologue

You might think that the culture wars of the 1960s and 1970s took place on the east or west coasts of this country, or in and around the great universities, or where the tie-dyed crowd congregated; that one would have had to smoke joints, drop acid, or join a commune to have experienced that momentous time of upheaval and change. Think again.

I

July 1967, Sunday afternoon

Mom and Dad, my younger brothers, Jeff, sixteen, and Kevin, fourteen, along with my son, Kim, also fourteen, gather at my parents' farmhouse on the high plains of far western Oklahoma—only my sister, Mary, who lives in Minneapolis, is missing. We've gathered to say good-bye to Clark, oldest of my three brothers. Drafted into the US Army only three months ago, he has been assigned to an infantry unit bound for Vietnam. Clark is a nineteen-year-old farm boy, frightened of going to war, trying not to show his fear.

The last thing he does before we drive to Oklahoma City, where he will board a plane on the first leg of his journey to Southeast Asia, is take his pet squirrel from a cage in the front yard. He is saying good-bye to the little creature, letting him run up and down the mimosa tree that hovers overhead. The squirrel leaps from a lower limb toward my brother's shoulder, misses, and hits the ground at Clark's feet. Simultaneously, a hunting dog, named Blue Bird (don't ask) and belonging to Jeff, pounces on the squirrel, and with one great snap of his teeth, severs its spine.

The only dry eyes are Dad's. He merely takes up his Sunday newspaper and says, "You people just need to get a grip."

Next day I call my mother to tell her Clark's plane has left. I expect tears, but she says evenly and firmly, "I've had enough! Everything I do from now on will be different."

She meant what she said. It was her declaration of independence.

II

August 1967, Monday evening

Mom announces that she is enrolling in vocational classes to prepare for a job, and that she intends to earn her own money to become "independent." This strikes my father as a sort of blasphemy. He, of course, forbids it. She states flatly to him, "You can't stop me!"

When he hides the keys to all the family vehicles, she catches a ride with a friend to the only used car dealer within forty miles. She finds an old clunker that suits her. The car dealer learns that my father has instructed the bank not to allow her to withdraw money from his account or to borrow money without his approval. He sells the automobile to her anyway. He extends credit to her with the proviso that she repay him within one year from the date of her first paycheck…from the job she didn't yet have.

These acts of "disloyalty" as he labels them, anger my father, but it soon becomes apparent that she will not back down. On the surface he seems to reconcile to their new way of living. He merely grumbles darkly to my brothers about having to prepare some of his own meals and to run the washing machine when he needs clean clothes. He does not complain to his friends. He doesn't want them to know he has lost absolute control over his household and doesn't want to look like a wimp to his contemporaries. Perhaps he also fears she might leave him if he becomes too insistent.

III

October 1968, Friday night

Sixty or so people, including me, sit in folding chairs in a small auditorium on the campus of a vocational technical school in the miniscule town of Burns Flat, Oklahoma. We are here to see members of our families receive certificates denoting completion of training courses. It's a rather motley crew—I count twenty-six graduates—mostly girls and women trained as nurses' aides or licensed practical nurses, and a few gangly young men in clean but permanently oil-stained coveralls who will become mechanics, most likely repairing farm machinery and trucks in the farming communities of western Oklahoma.

All are recognizable as products of this dry, windswept country-side—Dust Bowl survivors and their descendants, people who work with their hands and do the best they can under harsh conditions.

The audience is of the same demographic, except they are a generation older than those who rise to receive the rolled certificates tied with blue ribbons. Except me. I have driven here from Oklahoma City to see my fifty-four-year-old mother (her graying hair and farm-woman clothing betraying her as the most senior student) rewarded for more than a year of hard work under near impossible circumstances. She has come here five days a week for fourteen months, driving her old, second-hand car eighty miles each way, each day. She has labored long and hard to decipher the printed course materials with her seventh grade education she had abandoned forty years ago to work in her father's fields.

She has endured the wrath of my father, who has berated her

daily for doing this. She has surmounted the stumbling blocks he placed in her path. She has accomplished her goal: she is now a certified dietetic technician. This means she is qualified to plan and prepare meals for persons confined to health care facilities, like nursing homes and hospitals. It also means she is employable. Someone will pay her money for her work. She has a piece of paper attesting to the fact. She has value. She is her own person.

I am her witness.

As we drive home, we see an Indian powwow in progress on the outskirts of Elk City. Dancing figures cast wild shadows as they circle round a fire.

My mother says, "Oh, let's stop and watch. I need to see this."

The night is cool but not uncomfortable. It is pleasant to listen to the drums and singing of the Cheyenne and Arapaho peoples. When the "inter-tribal" dance is announced (which means that non-native people in the audience may participate), my mother and I, with only a knowing glance between us, wordlessly join the Native American women and dance a circuit around the fire.

We are both euphoric. It is a shining moment.

IV

March 1971, Sunday morning

Sunlight floods Mom's kitchen and dining room. Dad sits at the dining room table reading the livestock market reports in the Sunday *Oklahoman*, drinking his third cup of coffee. Kim and Kevin, both eighteen now, watch TV in the living room, the sound turned down low, their heads together murmuring to each other so quietly I can't distinguish their words. In the kitchen, Mom and I peel potatoes and chop carrots for the pot roast she is making for Sunday dinner, as she calls the noon meal. She tells me her plans to remodel her 1940s kitchen and to install new appliances as soon as she saves enough money.

I interject, saying, "I'll loan you the money, Mom, if you want to go ahead with your plans right away. You can pay me back later." My father still won't give her any money from the farm and ranch income since she insists on being "independent."

"No," she says, "I prefer not to borrow money from you because you never let me repay the money you loan me."

I say to her, "I probably can't afford to be that generous in the future since I am toying with the idea of going to law school. If I do, I will need the money repaid since I can't work full time."

These words are no sooner out of my mouth than Dad, who apparently has heard the whole conversation, stands up from his chair and in a split second moves to where I stand, grabs the collar of my blouse at the throat, almost lifting me off my feet. His face is so close to mine I can feel his breath on my face. I can see the anger and what looks like pure hatred in his eyes.

He says, "I have had enough of you! Enough of your marching in the streets pretending to know more than the men who run this country, claiming you are as good as a man, claiming the coloreds are as good as whites! Thinking you can be some big-time lawyer, somebody better than the rest of us! And worst of all, your meddling in my marriage. You have ruined my life putting ideas in your mother's head. You think I don't know that you put her up to defying me, her own husband? Put her up to thinking she can leave this house, go to school, get a job, be independent, and leave me here to look after myself? You think you are so smart that you can ruin my life with your big ideas? Is that what you think? Well, I've got something to say about that. She is my wife, this is my kitchen; I own both of them. I will say when either one is changed! It's none of your damned business!"

My anger almost matches his. I snap back, "You may be her husband, but that's a mere legal fiction authorized by a few words spoken before a judge and written on a piece of paper. I am made of her flesh and blood. Your legal relationship to her can be reversed by another few words and another piece of paper. My blood kinship to her can never, ever be changed. We will be of the same flesh until we die. You can't change that one iota no matter how much you bully and bluster."

He looks ready to strike me, but Mom's screams bring Kim and Kevin. They restrain Dad physically, but his verbal assault continues, his eyes wild, his face contorted in rage. As I gather my things and hurry to my car, my father calls after me, "Never set foot in my house again. Never speak to me again. I forbid you and your mother to speak to each other. I never want to hear your name again as long as I live. If you ever try to come near me or my property again, I will harm you."

Kim drives us home as I sit huddled in the passenger seat trying to understand what had happened. I know only one thing for sure. My life is irrevocably altered.

That day I knew my relationship with Dad had taken a turn, that his paradigm could not tolerate my bold defiance without striking back. I also knew I could not have reacted otherwise. Throughout the exchange, Mom cried but never uttered one word in my defense. She would not choose between Dad and me, though at that moment I desperately wanted her to choose me. Dad and I had clashed many times before, but not so explosively. Never with such personal implications. Never had the shifting sands of social change penetrated so deeply into our remote refuge.

Though we lived in the rural heartland thousands of miles from the Tenderloin, Haight-Ashbury, Stonewall, Kent State, and the street protests against war and in support of racial and gender equality, we could not escape the rending of the social fabric any more than those living near the epicenter. All our lives were touched in one way or another. Perhaps those like my father, who couldn't conceive of any way other than the one they had always known, had the hardest time dealing with it. But deal with it they did. There was no going back no matter how much they wished otherwise, nor how much they fought and raged against it.

From the distance of forty years, I see that morning as the apex of those decades. The top of the bell curve.

Epilogue

Mom found a job as a dietician and took much pride and satisfaction in her work until she retired at age sixty-five. In the late 1970s, the discovery of oil and natural gas underlying the farm brought wealth that gave her the security she had always dreamed of. She died in 1992.

Dad maintained his anger toward me and refused to speak to me until 1975 when I graduated from law school. At my outdoor graduation exercises at the Oklahoma City University, I saw him standing alone on the outer fringe of the crowd. I waved him to where the rest of the family gathered and he came to us. We never again mentioned that day in 1971, nor the angry words we each had spoken. He did ask me to draft deeds placing my Mom's name on the land titles when the oil and gas money started coming.

Clark served three tours of duty in Vietnam, once escorting the body of our cousin, Michael David Howard, home after his death in Tay Ninh Province in 1968. My brother came home without serious physical wounds, but he was an emotional wreck. His psychic wounds are still with him. At times he reminisces about his pet squirrel. He finds that easier to talk about than the sadness of war.

My son, Kim, went to military service in the last ever draft call made in this country in 1972. He returned safely, attended the University of Oklahoma, majoring in mathematics. He died of complications from HIV/AIDS in 1989.

Jeff and Kevin are the only members of our immediate family who still live and farm in western Oklahoma.

I was admitted to the practice of law in both Oklahoma and Texas, and maintained my private practice as a country lawyer until retiring two years ago. I have been the municipal judge of a small western Oklahoma town for more than thirty-one years. I still maintain a home in my little community and have, for the past seventeen years, lived openly as a gay woman with my partner. We both participate in local civic activities, like the genealogical society, the arts and humanities council, and operate a small poetry publishing press and art galleries.

Although my community remains ultraconservative in a political sense, it has not been immune to the social transformations that began in the 1960s. I like to think that by remaining a part of the community while holding my head high, in spite of my son's openly acknowledged AIDS and my own lifestyle, I've shown that change, even dramatic change, is not to be feared.

Mrs. Lieutenant

Susan Tornga

I fell in love in 1967, during the Age of Aquarius. Or rather, I fell in love with the idea of love. I simultaneously said "I do" to a spit-polished Army Lieutenant and "good-bye" to my Tucson home. At eighteen years old, I was too naive to be afraid. A marriage license and a passport were my tickets to adventure, but life's lessons tend to sneak up on us unannounced and unwelcome, and all too soon I discovered that adventure presents itself in many forms: The Good, The Bad, The Ugly.

The first airplane flight of my experience-starved life landed me in what was then West Germany. With wide-eyed enthusiasm, I took in the German countryside, the pomp and circumstance of military reviews and parades, and an ordered symmetry to life far removed from my blue-jeaned existence in the Arizona desert.

My first taste of this new reality centered on those very Levi's. Shortly after our arrival in Karlsruhe, West Germany, my husband invited me to a parade. The afternoon was sunny, so I donned my go-to wardrobe of jeans and a T-shirt. I'll never forget the horror I felt when I saw the other wives attired in what appeared to be cocktail dresses, accessorized with gloves and hats. In the texting age, it would've been an OMG moment. I turned around and ran back to the nonjudgmental safety of our apartment.

Someone must've seen me, though, because the next day the wife of my husband's commanding officer (CO) came calling. I forget her name, but vividly recall a formidable woman forever imprinted in my mind as THE COLONEL'S WIFE.

She said nothing about my faux pas, but rather welcomed me with the gift of a book, titled *Mrs. Lieutenant*. I'm not sure what I expected of *Mrs. Lieutenant*—perhaps the swashbuckling experiences of a female superhero. I couldn't have been further off course. One look at the Table of Contents and the purpose of TCW's visit and gift became clear.

I was not long into the narrative when I realized I had tumbled, Alice-like, into a nineteenth-century rabbit hole. With its references to wrist-, elbow-, and full-length white gloves, calling cards and acceptable social behavior, a more apt title for *Mrs. Lieutenant* would have been *Pride and Prejudice, Redux*.

A sentence on page 5 stopped me cold. "Play the game according to the rules and do not try to change them." What? Had not our beloved John F. Kennedy urged young Americans to help make the world a better place?

It was impossible to be a woman in the '60s and not feel the winds of change blowing briskly across the country. I didn't consider myself an activist—more of a supportive observer—as the sixties counterculture developed around me. I cheered the women's libbers, but didn't burn my bra; cried for the civil rights marchers, but didn't board a bus.

I continued to read *Mrs. Lieutenant*, waiting—in vain, as it turned out—for a punch line or a "gotcha" moment when the joke would be revealed. Words and phrases cited with Biblical reverence puzzled me.

I thought tea was a beverage, not an event steeped in more rules of behavior than an Emily Post guidebook. My mother never told me that an afternoon tea was "one of women's greatest pleasures," but there it was in black and white on page 18.

As I read further, anguish gave way to relief. It seemed I would never be required to host one of those ghastly functions, replete as they were with opportunities for social gaffes, because, the paragraph continued, "do not attempt to give a tea unless you have a lovely cloth for the table and a tea service."

I had no cloths, lovely or otherwise, and certainly a tea service was not in my purchase plans. My husband and I had been starving students until our marriage. If we didn't receive it as a wedding gift, we didn't have it. And why would I need a cloth, anyway? We had no table.

Mom may have neglected my social instruction, but she had warned me, "Never say never." In that, as in many things I would discover over the years, she was right. Shortly after we settled into new quarters—fully furnished, including the requisite table—I was *asked* (i.e., *commanded*), to host one of those dreaded teas.

No doubt about it, I was terrified. *Mrs. Lieutenant* devoted an entire chapter to the execution—an appropriately foreboding word—of the afternoon tea. There is a specific time range for a tea. If it is held earlier, the hostess must give it another name. I meekly hosted the "tea" at 1600 hours (4 p.m. to the layperson). By the way, per page 8, all formal invitations must be given and accepted in the third person. "Mrs. John Doe (never Mrs. Jane Doe or, heaven forbid, simply Jane Doe) requests the honor of your attendance..."

As hostess, I must choose my pourers with care. "To be asked to pour at a tea is a great compliment." Any faux pas in the selection process will reflect poorly (no pun intended) on the hostess' unsuspecting husband. See page 19. The ranking officer's wife is Pourer Number One and so on. If both tea and coffee are served, Wife #1 is the coffee pourer; Wife #2 pours the tea. "[C]offee outranks tea and tea outranks punch." That would be Wife #3.

The rabbit hole was now a polygamists' colony.

This VIP (Very Important Pourer) must be ever mindful of her posture, sitting erect with both feet on the floor. Oh yes, and when she is not pouring, "she should place both hands in her lap."

This paragon of minutiae comes complete with Q & A pages. One distraught wife, agonizing no doubt over her first foray into this social minefield, asked, "Is it permissible to put my cup and saucer on the tea table when I am through?"

Our author admonishes, "Heavens no! The hostess has given much care to see that she has a lovely table and certainly would not appreciate your ruining its appearance with your soiled cup and saucer." No doubt she wants to protect her "lovely cloth."

Before the new lieutenant's wife leaves this most pleasurable event, she must place her card—more about that follows—on the card tray that the thoughtful hostess, who of course has read *Mrs. Lieutenant*, placed on a "small table near the entrance." Enough with the tea…it's time for a stiff drink.

To a girl from the American West, the term "calling card" conveys visions of cow patties and bird droppings, as in "the pigeon left his calling card on the picnic table again."

However, as a Mrs. Lieutenant myself, I was required to possess calling cards of a more urbane ilk to place in the ubiquitous tray at the close of any social function. Not surprisingly, I had arrived in Germany totally unprepared.

Fortunately, *Mrs. Lieutenant* had the solution. Page 12 told me to "Make your call and say nothing about not having them [calling cards]. Order some immediately." Just don't order any old calling cards. "Engraved ones are considered socially acceptable."

Protocol required the caller to place a certain number of cards in the appropriate tray. The number of cards deposited was dependent upon the count of males and females present in the called-upon household.

I was now certain that Jane Austin had written this book almost two centuries earlier. Per page 15: "Remember, a gentleman calls on all adult members of a household, but a lady never calls on a man, so she is calling only on the female members of the family." My opinion to the contrary, this was no joke.

Soldiers were arriving from tours in Vietnam, and others never knew when they would be transferred into that nightmare. Yet the wives were supposed to worry about whether doilies or a cloth should be placed on a sandwich tray. For the record, per page 17: "Neither. The sandwiches should be placed directly on the tray."

Or, worse yet, that phone calls should be restricted to five minutes. Page 63: "Having long conversations on the telephone is a bad and hard to break habit, but your accomplishments will certainly be greater if you can overcome it."

Boys were dying in the rice paddies of Southeast Asia.

On the advice of *Mrs. Lieutenant*, I acquired three pairs of white gloves in the aforementioned short, medium, and full lengths. The ideal was to wear gloves the same or one length shorter than the ranking officer's wife. Never, ever, longer. At first, I would join other wives in surveying the receiving line at any function, determine the benchmark length and then dig through my purse for the appropriate pair. It didn't take me long to figure out that short gloves would never offend. I eschewed chic in favor of expediency.

Despite my best efforts to walk the fine line between the inane and the rational, eventually I did offend, earning Mr. Lieutenant a reprimand regarding his renegade wife. At one outrageously fancy reception, I responded to a general's wife's inquiry into the welfare of my children by saying that I had none. Apparently, I should've spared her the embarrassment of her error by saying the nonexistent babes were "quite well, thank you." That's when the gloves came off, figuratively and literally.

Life was getting a little dicey for me by this time. Feminism stirred, then woke from hibernation, ready to feed on nonsensical maxims. My first act of aggression was to get a job. This was unacceptable behavior for an officer's wife, but frankly, Scarlett…

Because I worked in an office staffed by many local residents, I gained firsthand knowledge from those who had lived through the horrors of the Hitler era. I began to learn about the world, the real world, far removed from dinner party seating charts and the correct way to answer the telephone.

Spurred on by the How Are Your Children incident, my husband grew more supportive of *Mrs. Lieutenant*, the book, than of Mrs.

Lieutenant, the wife, a harbinger of things to come. Ever penurious, however, he welcomed the second paycheck. Eventually the cutting remarks ceased. Similarly, the tea ladies decided I was not worth saving, so off they went, after bigger fish. Or perhaps crumpets?

Unfortunately, I didn't escape the watchful eye of *Mrs. Lieutenant*, who must have known reactionaries like me existed. "Even if you can't participate it is still your duty to join the Officers' Wives' Club and pay dues." (Page 57) 'Twas a tiny ransom for a modicum of freedom. Short of divorce, total escape was impossible.

Certain activities were "Command Performances," (i.e., attendance was mandatory). The New Year's Day reception at the commanding officer's quarters was one such event. The monthly "Hail and Farewell" dinners were another. When my husband was hospitalized with appendicitis, I elected not to attend one such event. Another black mark for this lieutenant's wife.

Had I studied my trusty guidebook, I would've discovered that *Mrs. Lieutenant* had addressed such an occurrence. Page 11 dictated, "When a woman attends a social function at night without her husband, she should arrive and leave with another couple." As if driving sixty miles each way on the notorious German Autobahn wasn't proof that I was competent enough to find my own way into and out of the Officers' Club.

I spent my days at my job and thus missed the chance to advance my social skills at those most pleasurable afternoon teas. Consequently, I was clueless as to the rank of the other officers, with the exception of the CO, whose wife always referred to him as "The Colonel." This gap in my education presented quite a dilemma at Command Performances.

The etiquette for arrival and departure required that we "pay [our] respects" to the other officers and their wives in order of their rank. Well, *everyone* is senior in rank to a lieutenant. "This procedure is reversed upon leaving." As *Mrs. Lieutenant* so accurately stated on page 9, "This means lieutenants [and their wives] will be especially busy." Or dizzy.

Twice, my husband received counseling from his commander regarding the behavior of his wife and his inability to control same. Had we had children or had I not worked, which effectively removed me from many opportunities for socially unacceptable behavior, I'm sure there would have been more such reprimands. I most certainly would have violated the dictum on page 60 that read, "Never ask an officer to push a baby carriage or hang out the laundry." Excuse me, just how did that baby get there in the first place?

Not surprisingly, the marriage did not survive. I often ponder those years in an attempt to understand why we never became a couple. The Army and its archaic attitude toward women set the stage. When we wed, my husband was twenty-five to my eighteen. I was a baby boomer, the first of that paradigm-shattering generation. He was raised on *Ozzie and Harriet* and graduated macho-cum-laude from The Little Woman Stays Home and Keeps Quiet School.

Eight years later, before the divorce and after seven moves at Uncle Sam's behest, my husband was told that he would be part of a reduction-in-force. In other words, the Army fired him. When he received the news, he called to tell me it was my fault. I was far too radical in my wifely behavior. I hadn't supported his career. In fact, I ruined it. In many ways, he spoke the truth. What I could never buy into was the underlying tenet from *Mrs. Lieutenant*, found on page 25: "Always remember a wife's identity is that of her husband's." It wasn't true for me in 1967, and it isn't true today.

Fortunately, for today's military service men and women, somewhere along the line, the rules of the game did change.

So did I.

Fear and Loving

Patricia Helmetag

The photo of a student couple walking to a laundromat near the University of Wisconsin accompanied an article in the *Philadelphia Bulletin* about cohabitation on college campuses. The bearded boy and unkempt girl, both in wide bell-bottom jeans with unruly tresses, labored under heavy sacks of laundry on their backs. It was August 1967, a few days before I left my Bryn Mawr, Pennsylvania, home for my freshman year at the University of Wisconsin–Madison. For the past nine years, I had worn a uniform to my strict girls' school, but now I wanted desperately to look like the hip girl in the photo, to have a shaggy boyfriend like she had—to be as free as she looked. My parents disapproved of cohabitation under any circumstances, and were appalled to find that it thrived at UW. They had signed me up for a private girls' dorm, and I was enrolled in the small school-within-the-school Integrated Liberal Studies program. This, at least, gave them some relief. As for me, I couldn't wait to get to where no one would be looking over my shoulder ever again, lost amid 36,000 students.

As it turned out, sexual freedom would be just one of their worries. War protests would be another. That fall, the rising death toll in Vietnam was announced nightly on the news, and the threat of the draft loomed over the male students. On October 18, Dow Chemical, the maker of the deadly chemical agent napalm sent recruiters to the UW campus for a job fair. Three hundred student anti-war activists protested with a peaceful sit-in outside the chancellor's office.

Chancellor William Sewell summoned the Madison town police, who battered the protesters with bully clubs. Tear gas wafted in my classroom window, burning my eyes, making it hard to breathe. Frightened and seeking fresh air, I escaped Bascom Hall into the middle of the riot and bolted down the hill to my dorm, away from the fray. The rioting surged on and off for several days. Classes were cancelled. When the rioting ended, sixty-five students and three police officers had been injured. The resulting rift between students and the administration consumed the university, the national news, and the den where my parents watched TV in the evenings. Alarmed at what they were seeing, they phoned to advise me to stay safely away from the action. The National Guard was called in, and the rioting and tear-gassing continued. Armored, helmeted men marched down Langdon Street under my dorm window. I was shocked to realize that I was living at the epicenter of an historic storm.

Horrified by the brutality I witnessed daily, I began to question my parents' worldview. Like many other students, witnessing the violent reaction by the police and Guard to what began as a lawful, peaceful "sit-in" coaxed me into reexamining my beliefs. Something important was happening, and the chants provided the score.

"Hell no, we won't go!"

"Hey, hey, LBJ. How many kids did you kill today?"

"Ho Ho Ho Chi Minh!"

I had grown up with my father's war stories. He'd served almost three years in India on the Burma border in the Second World War as an Army doctor-major with 20th General Hospital, the University of Pennsylvania's base hospital. He had reason to be proud of his service and of America's role in that war, but my friends were against the Vietnam War, and I was beginning to see how this war was different. In 1967, Dad didn't see it that way. At his insistence, I stood on the sidelines of the protests, but as the conflicts escalated,

I became more and more convinced that this war was the business of my generation, not his. His generation had it wrong this time.

When I returned home for winter break, the "generation gap" came along with me. My parents and I argued for the first time. I felt strangely powerful in my indignation. Their frustration at my intransigence was palpable.

When I returned to school, tragedy poisoned the air. Christine Rothschild, a freshman who lived on the first floor of my dorm, was found dead in the bushes—murdered on her early morning jog, twelve stab wounds piercing her chest, her own gloves shoved down her throat—and we heard about two other attempted assaults on women. Female students were told never to walk alone. I didn't need to be told. Nowhere felt safe.

There was death on the campus, death in Vietnam. I changed with the leaves that year. I grew my hair long, put aside my pretty clothes, and dressed all in brown. I dropped my sorority. I drank 3.2% beer at the Student Union between classes, and shared "grass" on seedy apartment floors with boys discussing their service options: the draft, ROTC, or Canada. We listened to Simon & Garfunkel, Joan Baez, Dylan, Phil Ochs, Donovan, and the Stones. We read Ginsberg, and we talked about women's liberation.

I'd never really given it much thought, but girls began to check each other in action and deed. When I asked a boy to help me lift something, my friend reprimanded me.

"You can do it yourself. Why do you have to ask him?"

It was a little thing, but it was an empowering realization. That was the moment that drove it home—what we now call an "ah-ha" moment.

When Lake Mendota thawed, I fell for a handsome boy named Chuck whom I spied across a smoke-filled room. On our first date I explained to him I was destined to marry my hometown boyfriend. This would be just for fun. He rented an eight-by-ten room above The Pub, across the driveway, behind my dorm. True to my parents' fears, I soon spent passionate weekend nights there, while back in my dorm room two pillows under my covers served as my surrogate in case of a room check. Chuck smelled of English Leather and smoked Camels. His slick, straight black hair was as long as Navy ROTC would allow, and he talked with a thick Milwaukee accent. He was dark and muscular and foreign. Ecstasy stuck with me on my trek to classes and throughout the day. And, like the photo in the *Bulletin* the summer before, we sometimes did laundry together.

Soon after Christine's murder, the Madison police visited the floor above The Pub to ask residents if they knew anything about a man who had lived in the garret apartment upstairs. Chuck gave them a description. Later, he held my hand and led me upstairs—so I could see what he had seen. The wooden stairway was dusty and bare. My heart throbbed as we entered a dark, wooden room. There were Nazi signs, and a dead, dried-up bat splayed on a crude target, surrounded by darts. Standing at the window we looked across the driveway, just as the man must have. We looked at the half-opened shade in my dorm, just as he might have. We could see directly into Christine's room on the ground floor of my dorm. I felt a chill go up my spine and down my arms.

❦

The police told us nothing. I don't know if the man who disappeared was the murderer. The murderer was never to be found.

The naive girl I had been in September had seen a lot in nine months. The war protests had opened my eyes to different ways of thinking. The women's movement gave me a new way of seeing myself. The death of Christine Rothschild had exposed me to the threat and horror of violent death—a constant drumbeat to men confronting the draft. Love had blossomed despite these difficult times. I wanted always to remember that.

On the outside, I became the girl in the photo, but not just her clothes, her hair, or her boyfriend. I had changed on the inside, too.

Rice-Jungle War

Mary Pacifico Curtis

Inspired by Barbara Sonnenborn's film, Regret to Inform

Green, it's very green here
paddies under mist
shrouded mountains
soft as whispers

in the distance—people, so tiny
they look frail but they're iron
frought
with grit and mettle

stories particle the soil, souls
lost in mud and brush
death on a delta, more death
of shame on soils at home

they named it our war we named it theirs
amid cries a woman between wounded
neighbor wounded cousin she decides
with what she has one lives one dies

women, all of them together now
ones from distant shores as one
wives, mothers, widows, whores,
betrothed ones, sisters now who lost

lost husbands fathers brothers sons
they carried on carried babes in arms
carried family to new days carried
grief carry their man in their hearts

green, it's very green here in this land
of two tongues rice fields humid jungle
war talk hanging thick here
making killers of young men

the stories are different
so much the same
here

shroud decades that follow
as life insists
the women

carry on wondering still
what each man met
on his own rice-jungle road.

Round-Eye in a World of Hurt: Vietnam, 1968–1969

Cathleen Cordova

When people hear that I was in Vietnam during the war, they usually say things like: "How did that happen? Are you a nurse? You must be brave."

No, I was not a nurse. I was a Department of the Army Civilian (a DAC) assigned to Army Special Services. In 1968, I had just graduated from the University of California–Davis with a degree in Sociology/Psychology, and had spent the previous four years working two part-time jobs and going to school full-time on a Regent's Scholarship. By the time graduation came around, I was more than ready to leave school, have some fun, and see the world. I chose civilian service to the military as my way of supporting my country and as my ticket to adventure. Little did I know what kind of adventure it would turn out to be.

Unlike the military nurses and doctors who were in Vietnam to care for the soldiers' physical wounds, we were sent to care for their psychological well-being. At the time, the Army was specifically recruiting psychology and sociology majors to run their morale programs overseas. Many of my friends, classmates, and family members had already been drafted. Despite anti-war sentiments at the time, I felt it was my civic duty as an American to do what I could to support our troops. And no, I wasn't brave, perhaps just too young and naive to be afraid.

Female civilian service to the military is nothing new. It's a long-standing tradition that dates back at least as far as the Revolutionary War. Women have always participated in the defense of our country and in support of our troops, even if only in an unofficial capacity. In fact, much of the advancement and opportunities for today's women can be attributed to the contributions and sacrifices of the military and civilian women who came before them. When I volunteered for service in Vietnam with Army Special Services, I was following in the footsteps of tradition and of intrepid women, whether I realized it or not.

I was only twenty years old at the time and I had never been around the military before, so it was a new experience for a naive country girl. After talking with the recruiter at the university and signing up for a year, I then returned home to tell my parents what I had done.

My mother took it surprisingly well. She was obviously worried, but said if that was what I really wanted to do, she was proud of me and would support my decision. My father, on the other hand, was furious. He was a flag-waving patriot, but he ranted and raved that no daughter of his, especially a proper young Hispanic woman, should run off with the Army, to a war in a country he knew nothing about. He disapproved and was so angry that he disowned me, and refused to speak another word to me. I remember calling home from school and asking to speak to him, hearing him in the background: "Tell your daughter I have nothing more to say to her."

To this day, I still do not talk of those times with my father. However, several years ago my sister told me that my father was actually proud of me, but was very worried for my safety. Perhaps he coped with that fear and anxiety by being angry at not being able to protect me.

Later the Army instructed me to go to the Sierra Army Depot in Susanville, California, for my physical. I soon found myself in a room full of young men standing in line holding small urine-sample bottles. They looked surprised to see me there; one of them finally said, "Hey lady, aren't you in the wrong place?" Unfortunately I wasn't, and the thought did cross my mind that he might be right, but it was too late. I was committed and on my way to Vietnam.

I never saw the recruiter again; everything following the physical was done by mail. Even my uniforms came in the mail with instructions on when and how to wear them. The uniforms were a shock to a young, 1960s woman. They were WWII leftovers, designed with long pencil skirts and peplum blouses. The instructions said I was to wear the uniform with black high-heeled pumps, uniform hat, and white gloves; the hemline was to be three inches below the knee. Women in the '60s wore wide belts and called them miniskirts. I cried. I could not believe they were going to make me go out in public looking like that. But wear it I did, and several weeks later with no orientation or training of any kind, I boarded a plane at Travis Air Force Base full of young GIs and only one other woman dressed like me. Bobbie and I became fast friends and still are to this day, due in large measure to that ugly uniform. Once we got to our first duty station, the women there said, "Roll up that skirt. Get rid of the gloves and heels. You won't need those here."

The flight from Travis took eighteen hours. We landed in Saigon, a shock physically, culturally, and emotionally. It was extremely hot and humid; the air was heavy and pungent. We were exhausted and somewhat confused—jet lag, I guess. Bobbie and I were separated from the troops and sent to a military hotel for three days of orientation before being assigned to our units. We spent hours filling out a mountain of paperwork, getting our military IDs and travel orders, and declaring our next of kin in case of emergency. It wasn't until a clerk handed us our noncombatant card that I started to get nervous. He told us to guard those cards carefully. In the event we were captured by the enemy, we were to turn the card over to the VC (Viet Cong) so they would know we were noncombatants. That recruiter never mentioned the possibility of being taken prisoner. She said we'd be assigned to safe locations. That little white card printed in English with my photo didn't do much to make me feel any better. When the clerk handed me my card he said, "Welcome to Vietnam, Cathleen. The circus is just beginning."

After orientation, Bobbie and I were sent to different locations. My first assignment was as a Recreation Specialist to the Free World Service Club in Tay Ninh. Tay Ninh is situated along the Cambodian border near the infamous Ho Chi Minh Trail, at the foot of Nui Ba Dinh Mountain, which in those days was known as "Rocket City." So much for safe locations. Tay Ninh base and airfield were carved out of the surrounding jungle, so that any area that wasn't covered with blacktop became a dust bowl in dry season, and a sticky, muddy mess during the monsoon rains. I arrived in Tay Ninh in a "Huey" helicopter, in a cloud of dust during the dry season. I soon learned that Tay Ninh was called "Rocket City" because the Viet Cong frequently fired rockets and mortars on the base trying to destroy the airfield and other military targets. My first view of the base from the air was sobering. It looked like a scene from the TV series *MASH*, but I already suspected this would be no comedy—no Radar, no Hot Lips.

I lived in a bunker for six months with two other Service Club women and a puppy named Chiquita. The bunker was our home or "hooch," as they were called. It was constructed of lattice and wire: our protection from incoming mortar rounds. Of course, if we got a direct hit on the bunker it was all over, but the sandbags that were piled four feet high all around our quarters and on the roof would supposedly protect us from flying shrapnel.

The hooch was a three-room "dorm" with a bathroom and running water from a storage tank outside warmed by the sun. Inside we had a tiny "kitchen" area with a sink, nothing more; outside, our hooch was surrounded by a high metal fence, topped with razor-sharp concertina wire, with an armed guard twenty-four hours a day. Our hooch was located near the Philippine Army's mortar platoon that fired rounds into the jungle at all hours. But we soon learned to differentiate between incoming and outgoing rounds and could sleep through the noise. The hooch was nothing fancy, just a safe place to sleep. We spent most of our days working at the Service Club.

We worked with the troops from the Twenty-Fifth Infantry, the Philippine Civic Action Group, and the First Cavalry units. Later, I would be transferred to Di An with the First Infantry, and then to the Mekong Delta to Vinh Long with the 365th Aviation Battalion. We were purposely transferred frequently because there weren't enough American women to staff all the clubs, and because they didn't want us to become overly attached to any one unit. Service Clubs were initiated by the Army during World War II, and were traditionally staffed by women in order to free the men for the more hazardous military tasks. It was the same in Vietnam.

My job was to run a Service Club. They no longer exist as such in today's Army, but can best be compared to community recreation centers. They were meant to be safe, clean, "homey" places, open 10 a.m. to 10 p.m., where soldiers could come to relax, read, listen to music, play pool, write letters home, or just get away from it all for a while. We were supposed to have three women assigned to each club, but often there was only one American woman there. Soldiers would frequently come to the Service Club just to talk to the "Round Eye" who worked there. The GIs called all American women "Round Eyes." They did a lot of talking, and we did a lot of nonjudgmental listening. We heard more than we ever wanted to know at times. They would tell us exactly what they'd been through in combat, what had happened to their buddies, and what they had done to the enemy.

The GIs called Vietnam the "World of Hurt," and after a while we began to hurt with them. We felt like sponges soaking up all their stories, their hurt, their pain, their fears, and their anger. We had to learn to shut down emotionally in order to maintain our own equilibrium and get our job done. We learned to deny our own feelings and fears. We had to remain aloof or run the risk of being hurt ourselves. We learned that getting too close to anyone meant that they could be lost in the blink of an eye. Death was an everyday occurrence in the World of Hurt.

Many times the soldiers were brought directly out of the field and literally dropped at our Service Club doorstep. They would be armed to the teeth, tired, dirty, and smelly; some were still shaking from their adrenaline rush, unable to hold the cups of Kool-Aid or coffee we offered them. Others were still in shock from whatever it was they had gone through that day and just wanted to be left alone. Our job as caregivers was to be positive, cheerful, and supportive at all times; to smile and provide diversion to the death and destruction that was part of their existence. A tall order for any twenty-year-old with little life experience. One young soldier I tried to console looked at me and said, "What do you know about anything? You're just a war cheerleader!" I was stung and hurt by his harsh words, but I learned that sometimes there are no words that can console and it's best to just be quiet and empathize.

In today's jargon, our civilian mission in Vietnam could best be defined as "stress management" under the ultimate stressor: war. A Red Cross "Donut Dollie" friend, Sara Haines, puts it this way: "We went there to be life affirming in an arena that destroyed life. We listened, suspended judgment, and tried to cheer and console the best we knew how."

Of course, there were the "other duties as assigned," which could range from working in local orphanages and military hospitals, to searching for female prisoners of war. We also frequently hitchhiked on helicopters to fire-support bases, bringing hot food and mail to the troops to provide them some rest and respite from their stress. Another Red Cross friend of mine describes our work in her poem:

Genie

I flew to desolate fire support bases
Home of the tools of war
And the men who used them

It was my job to perform the miracle
Of making war disappear (however briefly)
For boys who had been trained to kill

It was my mission to raise the morale
Of children grown old too soon
Watching friends die

It was my calling
To chase away fear and pain with hope
To return sanity to a world gone mad

I was the "genie," the master of illusion
I pulled smiles from the dust and the heat
The magical genie of "back-in-the-world"
Creating laughter from the mud and the hurt

But when my day's work was done
I crawled back into my bottle
And pulled the cork in tight behind me

That, in a nutshell, was my civilian service in Vietnam. I can sum it up as the best and worst year of my life. It was a life-altering experience. I was fortunate. I came home changed but relatively unscathed. Some of my sisters were not so lucky. Of the estimated 11,000 military and 20,000 civilian women who volunteered for service, eight military and sixty-five American civilian women died in Vietnam during the war. Many more came home with Post Traumatic Stress Disorder and exposure to Agent Orange, and have had their lives forever damaged by that experience.

I certainly don't regret having done my part in Vietnam. I did the best I could for those who had to be there. Then like the Genie of Back-In-The-World, I came home and pulled the cork in tightly behind me.

**Author's Note: Poem "Genie" reproduced with permission
by Emily Strange, Donut Dollie, Vietnam.*

Earth's Children

Julie Ann Schrader

Verse One

I am the youngest of all earth's children
I need time to learn
of lovin' safely under cover
where a fragile mind can turn

Chorus:
Oh, spare me from the people
who surrender all their dreams
who take what's easiest to get
though it's never what it seems

My bedroom is tiny, windowless, and boxy. Cracks meander from one corner of the concrete walls to the next, threatening to bring them down. A double mattress claims the floor, leaving a narrow path around it for my clothes and my guitar. I pay only $10 rent per month. I don't require much room. Ben and I threw away all our extraneous belongings, like deodorant, makeup, razor and shave cream, my bra and his briefs, in an act of solidarity, declaring our resistance to materialism and superficiality. We are long-haired, bell-bottomed, and full of idealism. I float within a matrix of kindred spirits, "furry freaks" who inhabit the rooms in our house on the hill. Out back, an elongated workshop extends down the sloping driveway. It serves as a spare crash pad, with makeshift bunks, running water, and the musky stink of draft dodgers. It's 1970, I live in Berkeley, aka "Berserkley," where the vibes are "far out and anything is possible."

Twins, Linda and Lorelei, inherited the house, and opened it to truth-seekers of every shape and hue. We are guitarists, drummers, dancers, singers, and philosophers. We cook and eat brown rice and tofu together, listen nonstop to the Moody Blues (*Threshold of a Dream*), Led Zeppelin (*Whole Lotta Love*), and the Beatles (*Sergeant Pepper's Lonely Heart's Club Band*). I panhandle on University Avenue decked out in a fringed poncho and a peace sign I've embroidered on the front. My wardrobe comes to me courtesy of the "free box" on Euclid Avenue. My favorite skirt is an East Indian mirrored cloth sewn onto a corduroy waistband, with a hem of orange and red diamond shapes and bangles that tinkle as I move. I weave flowers into the love braids that decorate my long wavy hair.

One day I find a weathered wallet on the sidewalk. I finger through it and count $360. I wait, pondering the Golden Rule. A guy with a halo of wiry hair runs up, searching the ground.

I hold the wallet out to him. "Yours?"

He bear-hugs me. I catch a whiff of patchouli. "Outta sight, man. This is my rent money!"

Life's actions send out ripples like stones dropped into a pond.

I left my home in Wisconsin for the unknown, inspired by an article in *Life* magazine depicting a group of people wearing big smiles and little else at a love-in. They were "turning on, tuning in, and dropping out." If I remained in Wisconsin, I would marry my college sweetheart, teach Sunday school, have a family, and live the life my parents lived. My future was locked in. The thought of it terrorized my spirit. Not long after I read the article, a portentous "waking dream" gave me the final impetus I needed. On the University of

Wisconsin campus, during a particularly unforgiving winter, I glanced out my window and saw palm trees and ocean in place of snow and sleet. I rubbed my eyes. Then hail hit the windowpane, and "California Dreamin'" had vanished. My heart was telling me to go.

I dropped out that semester and made my way cross-country with my Martin guitar and my knapsack slung over my shoulder. Later I would write a song called "Wisconsin," in an attempt to ease the pall of abandonment written across my parents' faces when I said good-bye.

৯৮

Who are we? We are freedom crusaders, spiritual seekers, love revolutionaries. We've ripped the reins out of the hands of our parents, teachers, churches, established institutions. We come together in answer to a universal call to create a better world. Our building blocks consist of peace, love, and mutual understanding, blended against a backbeat of rock 'n' roll. Our mass movement raises consciousness as well as eyebrows. Our outer world mimics our inner. We don't know where we're headed, or how long this will take. We thrive inside the Mystery.

৯৮

I lean forward to kiss Ben. We've finished our meditation, in Eastern posture, sitting cross-legged and staring into each other's eyes. This time his face crumbles away and an inner landscape opens before me.

"I'm heading out to write," I say. He smiles and squeezes my hand. He will continue to sit, I know, until his legs cramp. I can't last as long as he can. I braid his dark ponytail before I leave. Friends tell us that we look like we could be brother and sister. We are close enough that we send messages through our dreams.

⋆ℰ

Lights. Blue. White. Spinning, they bounce off the outside of the workshop windows, pulling me back from my writing. After leaving Ben in meditation, I spend the afternoon sequestered here with my Martin, paper, and pen, laying down the verses and chords to "Earth's Children," my latest song.

The sun sits low in the sky. I close the workshop door behind me as I start up the driveway, my Martin in hand. The lights again, whirling brighter now. I startle, staring at a half-dozen police cars fanned out around the house, their grills pointing toward the front door like weapons aimed. A panic weakens my legs. I drop low and peer through the living room window. Inside, Ben and my housemates kneel on the floor, hands cuffed behind them. Papers, pipes, and bags of pot are dumped into a pile. Numb, I force my clumsy feet to move down the hill. I don't look back. Shaking, I walk to a familiar dormitory a few blocks away. Alone in a strange bed that night, I hold onto my Martin like I would a lover.

⋆ℰ

Ben. I first saw him at a Berkeley student union hootenanny. Across the room, his back to me, he worked his twelve-string guitar. A tingling sensation seized the center of my forehead. All of my senses sharpened into focus. A rushing sound, like a waterfall, came into my ears, drowning out the chatter of people sitting around me. Every nerve cell demanded that I pay attention. The outer world faded to background as a light, subtle and soft, gathered in front of my vision. A soothing calm washed over my body. My breathing slowed. The light drew more light to it, forming into a luminescent globe. It extended into a beam, white with a bluish tinge, shining out from my brow, across the room, and into the back of his head.

Spellbound, I reached over to my friend.

"See that guy?" I pointed at his back.

"Uh-huh?"

"We're going to be together."

He stood up and walked past us. He was tall and wiry, his long dark hair reached his shoulders. Green, almond-shaped eyes. Zowie. And he played guitar! I overheard him telling some friends that he was going backpacking in the San Bernardino Mountains. Then he was gone.

I scanned the avenues for him, based on that beam of light and my certainty that we were meant to be together. Two months later, he passed me on the street, wearing a navy-blue peacoat with his guitar over one shoulder. I had to act quickly. His stride was long and he would disappear again if I didn't do something.

I touched his arm. He turned his kind eyes on mine, and said, "I've been waiting for you."

✤

The arraignment is scheduled for the following morning. I will do whatever I can to help. All I own of any value is my Martin, although I have no idea of its actual worth. This night, there are no dreams from Ben.

I ride several buses to get to the courthouse and sit behind the banister as my bedraggled friends stand before the judge. They are held on charges of possession of illegal substances. Bail is $50,000. There will be a trial.

As they file out, Ben sees me. He frowns and shakes his head. His look tells me that it isn't safe for me here. I shrivel. Of course. They would have collected my driver's license during the raid, and there must be a warrant out for my arrest. My heart rises to my throat. In that instant I am demoted from "flower child" to felon. My face flushes as I slink out the door.

Verse Two

I am the oldest of all earth's children
I've had my time of pain
Of one too many wooden lovers
And growin' half insane

Chorus:
Oh spare me from the people
who think they've found the cure
who publicize their empty lives
and then die from exposure

My morning ritual: I wake up and record my dreams in a note-book next to my bed. I grab a mug of coffee, my Martin, and sit on a braided rug near the sunny window to craft songs. Hours go by. I forget where I am. I don't eat, nor do I take a break. For me, this generational shift in consciousness is centered around music—my own, and all of the artists who are instruments of the message.

Locked away, my friends are depending on me. Isn't that what we're about, all for one, and one for all? I must step up. But my Martin! She was a gift from someone who believed in my music. With her I share my songs with the world. Her smooth tone that drips honey keeps my songs sweet. Her glossy rosewood insists that I write to inspire Truth. Smaller than average, she fits comfortably in my arms while my fingers fly over her frets. Selling her would not be a sacrifice if I didn't love her so.

I spend several nights at the dorm, tasting falafels and tahini, downing cups of coffee, and waffling with my decision. When dawn breaks on the third morning, I know what I must do. My eyes sting as I make a "For Sale" sign and head out to a favorite spot in front of the Berkeley Free Clinic. Wearing my patchwork jeans, big brass hoop earrings, and a fuchsia scarf around my forehead, I open up my guitar case and prop up the sign. I half hope no one will see, all the while knowing my guitar is the *only* hope we have.

In the middle of singing "Earth's Children," a well-dressed woman lingers nearby. She looks older. I remember the hippie rule, "Don't trust anyone over thirty." She wears nylons, high heels, and a lovely silk dress. Her hair is swept up, leaving a few tendrils framing her face, on which she wears soft powder and pale lipstick. A tiny heart-shaped pearl hangs from her neck. She listens to another song. I smile at her. She steps forward, her eyes on my Martin.

"How long have you been playing?"

"Since I was a little girl."

"Did you write these songs?"

A slight nod of my head.

"You have a lovely voice."

I blush and look at my feet.

"I notice you're selling your guitar. May I ask why?"

I hesitate. Should I tell her the truth? I look into her eyes.

"I'm trying to raise money to get my friends out of jail." There. It's out. Maybe she'll leave. I hug my Martin a bit closer.

She offers to buy me a cup of coffee. We talk at the Mediterranean Cafe.

"I've always wanted to learn guitar. Yours is a real beauty. How much are you asking?"

"I'm not sure. Enough to free my friends. To get their charges dropped."

Her eyes shine. "Well, my husband happens to be a lawyer."

Those familiar tingles again. Like seeing Ben for the first time.

"Could he help my friends?"

She digs a business card out of her purse, hands it to me, and smiles.

"He specializes in illegal search and seizure cases. From what you've told me, I'm pretty sure he can."

"What does he charge?"

She cradles my Martin in her lap as tenderly as she would her own child.

"How about a trade?"

Verse Three

I am youngest, I am oldest
I am a woman-child
I need a man who's wise with age
And still young from keepin' faith

Chorus:
Oh spare me from the people
Who've stayed outside too long
Who first confront the coldness
But then welcome it along

I pace the sidewalk outside of the courthouse while the lawyer whose wife now possesses my Martin argues before the judge in defense of long-haired, pot-smoking radicals. I linger on the precipice of the unknown, and time slows as it does while waiting for fate to announce itself. I feel disenfranchised, without my home, friends, lover, clothes, identification, and most of all, my beautiful Martin. My arms are so empty without her. Was I crazy to trust my beloved guitar to a lawyer whom I don't even know? And yet, the way his wife and I met, how she walked by just as I was out there—was that random, a coincidence, or was it an answer to my prayer?

The heavy doors open. One by one, my friends depart the dull interior and emerge into the sunshine. They walk along the sidewalk, brightly feathered birds of every persuasion, heading in my direction. My chest expands and the tears finally come. Ben reaches me and puts his arms around me. I know it then. Trading my Martin was worth it. As I look into Ben's eyes, I make a promise to myself. I will always live my life with the freedom I feel in this moment.

❧

Today, as I page through my "Berserkley" photo journal, I smile. We did change the world. Over time, life became more complicated, but I kept my promise. Through it all, I've followed my heart. Deep down, I'm still that wild Midwestern transplant in her peace poncho. The years have played their mischief, but I still wear capes, my hair still falls in waves to my shoulders, and wherever I happen to be, I know that anything is possible.

Hold Your Head High

Della Barrett

My dad always said, "Don't take any wooden nickels," and I often wondered what he meant.

On a warm evening in the spring of 1972, my two girlfriends and I stood outside the Hilltop Café in our small town in British Columbia. We were sipping soda pop and hooting about the basketball game our team had just won, and, of course, discussing the cool guys who had been watching us play. We were fifteen years old, with nothing better to worry about than sports, clothes, and boys.

Mickey, already sixteen, tall and broad-shouldered, pulled up beside us in his dad's new Pontiac. He barely glanced at me, but focused on my friends, Mindy and Gwen, and asked if we'd all like a ride down the hill and home. Laughing, they were ready to jump into his car, when I tugged on Mindy's sleeve and pulled her aside. "I don't want a ride from *him*! Remember..." I stared up into her face, bouncing my head, eyes wide with urgency.

She shrugged me off and shook her head.

I could feel my cheeks flush. "I told you about it, Mindy," I whispered, glancing at the car. "He jumped at me the other night in the dark...remember? He popped out from behind that shed in our alley, then...then he tried to talk me into having sex with him in the plum orchard." My whisper became a hiss. "I was lucky to get out of it."

"Oh, it was no big deal. Really! He was probably just fooling around." She rolled her eyes and adjusted her smooth hair so it tapered precisely to frame the face she'd spent ten minutes fixing after the game. "Besides, there's three of us. He can't bother three of us! And I'm tired. I don't want to walk all the way down the hill and across town in the dark—do you? Come on! Don't be a weenie."

I shut my mouth and followed the two girls into the Pontiac, climbing into the backseat behind the driver, where I could, hopefully, shrink into obscurity. With the windows down, Mickey turned up the tunes on the radio. Carole King belted out, "I feel the earth move under my feet..."

"You girls like this one, I'll bet." He smiled and chatted lightly all the way down the hill and through town. First, he dropped off Gwen at her house and then, as we turned another corner, something shifted uneasily in the back of my mind. He was taking a roundabout way past my house to drop Mindy at hers. When he pulled up in front of Mindy's house, I opened the door and began to climb out. Mickey called my name. "Stay in the car. I'll give you a ride home."

"It's okay," I squeaked. "My place is only two blocks from here." I jumped out to join Mindy who stood near the car listening.

Mickey motioned with his hand and in a softer tone added, "Come on. Why don't you climb in the front seat?" I glanced at Mindy, who nodded her head and turned, offering up a half wave as she walked away. I felt foolish standing there in the dark, so I slumped into the front without making eye contact with him. His window was up now and the air was suddenly heavy, thick with the scent of bad cologne.

We had gone two blocks before it dawned on me to protest. "Hey, where are you going, Mickey?" Pointing to the right, I added. "I live over there."

He didn't say a word, but another block south, he turned left. "Thought we'd go to Pine Park for a few minutes. You'll like that, right?"

"Uh, no...I—I don't think so...it's getting late." I brightened as an idea formed. "My folks know I'm on my way home from the basketball game. They'll be waiting for me." I gave him a solemn look, as if to complain about those darn parents. A similar line had worked well two weeks earlier when he had stepped out from behind the shed near the plum orchard.

Mickey stopped the car at the grassy edge of Pine Park. Reaching across the seatback, he dropped his hand on my shoulder. A cloud of cologne drifted along his opened arm. Brut was my guess. He lifted two fingers to caress my neck. I wondered if he could feel the revulsion tremble down my spine.

With his free hand he undid his belt buckle and the top button of his pinstriped hipster bell-bottoms. I grabbed at the door handle. "Yes, well…I gotta go now. See you later." I lurched out headfirst.

"You're not going anywhere," he growled, attempting to grab my leg. His big hands got my ankle and held on. I kicked and squirmed. When I finally broke free, I landed on my face in the grass. He must've slid across the car seat behind me. Suddenly, he was on top of me, crushing me into the cold, wet grass. Pinned down, panic rose like bile. It was a dark, isolated spot, with no one around. He yanked at my pants, trying to pull them down. They were tight and wouldn't budge, so it hurt. He cursed and pulled my shirt up.

Anger washed over me. With a rush of adrenaline I fought. Scratched. Screamed. Rolled. Torqued my body as best I could. Finally, he slid to the grass. I rammed my knee up between his legs. Hard! He crumbled away, moaning in agony. I scrambled to my feet and ran. Ran across the parking lot. Ran across the empty, dark street. When I saw a row of bushes, I ran to them, hoping to avoid the streetlight, hoping to hide. *Wham!* I hit a barbed wire fence, full force, face-first. Pain shot through my chest and arms in hot, sharp sparks. As I bounced back, screaming, my shirt snagged in the barbs.

I scrambled to get my shirt untangled when I heard him calling from far behind me. Glancing over my shoulder, I saw him standing next to his car hollering, "Get back here!" He was pointing to the ground. Pointing and stamping his feet like a spoiled child. "Come back here right now, bitch."

For the first time in my life, I swore, "Fuck you!" It gave me a surge of power. I shouted it again, louder. I turned and ran toward home, tears streaming down my face. How could I have let this happen?

Six long blocks later, at my backyard, adrenaline still pounded in my ears and a taste akin to hot metal lingered at the back of my tongue. At the back porch door, hidden from the street, I bent forward and heaved onto the lawn. After a minute I wiped my mouth with my shirtsleeve and hung there, bent over, until my breathing slowed. That's when I noticed it—my favorite shirt was ripped. Damn him! My favorite blue shirt! All the girls in my classroom had admired this shirt. With urgency, I dusted it off and patted it smooth. I turned to the house and, still trembling, pushed open the door. The kitchen was empty. All was quiet. My parents must be asleep. Thank Heaven. I slipped out of my muddied shoes, tiptoed to my bedroom, and released a sob, a muffled cry. If they heard me, my parents would surely say I asked for it. They would never understand.

The next day at school, I told no one. I held my head down, trying to melt into the furniture, unseen, and was relieved to learn that Mickey was absent. When I saw Mindy near the lockers, I choked. She had been a lousy friend last night. It took me a moment to figure out how totally pissed I was. She had been my idol. She should have supported me, helped me avoid Mickey. She strolled into the classroom before I could formulate an argument. At lunch break, I walked with her to the Hilltop Café, offering her bits of what had happened at Pine Park. She blew it off as trivial. A girl like her had more important things to worry about. She simply smiled at the cute boy holding the door for us. He gazed at her perfect hair, clothes, and makeup and didn't seemed to noticed me. I was happy about that.

Over the next few weeks, I avoided Mindy and my other friends.

I stayed in my room where it was quiet. When Mom asked about my scratches and the torn shirt, I admitted to landing on the barbed wire fence, but that was all. I swallowed my secret whole and hard and, like a boiled egg, it stuck in my throat. All I could do was gasp for air.

I wondered why Mickey had chosen me as his victim. A thousand times a day, I reprimanded myself for being a wimpy girl and an easy target. This would never have happened to a strong girl like Mindy, I thought. All I had wanted was to fit in with the other girls, to go along with the crowd.

And that's when it came to me. I had been trying too hard. I had become a follower. If I had stood tall, Mickey might not have forced me into anything, period. I did not deserve this. I wished I had gone with my gut feeling that dismal evening and walked home regardless of what the other girls were doing or saying.

One day, alone in my bedroom after school, I overheard my father on the telephone. He was talking to one of my older sisters at college. As he was about to hang up he said, "Don't take any wooden nickels."

Later I asked him what he'd meant. He said, "Don't be a sucker for trouble. And," he added, wagging his finger, "that goes for you too." The heat rose to my cheeks. I turned and hurried back to my bedroom. There among my favorite records I found an album by Neil Diamond. It was the only sound that could soothe me.

A month later, the word was out: Mickey had been charged with rape. He was going to jail for the rape of a girl who lived just down the street. Some students were sneering: "*She asked for it.* She wears short shorts and halter tops! Ginnie's nothing but trash!"

"No!" I blurted, and quickly covered my mouth, my heart racing for being so bold. "NO!" I repeated. "Mickey is the jerk." I said, gaining momentum. "Mickey is the asshole!" They all looked at me, shocked by my language. I was the girl who "wouldn't say 'shit' if she stepped in it."

I stood still. I knew then that I should've spoken up a month ago.

Poor Ginnie. Shame washed over me once again, but this time it was not for being a weak girl, but for being too quiet in the face of evil.

It hadn't crossed my mind to report Mickey to the police on that dark, horrific night at Pine Park. This was the 1970s—the police surely wouldn't have listened to a schoolgirl. And what had really happened, after all? Nothing but a struggle. Mickey would have smirked and denied everything. And I'd have been labeled the liar.

Today, victims can speak up and be heard. Today, the police have been trained to listen. Today, if anyone complains of being bullied or assaulted, we tell them, "Report it."

For my part, I will always encourage young women to just say no, to keep their heads high, and, above all, not to take any wooden nickels.

Headed North on a Southern Highway

Julie Royce

On college campuses across the country students joined marches, flashed peace signs, preached tolerance, and grooved to Bob Dylan and Peter Paul and Mary. But one harrowing night in 1968, as I sat alone in a car, stranded on the side of a deserted freeway, the lyrics that ran through my mind were sung by the Youngbloods and warned, "Love is but a song to sing. Fear's the way we die."

Gloom had hovered around the snakelike ribbon of Highway 10 in Louisiana. Its darkness provided cover for white-sheeted monsters who hid their faces and flaunted intimidation. I worried that approaching headlights signaled Klansmen bearing down on us. My heart rate sped to the frenzied pace of dogs attacking peaceful demonstrators.

The '60s was dubbed the decade of discontent, and peril paraded in more than bleached bed linens. Danger sometimes dressed in blue uniforms with shiny gold badges pinned above the left shirt pocket. A southern freeway in the dead of a December night wasn't the place for a newly married white bride and her black groom to be stopped by the police.

"Slow down," I begged. "Cops look for out-of-state plates."

But he was cocky—a Cincinnati Bengal running back who had adoring fans. He had completed his rookie year with the new NFL expansion team coached by Paul Brown. Five years earlier he'd been playing sandlot football in segregated Beaumont, Texas, where a black kid was expected to know his place—and to stay on his side of town.

He pushed down on the accelerator, and the needle inched from seventy-five to eighty to eighty-five.

"Please…" I turned my head, unable to watch how much higher the odometer of the Olds Ninety-Eight climbed.

Maybe he was proving to me, or to himself, or to the South, where he had chafed under the yoke of racial separation that the rules didn't apply to him. I didn't suggest that on this godforsaken stretch of concrete he wasn't a pro football player, but a dark-skinned man who threatened decades of status quo.

A lethal mix of hate and misunderstanding, racial pride and racial fury, had exploded six months earlier when James Earl Ray assassinated Martin Luther King Jr. Detroit and Watts burned. Chicago and Cincinnati became war zones. Washington DC and Baltimore reeled with broken windows, smashed cars, and rioting. In the Deep South, the backlash against the civil rights movement was palpable, a nervous sweat that clung to your skin and clogged your pores with its gritty taint. It cautioned outside agitators who spouted integration that they should be very, very afraid. A black man, especially a brash black man who ignored local prejudices, was not welcome in Louisiana. Neither was a white woman who had the audacity to fall in love with a man of color. Their going-away party might leave them hanging from the sturdy branches of a bald cypress.

My stomach lurched. Shivers crawled along my arms and back. A small-town farm girl, who'd experienced four years of culture shock at Michigan State University, I was less brave, or had fewer scores to settle, than my husband. I didn't think baiting local law enforcement was sporting entertainment. I harbored no urge to become a martyr on an inky, starless evening in an isolated spot where there would be no witnesses and no justice.

As he drove us along that desolate interstate, I thought back to how we'd met four years earlier. I didn't watch football, and didn't know a first down from a fumble. I had no idea who he was. All I knew was that one night in 1965, on my way back to my dorm from my waitressing job, I walked from Grand River Avenue, across campus to Wonders Hall. Recent attacks on female students made me nervous, but I had no one to accompany me. I did my best to be alert to my surroundings. I got as far as the bridge over the Red Cedar River when I sensed someone behind me. I turned to see a solitary figure step from the path and blend with the trees. I quickened my steps. My shadow emerged and paced his steps to mine.

Ahead of me, outside the Men's Intramural Building, I recognized a student from my dorm unchaining his bike. I strode up to him and said, "There's someone following me. Do you mind if I walk back with you?"

Intense black eyes studied me. "I've seen you in the grill." A close-cut Afro framed his chiseled ebony-colored face. He didn't smile, but looked pleasant, more curious than thrilled to meet me. "What's your name?"

I told him and he introduced himself as Kelly Valery. During the first two weeks after meeting him, I wasn't aware that he'd given me a phony name. Maybe he was toying with me. Maybe he thought I was a football groupie and my story a pretext to approach him. Either way, I was disappointed when he called, asked me for a date, and then admitted he wasn't the fictitious Kelly Valery, but a Spartan football player. I subscribed to the stereotype that the athletic department handed out egos along with green-and-white jerseys.

But he was soft-spoken and polite, charming and funny, not what I expected of a campus jock. Ours was an off-and-on relationship for the next three years. My feelings zigzagged the emotional spectrum. My parents voiced loud objections to the relationship and refused to meet him. But I loved him, though I feared graduation and pro ball would deliver a deathblow to our romance. I was surprised and euphoric when he called me from Bengal training camp and asked me to join him in Cincinnati. We married at the end of the season and packed for a trip to Texas to introduce me to my new in-laws.

A blaring siren halted my reminiscence and flashing red lights gained on us. I gripped my husband's arm. He pounded his fist on the steering wheel, pulled to the shoulder, and turned off the engine. The siren quieted as our pursuer stopped behind us, but the strobe continued its eerie illumination. A beefy, uniformed man approached our car. In the backlight I saw a tight-scowled angular face. Thick neck wattles should have sheathed an Adam's apple too prominent for a man with thirty extra pounds padding his frame. Broad knuckles rapped the window. My husband rolled it down.

"Get out," the stranger said.

My Pavlovic fear response kicked in when I heard his drawl, my bigotry as transparent as the cop's. I started to exit on my side of the car, but he stopped me, "Not you. You stay there." He shined his flashlight on my face. In its backlight, I watched his eyes fill with a look I'd never seen before. Power mixed with disgust. I prayed it was just my imagination, but my body tensed, telling me otherwise. The air in the car was stifling, and I felt dizzy.

My husband stepped out with no jerky movements that could risk misinterpretation. I couldn't hear the conversation between the two men as they walked back to the police car. In the rearview mirror, I watched the officer open the passenger side door and my husband slide into the vehicle. The cop returned to our car, reached through the rolled-down window and yanked out the keys. "I'm taking your husband to the station." He spat the words with such force they sounded more like a threat than a mere statement of fact.

"You stay put."

I slumped further down in the car seat, wrapped my arms around myself and wished I could disappear. Abandoned on the side of the road, questions raced through my mind faster than the speed we'd been driving. *What would happen to my husband? What about me?* It wasn't safe to be left on the side of the road in the middle of the night. Louisiana offered no safe time or place for a white woman married to a black man.

Miscegenation had been a felony there until a year earlier. In 1967, the United States Supreme Court struck down antimiscegenation laws, but the local statutes hadn't disappeared from the books. Unconstitutional and unenforceable, they made the point that a bunch of black-robed old white men could overturn discriminatory laws, but they were powerless to legislate people's hearts.

My terror grew with the ticking minutes. Grimmer thoughts replaced my earlier reflections: In 1964, the year I graduated from high school, three young men were burned by the Klan in Mississippi. In many parts of the South, lynching was a socially condoned method of dealing with uppity black men who threatened the virtue of white women. Beatings, torture, murder. How many, no one knew.

The pretty young face of Viola Liuzzo from a newspaper photo popped into my mind. I had tried to discuss with my mother the tragedy of the thirty-nine-year-old Detroit woman murdered by the Klan. Liuzzo left behind a husband and two children.

Mom had asked, "What was she doing down there, sticking her nose into something that's not her business?"

"That was Liuzzo's point, Mom." I needed my mother to understand. "When Liuzzo left for Selma, she told her husband that the battle for civil rights is everyone's fight."

The generation gap between my mother and me had widened to the point where words couldn't bridge it, and we both mourned a grievous loss.

I traveled the roads of many memories that night as I waited. An hour after I was ordered to stay put, I thought about getting out of the car and running for help. Ridiculous! Where would I run and who would help? I grew frantic, gasped deep breaths to calm myself. Maybe I could lie in a ditch and wait for morning, walk to the nearest town—wherever that was—and call for help. I clutched my purse like a lifeline. It contained a credit card and twenty dollars in cash.

Alone, I wouldn't be accused of trying to mongrelize the races. Guilt played a damning game with my brain. *I was safer without him. Safer if I didn't admit I was his wife.* If I ran without summoning help, I would be deserting him. I had no moment of clarity that suggested a more noble alternative.

I might never see my husband again. Tears streaked down my cheeks for a man whose fate I didn't know. I considered my own precarious position, and a second wave of tears followed. *I am too young to die.* I'd give it ten more minutes and if he wasn't back, I would head into the fields or the swamps and take my chances with alligators or dogs. It seemed preferable to remaining in a car, a waiting victim.

During those ten minutes, I relived the Christmas we had celebrated three days earlier on the *colored-side* of segregated Beaumont. My new in-laws had welcomed me to their smallish three-bedroom, one-bath home and insisted my husband and I take the largest bedroom, the only one with a double bed. My father-in-law collected pecans from a tree in their yard and my mother-in-law baked me a syrupy-rich, gooey pie. In the trunk of our Oldsmobile nestled a bag filled with nutmeats so my husband's northern wife could bake him a proper pecan pie.

My stay in Texas had included a football game between Charlton-Pollard and Hebert. It was held in a stadium disproportionately large for a high school game. Southerners take their football seriously, I was told. I looked around me. I didn't see a white face in that packed 20,000-seat stadium. I hadn't seen another white face the entire week since our arrival. An excited fan a few rows behind me was incensed when a running back fumbled, "You's playin' like a damn white boy," he screamed. He caught sight of me and said, "No disrespect meant, ma'am." I stifled a laugh.

Christmas dinner was barbecued ribs and collard greens. I took a bite of pumpkin pie and wondered who screwed up the recipe. The taste was off, and the strange texture couldn't be camouflaged with whipped cream. When my father-in-law asked for a second piece of sweet potato pie, I realized that what I was eating was only a close cousin to pumpkin pie. My new brother-in-law bought me a leather coat. In a family where every dollar counted, it was a magnanimous gesture.

If my husband didn't return unharmed, how would I explain to his warm, loving parents that because of me their son had been put in danger, maybe gotten beaten or killed. Two tons of blame settled on my thin shoulders.

Before the ten minutes had passed, I saw a car pull up behind me. I didn't know if it was the police, and if it was, whether they had my husband with them. If it were a stranger, how would I explain my situation? The fear I had gotten under control moments earlier resurfaced, and I clasped my hands together to stop the trembling.

A figure emerged from the passenger side of the car: tall, broad-shouldered, the size of a football player. I exhaled my relief as my husband climbed back into our car. He turned on the engine and used the turn signal as he drove away. He kept his eyes on the odometer, and our speed below posted limits. He didn't say a word. He looked unhurt, not a cut or a scratch that I could see.

After twenty minutes I found my voice and whispered, "What happened?"

"Nothing important. They called Coach, and he vouched for me." I had questions, so many questions, but he refused to say anything else about it.

My words keyed into a computer nearly a half-century later can't describe the angry prejudice that drove the civil rights movement. Frightening thoughts examined in the daylight after four decades aren't the same ominous threat they were on that moonless night. Until we headed north on that Southern highway, I had never confronted my own mortality. Never considered that the sun might rise the next morning, but I might not be there to feel its warmth. Never experienced panic so strong it gripped my stomach as though hate was a living thing that reached its ugly hand down my throat, twisted my gut, and left me paralyzed.

Once in a while, when I'm feeling particularly brave, I pull that nightmare from my memory bank and examine it. The times were changing. Not fast enough for some of us. I remain curious about what happened in that Louisiana police station. I believe my then-husband and I escaped unharmed because an NFL football player couldn't go missing. A country that hated a man for his skin color still loved its football. A game I had held in low esteem may have saved our lives.

Part II

Time Waits for No One

The Baptist Girl

Linda Joy Myers

Our bodies are like a photo-plate where images, words, and teachings are etched, a permanent record of where we've been. At times, pure light flows across these images, illuminating our memories into a full portrait of our experiences.

The Baptist Girl's anxiety coursed through my body and mind, despite my pretending to be cool, as I perched on the stool in the art room at the University of Oklahoma in 1969. Before me was a semicircle of students with drawing pads. I tried to appear casual and relaxed, but my face flushed the cadmium red dotting the floor like a Jackson Pollock painting. Grateful at least for the bikini bottom I wore, I questioned my reasoning, having talked myself into being here in the first place to be an art model for my friend Joanie's art class.

Joanie's husband and mine were both professors in the university's chemistry department, and when I met her at the beginning of the year faculty picnic, it was clear that we could be soul mates. She was wearing a poncho, weaving something on a small loom, and sported layers of turquoise and silver jewelry—not a typical professor's wife look. Though it was 1969, we were in the Midwest, where it was still 1959. But on top of that, we were in the Bible Belt state, which pushed us back to 1949.

Only two months before, I'd worn pants in public for the first time, the voices in my head jabbering, "You must always dress like a lady—with skirt, girdle, hose, and white gloves," and arguing with, "What's the matter with you? Just wear what you want like everyone else." I longed to wear pants, jeans, cut-off shorts. To just be normal. I looked around at the artists sketching and painting, wondering what people thought of me. Could I still be acceptable even in pants, even here on this stool modeling? Was I a decent person?

Now I was half-naked and blushing, and the voices had escalated to screams. Every other woman on the planet was comfortable with her body. I'd tried, but the truth was that the day that Joanie asked me to be a model a few weeks prior, I'd just ducked into another room to try on a dress so she wouldn't see me in my underwear— this extreme modesty despite the fact I was married and had a child. I knew I was out of step: Nakedness was the currency of the times; everywhere women were disrobing, freeing their bodies, having and discussing sex, and experimenting with the "rules" that used to distinguish good girls from bad—delighting in the upending of the rules and not caring about being one of the "bad" girls. Where I grew up, you would do anything not to be a bad girl. Bad girls were sinners to be pitied. Prayed for. Ostracized.

As I came out fully dressed to model the outfit for Joanie, she looked me up and down, smiling. "You'd make a great model. You should model for my drawing class. We need new blood."

"Oh, no, I couldn't," I said, sweating at the very thought of it, grateful for the privacy where I'd just changed my dress so my female friend would not see me.

"You'd be a great model! Just try it," she said, brushing back her straight dark bangs. Her silver earrings flashed in the light. Green paint lingered under her fingernails. I admired that—she was a real artist. No white gloves for her.

The voices in my head started arguing.

"You're so hung up. It's all that shame from your grandmother, from the Baptists—get over it."

"But it's evil to be sexy, to be naked. Wrong. Unladylike. Gram would kill you if she knew."

"She'll never find out. Come on—aren't you a modern girl? It's the sixties."

This argument went on for few seconds.

"Okay, I'll do it!" I said out loud, figuring no one would call me. There must be a lot of pretty girls willing to take off their clothes.

"Great, and you get five dollars an hour, too." She grinned and waved good-bye.

That night I told my husband, but all he did was nod and casually say, "Far out." I liked that he wanted me to be cool—we thought we were both as cool as Vietnam War protestors and readers of the *I.F. Stone Weekly*. We'd even tried marijuana a few times. He didn't know that I was still embarrassed to be naked, even with him. It was too shameful to tell anyone. Long ago, I'd learned it was best to keep your true thoughts and feelings to yourself.

My grandmother had rescued me when I was five after my mother left. I loved Gram with a submissive desperation—she was the only person who bothered to raise me, but she did it with extreme control and her own stubborn ideas about what a woman/girl was and wasn't. Born in 1894 on a small farm in Iowa, she was a combination of conservative Victorian woman and rule-bender herself. When my mother was a little girl, Gram left her behind to work in the big city of Chicago, and later sailed to England without her. But she always dressed like a lady.

I know now that her insistence on being a lady at all times had to do with her own proud shaping of herself from a barefoot Iowa farm girl to a sophisticated woman who traveled on fine ships to Europe and wore silk dresses and boas and strappy leather shoes. But when I was a girl, she seemed most unreasonable—never letting me play games on the floor. Ladies didn't sit on the floor. Ladies wore gloves, a girdle, dresses just below the knee; they had perfect makeup, deportment, and quiet voices. They pleased men, they fit in, they were perfect. Did I mention that she also swore like a sailor?

Abandoned by my parents, I was always seeking answers: Why did my mother and grandmother get so angry when mother visited that they broke dishes and yelled so loudly the neighbors looked at us funny later? Why did my grandmother and father fold their arms and spit curses and accusations at each other? Why didn't people just love each other?

At age nine, Gram allowed me to go with the neighbors to the Calvary Baptist church—I'd been wondering about church, about the Bible, and had been asking her questions. In Sunday School, I learned about the good women and the bad ones: the Virgin Mary and Mary Magdalene.

I squirmed in the hard wooden chairs, wondering why the children were kidding around, winking at each other, passing notes. I thought we were supposed to hear stories about Jesus and how he loved everyone and would make everything okay.

During the few years I went to the Baptist church with the neighbor family, I would get saved several times, tearfully coming up to the front as the gospel songs were sung; we were invited to leave our sins behind to become as new again. I thought getting saved would erase the stain of my parents' divorce from my soul. I was taught they were sinners, adulterers, and I believed that their tainted blood was part of me. I kept wanting to believe that I was saved and a good person, but it seemed to wear off. My parents continued to act crazy, and my grandmother grew cruel with her punishments and constant criticism. I shrank into a malleable pleaser and covered up uncomfortable feelings with a smile.

Shame gathered around me like a shawl—for being a girl, for being tainted, for not being perfect. A woman's body was shameful—that was a given. Why else would Jewish law say a woman could not be around men that time of the month? The world taught me that women were not important, subject to the whims of men. After all, men ran the world. Gram contributed to the shame teachings by making sure I was covered up completely—no standing around in my slip—though we lived alone. Legs should be crossed at the knees. From the Baptists, I understood that my body was not important, but also immensely important. That bodies were about sin and scary desires. That woman was about sin, temptation. Evil.

So how did I manage to get married, have sex, and have a child despite all this? The scared and shamed Baptist girl was locked in a closet. I pretended to be okay with sex and my body, trying to bury feelings of shame, but I was still embarrassed about my body, my sexuality, such as it was—and then ashamed of being embarrassed.

$$\mathfrak{F}$$

On the stool in the art class, sweat poured down my ribs. I burned hot with shame—hoping the students couldn't see my distress.

I knew that I'd compromised my role as a model by wearing my bikini bottom—the "real" models were nude, but the teacher told me it would be all right to wear the bikini bottom to class. I couldn't bear to be completely exposed to view. Every time I was scheduled to model, I wrestled with ghostly voices that sucked me into shame. Each time I perched on the stool, sweat streamed down my ribs while my face reflected various colors of the rose. "Down there" was to be covered at all costs, but I also knew that by covering myself I was exposing the very fears I wanted to hide. Every week I would plan to take off the bikini bottom, but shame burned hot inside me, the fears and familiar voices tumbling and swarming in my head. On the modeling stool, I pretended to be casual by sheer force of will. The students and teacher had told me that I was a good model—I could hold a position for a long time without moving. What they didn't know was that it was because I was frozen, afraid to move in any direction.

One day after class, Joanie and I had coffee with David, a friend of hers, who flirted me up. I'd dated only three boys before I got married, and didn't understand the language of men. A few weeks later, after several coffee dates, he asked me to model for him, privately, for a fee. I would be a professional with him as well as for the class.

Wanting to be cool, I said yes. After all, this was a moneymaking endeavor. In the tiny bedroom of the apartment he shared with his wife, he'd rigged a madras bedspread as a backdrop, and after tea, his blue eyes seeming to drill past my secret shame, he asked me if I was ready to pose. To my relief, he wasn't pushy. I kept the robe on until the last minute, but when I let it go, I was naked. My heart was beating fast, sweat was running down my ribs, but his gentle manner and encouraging murmurings helped me relax. With him, I could express my worries about being exposed, but he kept telling me that I was beautiful, that it was okay. He was a photographer, so I no longer had to stay frozen before the lens. I was moving, and he captured me in motion, smiling, moving to the songs of Judy Collins, Simon & Garfunkel. He kept clicking, telling me I was a good model. Perhaps it was possible to be naked and be good. In his eyes, I was both.

Over the following weeks, I continued to wrestle with the old voices inside my head as I bathed my baby boy and fixed dinner for my husband. At parties, I tried to be like those cool women who could do whatever they wanted. I wore an open-weave crocheted dress with a skin-colored body stocking underneath. In the dark, it seemed I was naked underneath, but I was not nearly that brave yet.

Finally, the day came when I decided to face down those voices in my head. If I was going to be a model, I had to do it right. If I was going to be part of this new era of womanhood, the new society my generation was determined to create with freedom of speech, a new attitude toward racial integration, an anti-war and pro-human world, I had to have more courage—to break with my past, to become who I was trying to be: an artist, a person with a voice. I had to start with me.

I set a date for my complete unveiling in the art class, not even telling David as I practiced pushing down feelings of shame. I dreaded the class all day, wrestling with yes and no, but I knew what I had to do. When it was time, I did my best to feel nothing as I stripped down everything and slipped on the robe behind the screen. Heart pounding, I walked to the modeling stool, trying to appear casual, not looking at anyone as I untied the robe and arranged myself on the stool. What were they thinking? They must have noticed—more than half the group were men—but they just bent their heads to their work. Grateful for no reaction, I let the sweat roll down, fierce blushing painting my face, breathing in and out, trying to let go of the old voices. The room began to groove on the sounds of Crosby, Stills, and Nash; the air filled with the sounds of charcoal, the smell of paint. For an hour, I breathed and sweated, doing battle with the forces of the past, still as a statue.

That day and the weeks that followed, as my new self was drawn into being through smooth charcoal lines on white paper, painted with the colors of spring and new beginnings, I sensed a mending of the Baptist Girl. It was only a start to something that would change me, though it would take many years before the transformation was complete. As I watched the lines and colors draw me into being, seeds were being planted for me to one day sit in a semicircle around a model and learn to draw (eventually getting my degree in art). I would know from the inside out what it was like to be up there on the stool, flesh exposed; to be more than a set of lines, dark and light spaces—trembling with life. More than a model, a whole person.

Story Without End

June Blumenson

What is dissociated or repressed—known then not known—tends to return, and return, and return.
—Carol Gilligan

"So where is the little bastard?" my oldest sister asked me as she stood at the end of my hospital bed rubbing my toes. She looked ghastly in the dim florescent lighting. I knew she meant to relieve the tension in the room with her bad joke, but I froze with shame. Unmarried—1965. I turned away to look out the window. Street lamps illuminated gently falling snow. It was Christmas.

My brothers, sisters, and their spouses had left their kids knee-deep in wrapping paper to visit me. Now, they gathered around my bed, too polite to leave before visiting hours were over. They kept their coats on, eager to get back to their homes where fake snow and tinsel hung from their trees, away from the problem of their youngest sister. I smelled holiday cheer on their breath, just like I did when Dr. Peterson had arrived midafternoon to deliver my baby and bring me a pony of whiskey. The nurses flirted with him. Everyone was in a party mood. Except me.

Shortly before my visitors arrived, I'd hobbled to the nursery, looking through the window like a kid outside a toy shop, nose pressed to the glass, searching the sea of bassinets. Which one was mine? High on drugs and hormones, a part of me wanted to shout, "Unto me, a child is born." Instead, I lingered in the stark hospital corridor, a pariah, silent, utterly alone, amazed that after the fullness of pregnancy I could be so empty. Everything gone. Any trace of milk in my breasts dried up, shot away with stilbesterol, the drug prescribed for unwed mothers. I had only the pain from the episiotomy. I asked a nurse if I could see my baby, but she quickly shuffled me back to bed. I started crying, screaming at them. The head nurse called the doctor to issue orders to sedate me. Heavily.

A few hours later when my family arrived to visit, I lay still. My lungs seemed filled with water. Blood rushed to my head. I felt hot, unfocused, disemboweled. I could see their mouths moving as I drifted away, alternating between hovering on the ceiling and swimming underwater like porpoises I saw in a cartoon. Bubbles floated from their mouths and one said to the other, "Although humans make sounds and occasionally look at each other, there is no solid evidence that they communicate."

What was my sister saying? Where was my baby? I was nauseated from the smell of antiseptics and floor wax. The bathroom door hung open, exposing the edge of the sitz bath. The painkillers had begun to wear off. My vagina stung. I needed to pee. My sister's words kept ringing in my ears, "Where is the little bastard?"

From some distant place my voice answered. Disembodied. "I don't know," I told my sister. "I'm not allowed to see him." So it began, the epidural deadening of my mind.

❧

The next day, a hospital social worker, stiff and exacting, arrived at my bedside carrying a clipboard. He flipped through forms and gave me a pen to sign on the highlighted spaces without explaining anything other than hospital policy. "You cannot see or hold the baby," he said, staring at my forehead. Clearly, unfit must have been written there. He scurried away with the signed paperwork, never giving me copies. In his world, I was simply a statistic.

The surrender rate for white unwed mothers in the early sixties was forty percent. I gave birth eight years before Roe v. Wade would be passed in 1973. Although the pill was available in 1961, only married women could get prescriptions. Spermicides, condoms, and quick withdrawal were pathetic choices for contraception in a time when mothers did not talk to their pubescent daughters about sex. We learned the hard lesson of shame. Our bodies were problems that every woman needed to figure out for herself how to solve.

At my last postnatal checkup, my doctor's advice was, "In the future, keep your knees together." His message was clear: deny your sexuality. Still, he was well meaning and advised me not to get involved in the medical details of pregnancy or labor since I was releasing the baby. He didn't inform me of the effects of smoking on the fetus. The Attorney General in 1964 warned that smoking caused premature births. I smoked a pack a day. Health risk labels didn't appear on cigarettes until 1970. Fetal alcohol syndrome wasn't recognized until 1973. Some studies today link breast and testicle cancers in adults to stilbesterol given to their mothers.

I was twenty-two, on the cusp of adulthood, and the cusp of a huge cultural change. These were the transition years, one foot in tradition, the other in the New Age. One minute we were kids playing jacks, jumping rope and chanting with girlfriends, "We like Ike." The next minute we were protesting the Vietnam War in the Age of Aquarius. It was the sexual revolution. Still, if a girl got pregnant, it was her fault. "Date rape" didn't exist, and "no" meant "yes." If the guy didn't succumb to a shotgun wedding, he wasn't chased out of town, his dreams weren't shattered. No DNA testing, no paternity suits, no postpartum blues. There were no good choices, only forced marriage, illegal abortion, adoption. Life as a single mother didn't seem possible. It was a culture of pretense and stupor. I made decisions given the circumstances of my existence, and looking back, it seems it couldn't have happened any other way.

It is 1965, summer stock, before my junior year in college. Back stage, after the performance of the historical drama, *The Lewis and Clark Story*, I remove the long black braid extensions that I weave into my hair each night transforming myself into the Indian guide, Sacajawea. Night after night, in a tightly choreographed scene, the brutal fur trapper Charbonneau viciously beats the Indian woman he has impregnated. He grabs me by my hair, raises a hand to hit me, and as he slaps his own palm hidden in my hair, the sound reverberates in the amphitheater. I turn my face as if he really strikes me. Then he throws me to the floor where I curl, stomach upstage, into the fetal position, and he quickly thrusts his boot under my knees, flipping me over. From the audience perspective, it looks as if he has kicked me in my swollen belly.

After the show is over, the great-granddaughter of Sacajawea comes back stage to my dressing room to meet me. She is elegant. Gracious. She asks me to sign her program and, to honor her, I ask her to sign a program for me. She writes. *Thank you. You have given me a beautiful portrayal of my great grandmother.* When she leaves, I stare at myself in the mirror. My eyes, accentuated by heavy eye makeup, are big and luminous. I notice circles under my eyes. I feel a strange affinity with the pregnant Indian maiden. Tomorrow on Monday the stage is dark. I won't strap on the pregnancy padding for a performance. I've asked fellow actor, David, who plays the part of Charbonneau, the wife-beating fur trapper, to go with me to see a doctor. In real life, he is a kind and gentle friend.

David sees the bad news on my face when I come out of the doctor's office. We drive in silence to the house he rents for the summer with other members of the cast. I am relieved no one else is around as I sink into his unmade bed and curl into a ball. Slowly, the tears come. He gently takes my hand. "What will you do?"

"I don't know. I'm scared." David doesn't know my boyfriend, who is also an actor, and is in a summer theater production five hundred miles away in a different state.

"I can't marry him. He is even more of a mess than I am. We both drink too much, but he is hardly ever sober."

Then in a spontaneous attempt to rescue me, David blurts out, "Maybe I should marry you." We laugh at his noble gesture, at the terrible confusion of what it is to live in a time of social upheaval, and at the sad truth that although I play the part of the Indian girl pathfinder, I am lost.

✤

My brother Gary, two years older than I, was the first person in my family I told I was pregnant. I was always his tagalong sister. Still in shock with my news, I hadn't formed a plan, but within a heartbeat, he offered to adopt the baby. He had been married for almost a year. I talked with his wife, and she said they were ready to start a family. It seemed the perfect solution. We agreed the child would grow up knowing me as an aunt. If the day came and he wanted to know who his parents were, it would be revealed. Four years later, they had a daughter of their own.

I didn't tell my best friend until late August before she went back to college. We drove to the Missouri River and crawled out on a piling under the bridge like we had done as teenagers. We'd sit and watch cigarettes, pitched from cars overhead, fall like shooting stars into the water. We'd belt out our watershed song "Summertime." Life was easy. The future was waiting for us to spread our wings and take to the sky. But on this day, things were different. My pregnancy was like a line drawn in the sand between us. Her future was flying high. Mine was dulled and uncertain. I could see fear in her face when I told her, and then relief. We both knew this could have been her; it could have been every friend we knew.

"So you won't get married," she said more as fact than question. She knew my boyfriend's drunken reputation.

"Every night he calls, dead drunk, and claims he loves me. The next day he's hungover, cold and distant. He's unreliable, an alcoholic. Neither of us are fit to be parents."

She put her arm around me and let me cry it all out. "What will you do until the baby comes?"

"Mom wanted to send me to a home for unwed mothers, but my sisters convinced her to let me stay at home. With conditions."

"That doesn't sound good."

"The story line is I've returned to college. I'm not allowed to answer the phone and when anyone visits, I have to hide in my room."

"Like you're in prison."

"More like invisible. I won't exist."

That was my future, like so many women from that era. We were ghost mothers, expected to vanish. A month after my son was born, I moved two thousand miles from my Midwestern home to Miami, found a job, and got on with my life, just like "the girls who went away" were supposed to do—to act as if our children never happened. It's difficult for younger people today with progressive attitudes toward single mothers, open adoptions, and legislated reproductive freedom to comprehend the trauma caused by the shaming culture and repressive laws that existed before the mid-seventies.

In the early sixties, the world was changing and I wanted to be part of that change. I didn't want to repeat the mistake of my oldest sister who had married an abusive man when she was sixteen because she "had to." I challenged the idealized domesticity of the '50s and '60s sitcoms, the degradation of women in television comedies. But mostly, I concluded from familial sampling that marriage did not mean happily forever after. It was more often the end—of education, of dreams, of independence.

No one in my family could foresee the way things eventually unfolded, the years of estrangement between me and my family. The first time I saw my son he was three years old. When he was seven, my brother and his wife divorced. My former sister-in-law got full custody. At the time of the adoption I was so relieved to know that my son would grow up in a stable home, and that I would always know where he was and could see him, that the warning of my brother's adoption attorney didn't register. "You have no idea," the attorney told me, "how desperate people become in these matters. How time can change everything. Think long and hard about what you are doing."

Under the circumstances there was no time to think long and hard. It has taken me decades to realize how marginalized I was during my pregnancy and in the adoption process. Everyone assumed I had no rights, no voice. I had no representation and was asked to sign papers without fully reading them and to accept the secrecy of my identity. After I left home, no one in my family contacted me for years. I was disposable. Irrelevant. Slowly over the years, my brother repaired his relationship with his former wife to the point that he was allowed to see the children a few times a year. But when my son, at fifteen, asked directly who his birth mother was, my brother disavowed our agreement and did not tell him. He had his reasons: his visiting rights were fragile, and I was perceived as a threat by my former sister-in-law, rather than an addition of love and support in my son's life. Although I revealed the origins of his birth to my son when he was twenty-one, the legacy of secrecy continues with his grown children. My son told me his allegiance will always be to his adoptive mother, and I will only be acknowledged as his aunt. At family gatherings, I am the elephant in the room.

It is human nature to long to come out of the shadows. Every spring, I want to receive a birthmother card from my son. I want to be more than a distant great-aunt to my grandchildren. I want to connect the truth between the lines on the family tree. I want my only daughter whom I gave birth to when my son was fourteen, to be acknowledged by her half-brother. Although I was at an age of legal consent when I gave up my child, I can see now how incapable I was of making a truly conscious decision. Traumatized by the loss, something essential severed inside me. The tremendous loss, the exclusion and silence over the years, left me emotionally thwarted, unable to heal completely because the wound has never been wholly acknowledged, nor have I been able to celebrate joyously the birth of my son. But back then, my family offered a solution, and the decisions we made seemed right to all of us. I have to believe this. It is the only way I can ever forgive myself.

Woodstock or Bust

Jasmine Belén

"Question authority!" a sista with beaded dreads yelled from a podium in Times Square. "Stop assuming the rhetoric of the warmongers is the gospel truth. It is not for God or our country's safety that we are fighting for. Bring our soldiers home from Vietnam! It's time for revolution. Are you ready?" She shook her fist high in the air. Her bellowing voice incited a roar from a swirling sea of tie-dyed hippies.

I leapt to my feet as fast as a pregnant sixteen-year-old girl could. "One-two-three-four, we don't want your fucking war!" I yelled at the top of my lungs.

Political unrest filled the air in the summer of 1968. The peace rally planted a seed of hope in my psyche. I swooned and grabbed my friend's arm. "Whoa, the baby's kicking hard. It wants to be part of the protest, too."

Kathy tenderly patted my exposed belly, which was plastered with peace symbols. We looked like sisters with our waist-length dark hair.

I told Kathy, "Before this war, I'd never even heard of Vietnam. My mother said war will always exist. When I told her our generation could change the world, she said my starry-eyed attitude would lead me to nowhere land."

Kathy responded, "Nowhere land? I wonder if she knows that's a Beatles song."

In August of 1969, nineteen months after my son, Bobby, was born, I rented a house with Kathy. We were ostracized unwed teenage mothers who wanted to tune out and defy our strict Catholic upbringing.

A few weeks later I burst into our parlor. "I scored two tickets to the Woodstock festival tomorrow and got us a ride in this cool VW van!"

"Far-freaking out!" Kathy yelled. "I'll get my sister to babysit."

Nabbing a ticket to the sold-out event was a major coup.

That night as I lay with the baby I felt pangs of guilt. I craved having three days of no responsibility, but hadn't been separated from Bobby for more than a night. I often felt cheated of the freedom that other teens had.

When the VW pulled up the next morning, my body tingled with excitement. Every inch of it was crudely painted with daisies and anti-war slogans. We taped up a sign that said "Woodstock or Bust."

The energy was contagious. Six people piled in, clad in their most outrageous hippie outfits: tie-dyed skirts, beaded headbands, and far-out looking shades. We grooved on the new song by John Lennon, "Give Peace a Chance." Surrounded in a cocoon of love with total strangers, the two hours to upper New York State passed quickly. A Jamaican guy with matted hair said, "Let's drop our acid now. We'd be totally stoked by the time we arrive."

Despite my doubts about tripping in the bus, I said, "Cool, lay it on me!"

After Kathy and I each swallowed a Purple Haze tablet everyone burst into a Jimi Hendrix's song. As the van made its way through the suburbs of New York, Kathy dug around in her knapsack. "Shit, man, I forgot my halter top! Can we stop at a store?"

"Sure babe. Be back in a half hour."

When Kathy and I entered the store, the first rush of the drug hit. I gripped a railing to steady myself. "Let's make this fast."

Kathy rifled through the halters while we laughed uncontrollably. "Just buy that one. It's cute. We need to split before I flip out," I said.

"The acid is scrambling my brain. I can't stand here anymore. I'm going to swipe this," Kathy whispered.

"Whatever," I said as she slipped it into her handbag.

We headed toward the exit but two stern-looking men stopped us. "Girls, follow us to the office."

I tried to charm my way past him. Sweetly I said, "You guys are sure cute but we're in a big hurry. Maybe some other time."

"I bet you're in a hurry. Open your purses."

Kathy swore. "Fuck off. I don't let anyone go through my pocketbook."

The man with the acne scars morphed into Satan. Fire shot out of his eyes. The chunky man's waxy face melted into a grotesque shape. The effects of the hallucinogenic had definitely kicked in. I struggled over loyalty to my friend or heading to Woodstock alone. After all, I hadn't stolen anything.

"You have no right to detain us! We didn't do anything."

The tall man snatched Kathy's purse, pulled out the top, and blocked our exit. He grabbed our arms and herded us into a small, windowless room. "You girls have identification?"

"No! But I'm eighteen and my friend is emancipated," Kathy sniped.

"Give me your parents' telephone numbers." The plump man towered over us. The room was unbearably warm.

They called Kathy's crazy mother, who could talk faster and longer than anyone I knew. Just listening to her made me dizzy. I avoided her whenever I could. "The police are on their way," the security man's voice boomed. The gravity of the situation hit me.

The devilish-looking man shoved me into a chair. "What am *I* being charged with?" I insisted.

"Being an accessory to robbery."

It sounded so harsh. I had no idea I'd also committed a crime.

"I was going to send money later," Kathy lied.

"Yeah, right, and I'm the pope, too."

The full effect of the LSD kicked in. We burst into laughter at the absurdity of being arrested by a pope who looked like a demon.

He growled, "You think this is funny? Wait till the NYPD lock you up and throw away the keys."

My drug-addled mind conjured up images of being shackled in a dank dungeon guarded by a humpback ogre who swallowed the key. "Could you please tell our friends to wait for us?" I pleaded.

"Like I said, girlie, you're going to jail! You'll have a whole new set of friends."

A wave of fear shot through my befuddled brain. What would happen to my baby if I went to prison?

Kathy gripped my hand. Her big brown eyes looked as forlorn as the velvet painting of the doe-eyed waif that hung on a nearby wall. After a short eternity of time we heard the sound of heavy footsteps outside the room. I overheard, "Thanks for apprehending them. That's two more dirty hippies off the highways this weekend."

A chubby officer who looked like a bulldog charged in and glared at me as if I were public enemy number one. He barked, "Stand up and put your hands behind your back." He snapped on the handcuffs. "You have the right to remain silent. Anything you say…blah, blah, blah." His words faded into an incoherent stream of nonsense. When they paraded us past the curious shoppers to the patrol car, I hung my head for the walk of shame.

"You can't keep us very long. I know my rights," I said in a feeble attempt to regain power.

"Hush," Kathy said. "Don't anger them. Maybe they'll still let us go."

In the cinderblock interrogation room we sat under wanted posters trying not to giggle at the hilarious faces that beamed down. The officers grilled us. "Have you been arrested before? Did you choose the Shop and Save store to rob for a particular reason?" An ancient-looking cop with bulbous eyes put his face shockingly close. "Have you ever taken drugs?"

His eyes were as penetrating as spotlights. I was almost sure he glimpsed the psychedelic circus performing in my irises as his features twisted into a kaleidoscope of animated images.

"No! Absolutely not! Can you please let us go? We're both mothers of small children."

"Some mothers! You should have thought of that before you committed a crime."

After we were fingerprinted, an officer led us to the cells. A dappled light shone through a small hall window and created a strobe effect against the shiny steel bars. "Wow! Kathy! You look so psychedelic with the light flashing off your tie-dyed skirt."

Kathy undulated her arms and sang a Hare Krishna song. I marveled at the colorful mosaic trails that crackled around her. After a while she became quiet and pensive. "Remember when we were young and braided each other's hair?"

"Scoot over here," I said. Kathy leaned her head against the bars and I braided her hair tenderly. Then she did mine through the bars. "I thought we'd be doing this at Woodstock. I hate to miss the peace-in."

We heard a commotion in the corridor that grew increasingly louder. "Oh no! Are the villagers coming to hang us for stealing?" I joked.

Three officers appeared with six young people in tow. The raucous group shattered the quietude of the jail. We flashed the peace symbol at them.

"Hey, what bogus charges are you girls in here for?" a long-haired man asked.

A cute guy yelled, "Let's not let the fuzz blow our trips! We'll have our peace-in here at jail stock!"

A resounding cheer went up, and we burst into singing our favorite rock and ballad songs. Kathy and I shook and shimmied our bodies as the men hooted their approval. One guy took off his shoes and beat them on the bars when we chanted protest slogans. "Make love not war," was my favorite. We had two hours of fun before an officer stormed in and demanded silence.

"You can't still our voices! Down with the establishment," a man yelled. The others leaped to their feet and chanted. "Nazi tyrants! Down with the filthy pigs!"

I lay on my cot with my pillow over my ears to drown out the din and visualized slipping through the steel bars that had melted like clocks in a Dali painting.

Around midnight an officer told us, "Since you're both minors you'll be released to Mrs. Paiva. Your arraignment is on Monday." The deputy's eyes spun like pinwheels as he spewed out all the rapid-fired information that Kathy's mother had barraged him with.

"She's lying! We're legal adults," I protested. Apparently Kathy's mom's addled brain could not keep track of how old her daughter actually was. The thought of her talkative parent coming to pick us up was more terrifying than being in jail. "Can't we stay here until our arraignment?"

"This isn't a hotel for minors!" he yelled.

The effects of the drug were still strong when Kathy's mother entered the station. She was an attractive, buxom woman with auburn hair. As she walked down the hallway towards our cells her lips whirred into a red blur. Mrs. Paiva babbled to the disinterested janitor who swabbed the hall, "These gray walls are too dreary. Can't you paint them yellow to uplift the prisoners? Also, the air is stale. You need windows that open."

As she spoke, her lips moved at the speed of light. The officer hastened our release paperwork and opened our cell doors.

Our new friends shouted good-bye, "Peace out, man. Have a groovy trip. Tell the people at Woodstock we're being held for speaking our minds."

Kathy grumbled. "Ma, you didn't need to pick us up. We were fine."

"You call that fine, being locked in a cage like an animal? I thought I was doing you a favor by picking you up. How ungrateful! What about your children? If you go to jail I'll place them in a good Christian home."

When we climbed into the backseat of her beat-up Chevy, Mrs. Paiva said, "Someone should sit with me in the front seat."

"No. We're tired and need to stretch out," Kathy sassed.

"Yes, I guess a life of thievery is exhausting! You girls pull out your Bibles and read up on what Jesus thinks of your actions."

"Ma, Christ hung on a cross next to two thieves and said he'd see them in paradise. Jesus was a freak just like me."

Mrs. Paiva groaned, as if her daughter had stuck a dagger in her back. "That's blasphemy. How dare you take the Lord's name in vain."

Kathy squinted her eyes as she slumped next to me. She yelled, "I didn't Ma! Don't rag on me. I hate you and everything you stand for."

Her mother hollered back. "It is bad enough to be rebellious, but anybody who curses their parents shall be cursed, and find themselves in obscure darkness."

Like dueling swords clicking in the air, the sound of their banter drove me wild. Within the hour, Mrs. Paiva must have said every word in the English language twice. When she ran out of English she lapsed into her native tongue—Portuguese. This was far worse than any night in jail. I wondered how my baby was doing and hoped the sitter remembered the tips I'd left for his care. "Can you stop at the next diner so I can check on Bobby?" I asked.

I whispered to Kathy, "I'm going to take off. Tell your mother I ran into a friend and got a ride home."

Kathy pleaded, "Please don't leave me with her."

"Sorry, I'm blowing this pop stand."

"Me too."

The Dairy Queen was the perfect distraction. Mrs. Paiva stepped up to order some food and overwhelmed the server with her chatter.

"Let's split!" I yelled.

We bolted down the street, laughing wildly. Kathy stuck out her thumb and a cute boy in a Mustang screeched to a stop. She leaped for the shotgun seat. That was cool. Romance was the last thing on my mind.

"We're trying to find a ride to Woodstock," Kathy said, hoping he'd offer.

"Good luck. The freeways are jammed."

My heart suddenly yearned to see my baby. "Can you take me home?"

Kathy's eyes widened with disbelief. "Are you sure? It's not often we get childcare. We can still party."

"Yeah, I'm sure. There'll be other Woodstocks."

During the two-hour ride Kathy chattered. I drifted in and out of consciousness. By the time I reached home the effects of the drug had lessened. I tiptoed into Bobby's room. In the dim light I stared at his moonlit face. I snuggled him close and with a feather-like touch traced his chubby cheeks and stroked his silky auburn hair.

I crooned, "Sweet baby, I hope my embrace is the only armed forces you'll ever be in." Bobby opened his sleep-laden eyes and smiled with delight. His cherub lips pursed and made a sucking sound. My heart swelled and my tough demeanor softened under his spell. I'd never felt love as sacred as this. "I'm going to be a better mother," I promised.

I inhaled Bobby's salty aroma. It was a drug more potent than anything I could ever take. He was the rainbow in my backyard and the love-in I yearned for. My own fabulous Baby-Stock.

Miles away from the festival's hullabaloo, I found my own peace. It was a feeling so divine a heart could mellow in it. The Beatles were right. All I needed was love.

Berkeley Raga

Judith Terzi

I

Mom, the fog is lifting and I can see the Golden Gate,
patches of orange peeking through. Edward Teller's
teaching physics next semester. What a lucky break.

No math problems, just book reports. A professor
from English got fired; he wouldn't sign the loyalty
oath: *Are you now or have you ever been a member*

of the Communist Party? My roommate's always horny,
she's Alabaman and dresses up for dates. Mom, no one
dresses up in Berkeley. There's one pay phone for thirty

girls. I'll be calling soon. I met a Sikh and a Persian.
I'm still a virgin, Mom. Twice you called me a slut—
the time I slouched in Jerry's Buick. (We weren't even

close to…You kept flipping the porch light on and off, but
we didn't care.) And the time I sat on Dave Freed's lap
in Daddy's big beige chair. Lately, we're Twist nuts—

eeh-oh twist baby baby. My pink top sheet just ripped,
I ironed on Bondex; it tore again in the washing machine.
Twisty twisty twisty. Do you think you could ship

some flowery fitted and flats? It rained. The air is so clean.
Did it rain down south? We walk everywhere. I'm losing fat.
Oooh yeah just like this. Having an apartment is my dream.

It would cost $50 a month each for three. Can you beat that?
Maybe next year? I'm losing weight, my shirtwaists are loose.
I don't have chicken legs anymore like in LA. How's Max?

Saw a cute doxie yesterday. Does Maxie miss me? Excuse
all the me me me me's. Have you read Vance Packard's
The Hidden Persuaders? Mom, it's terrible how we are used,

manipulated to purchase. "Lipstick red and ivory tipped"
used to be the slogan for Marlboro; it was a lady's cigarette.
I'm down to six a day. You? Tried Hillel like I promised,

saw schlumpy guys dancing, after ten minutes I split.
Got fixed up with a ZBT Saturday. He didn't even speak
to me, just kept vomiting into sawdust. What a let-

down. I walked back to Bennett Manor alone. Next week
We're going to hear JFK in the city. Found out I'm type O—
a universal donor. Don't ask me for blood. No need to pack

a food box next month. Right now I see San Francisco
from the Student Union. Had three dates on Sunday.
I'm still a virgin, Mom. The bay's shiny blue. Bye, gotta go.

II

Hi Mom. Sorry I haven't written. It's clear, no fog.
All moved into the apartment. Liz went back to Mobile
after our ceiling caved in. I went to hear Carl Sandburg

and stood in line to shake his big hand. I hope Marie will
work out as a roommate. She's not easy to get to know,
hangs with men in North Beach. I still like the Shirelles

but am branching out. Have you heard "Desafinado"
with Stan Getz and Charlie Byrd? It's whimsical, sexy.
Last night there was a mouse in our oven, though no

trace of it this morning thank God. The bay is glittery.
Marie and I saw *The Seventh Seal.* That was my first
foreign film. Didn't get all the symbolism. Having cherry

yogurt and a green apple right now. Went to the dentist,
but he couldn't find the hole in my molar. I met a guy
from Bakersfield. He's cool for being from the sticks.

How's work, Mom? I think Marie is unhappy, disguises
her sadness with sex. A guy came looking for her at 2 a.m.
last week. I was petrified, didn't open the door. She lies.

Each guy thinks she's seeing only him. He slammed
his fist into the door, called her a whore. She wasn't
home, but I got him to leave. This is a big problem:

When I got home yesterday, Marie was sitting in front
of an unlit, empty oven, her head inside. She attempted
suicide. Mom, can you believe my roommate is pregnant?

III

Can't wait until fall to move into a new apartment.
I'll have two roommates, both from LA. I'd like to study
intensive Italian over summer and work. I can rent

a room. Marie doesn't know who the father of the baby
is! I think she's rebelling against her upbringing
in Oklahoma. Mom, don't you? I've got a date Saturday

with my Bakersfield friend. The bay is sparkling.
He wants to hear Joan Baez. The birth control pills puff
me up like crazy, Mom. Oh, my new job involves dishing

up meatballs, corned beef and cabbage, beef stroganoff
in the cafeteria to Saudis and Kuwaitis. There are hundreds
of them here. I've got to finish a term paper for Goff-

Man's sociology class: "How I Got the I and the Me." Hard
stuff. The *I* is the self as subject, the *Me* is the self as object.
Wish me luck. Just paid $10 to get this typewriter repaired—

the *a* and the *t* kept sticking. Saw my very first French flick,
Breathless, by Jean-Luc Godard. I so want short hair
like Jean Seberg's. I understood her because she speaks

with an *accent américain*. My goal is to be fluent in a year.
There's a dry cleaning machine that cleans eight pounds
for $1.50. I think I'll try it. I need a French lover.

IV

I'm in the Bear's Lair now where I'm a cashier,
so I can't see the bay. Our apartment is the greatest.
We each get one day a week for dinner duty. We're

a long way from the slop at Bennett Manor. We roast
chicken and lamb and sauté chicken livers in white wine
with mushrooms. My Spanish prof is often a guest—

he's dating Sarah. I feel uncomfortable each time,
knowing he's grading my papers. Do I really
deserve the A's I'm getting? He's forty, Mom. I find
the age difference weird. When I don't have an activity,
I feel lonely sometimes. I take a walk or lie on the grass
near the creek that runs through campus. Went to a Ravi

Shankar concert. Have you heard of a raga? It lasts
forever and is very emotional. You could say it's a sonata
with frenzied improvisation. I finally bought a madras

bedspread (like Sarah's) at a store with stuff from India.
I can also use it for a curtain if I have to. Mom,
There's a guy who promotes the legal use of marijuana.

He stands right in front of campus. The cops arrest him,
but he always comes back. No, I haven't tried smoking
it, but now I know Marie did. Once when I got home,

she and some of her North Beach men were sitting
on the carpet. I thought I smelled cloves or another
spice. I'm down to three cigs/day. You? I'm practicing

French with an Algerian who came here in September.
Met him in the language lab where I monitor six hours
a week. His name is Boussad. That means luck in Berber.

JFK gave scholarships to Algeria after an eight-year war
with France. Mom, I haven't seen Marie around at all.
Some Kuwaiti guys invited Laurie and me for dinner.

We ate rice and lamb with our hands. You had to roll
the rice into a cylinder with your fingers and thumb;
otherwise it crumbled. We kept the talk superficial:

no mention of Israel. One guy was wearing a long robe
called a dishdasha. He looked like a sheik, I swear,
Mom. These guys have dough; they drink bourbon.

Laurie's signature dish is pasta, so we went next door
for a pan. Our neighbors told us the President had been
shot. We have no radio. I shook his hand, remember?

V

I remember where I was when it happened. That's what
Everyone's saying even now. Mom, were you at work or
out to lunch? Wonder what Daddy would have thought

about Johnson? Laur's interviewing for the Peace Corps.
Sarah's staying on for an MA in English. Are you ready
for a big change, Mom? I finally got my hair cut short

like Jean Seberg's. Sarah and I saw a play by Alfred Jarry,
Ubu the King (*Ubu Roi*). A crazy satire on the abuse
of power and bourgeois greed. Nothing like plays Daddy

and you took me to see. A complete collapse of values.
And crude language. You would have walked out, I think.
I want to come home in June, Mom, live with you

for awhile. I can get my credential later, maybe take
a couple classes at UCLA, find a job where French
is required. Today I can't see the Golden Gate—

the fog is way too thick. There's not a single patch
of orange peeking through. It sure feels like rain.
The wind is picking up. Is it raining down south?

My People's Park

Elise Frances Miller

As my senior year at UC Berkeley came to a close, the People's Park riots delivered the climax to the chain of violence I was practiced in avoiding. I had skidded around some sort of political action every quarter that year. Bomb squads outside Wheeler Auditorium. Lines of students snaking through campus with sticks and boards, breaking every window in sight. The People's Park riots were happening just outside my apartment cloister. All I wanted was to sever myself from the chaos.

That spring, I spent weeknights inside, studying my art history books, occasionally daydreaming to the strains of soft rock on KNBR radio. On weekends, I dated as many grad students as I could in a round robin of faux romance. Escape, and good times. In April, when the first neighborhood residents came up with the plan to transform the university's neglected parcel of land into a beautiful asset called People's Park, I was busy taking the bus to San Francisco, looking for work, an apartment, and roommates. When I finished up in June, I would skip the pomp and circumstance and head for the big city to continue my escape and good times.

My friend Karen had gone up to the new park, her enthusiasm sparked more by plans for the garden than by the politics. She joined the bunch to clean up and plant, kneeling in the mud with seedlings supplied by the organizers. But I had decided that I could not go along with a confiscation of private property. No matter that the university's plot had become a greasy, derelict space, full of drug dealers and vagrants, nor that residents and neighborhood merchants had joined the students in their takeover. I still regarded the action as theft from the university.

Then came May 15, 1969, called Bloody Thursday because a man died that day, another was blinded, and many were wounded with birdshot, buckshot, and bludgeoning. But I knew none of this, buried as I was under piles of class notes and books, until early afternoon when I got the call from Richard McKibbin, a guy I'd been dating for a few weeks. Like me, Richard was no radical. He was in the economics master's degree program, and his ambitions were as East Coast as his V-neck sweaters and neatly trimmed mustache. His voice on the other end of the line was tight and breathless as he described the scene on Telegraph Avenue.

"It's total bedlam," he said. "The cops and soldiers are chasing protesters in all different directions. Can't you hear the rioting from your place?"

I told him to hang on a minute and went to open the sliding glass door in our living room. Our third-floor apartment looked out on the green brick wall at the back of the gas station garage on Telegraph and Parker, just a block from the battleground. The unintended blessing of our terrible view was that it *did* deflect noise.

"Yes," I told him, "I can hear it now." I could smell it, too. With a few coughs into the phone, I shut the window. "I think I can hear them shooting something. Is that the tear gas?"

"Who knows what they're shooting?" he shouted hysterically. "Or *who* they're shooting…" He took a second to calm himself, then continued. "It's probably CS gas. That's worse than tear gas. It's the military issue."

I gasped. "Military?"

"Yes. Governor Reagan sent police to the Park in the middle of the night. They put up a fence to keep everyone out. The protesters and police went at it, so Reagan called out the National Guard to help the police. They're military."

Suddenly, I could barely hear his story. Soldiers against students, I thought, like Paris!

🙧

Exactly one year before People's Park, I had witnessed the historic French May Revolution, with its overblown government-instigated violence against college students conducting peaceful marches for both free speech and an improved educational system. Yes, there were other causes, other "elements" among the students, but on May 3, 1968, I witnessed soldiers with hooded helmets, batons, and bayonets—all eight-foot giants to my eyes—out to round up students for simply assembling in the Sorbonne courtyard.

I was not uninitiated after three years at Cal, but still, I had never seen real soldiers arrayed against masses of unarmed, idealistic, and hopeful students like those in Paris. I believed then, and up until Richard's phone call, that the French kind of overreaction could never happen in my country.

🙧

"Are you listening?" Richard was shouting into the phone. I refocused and apologized. "I was just thinking about the May Revolution last year. You know, I told you..."

"Yes, but I wasn't even a protester! I was making my way to class through that morass of fleeing students, when suddenly a trooper shouted 'Halt!' like a goddamned Nazi. I was just amazed at first. But then a minute went by and this guy was staring me down and I couldn't move forward."

"But I don't get it. Why wouldn't he let you move?"

"I don't *knooow*," he whined. "A power trip? He wore a gas mask, and his fucking rifle was pointing right at me! But instead of getting scared, I was getting kind of pissed off. I started thinking, like, fuck him. I haven't done a fucking thing! The gas was clogging my brain along with my throat, and I couldn't say a word. I guess I was out of control. My hand just went up and I gave the trooper the finger.

"So he pounced. It was like he was waiting for me to give him an excuse. He grabbed me and handcuffed me—shit, was he strong! I went into a paddy wagon. It took me the next two hours to get free!"

"Oh, Richard…are you okay?"

He laughed half-heartedly. "A few scrapes and bruises, mostly to my ego."

I ignored his bravado. "Weren't you scared to death?"

"Scared? Yeah, well, I've never come that close to real trouble before. But mostly angry and damned insulted. The worst was just the hassle!"

Arrested for giving the finger to a National Guardsman? Richard's story *was* dramatic, but I grew cynical when he asked me if I would come over that night to his place. Lately, he had been pushing the idea of our sleeping together. Now he told me that his nerves needed soothing, and I was the lucky girl he had called on for comfort.

He also urged me to avoid the danger. "Walk to class down Dana or even Ellsworth," he advised. "Or better yet, just stay home!"

⁂

That Bloody Thursday, I was not going to let them force me to skip class. Svetlana Alpers was the only female art history lecturer I had had at Cal, and she was my favorite. As I exited my apartment, I worried that my style was too hippie. Shedding my knitted poncho in the cool spring breeze left me in my peasant blouse, jeans skirt, and Birkenstocks. That would just have to do. Looking carefully around from the front door overhang, I snapped a photograph of two National Guard soldiers leaning back to back against a lamp-post right on our corner. The one facing my Instamatic held a huge rifle upright between his laced black boots. A camouflage helmet pulled down over sunglasses obscured his eyes and his humanity.

Across the street, two other Guardsmen paced near their corner. Beyond them were a black VW bug, the cut-rate, trendy shops on Telegraph, the Campanile, and the incongruous green, springtime Berkeley hills. I shuddered. Cynical or not—about the Park and about Richard's need for "comfort"—I took my boyfriend's advice and fled to campus in the opposite direction of those soldiers.

On my walk, I thought about how I was living in a Berkeley as occupied as Paris the year before. I did not want to see it, hear it, smell it. But once in class, I listened with the flag of my mind at half-mast. I was mourning the people I knew were going to be hurt. I realized that here, just as in Paris, the "spoiled" children of the bourgeoisie were allied with middle-class merchants and residents, wanting only to rid themselves of the unsafe abomination in their neighborhood. I could not believe that the university or Governor Reagan cared one iota about that little block of rotting land. Like Pompidou and de Gaulle in France, Reagan would do anything to make political brownie points with his absurd posturing. By the time I left class, I was afraid, but I was also angry.

❧

Outside, I heard the crowds and the whir of helicopter blades from down the hill in Sproul Plaza. Surely, I reasoned, the demonstrators had been quelled by now, probably corralled into the Plaza. I headed down to Telegraph.

And then, just like in Paris—it was impossible not to see it, hear it, smell it—the attacks and violence were all around me. Telegraph was filled with bellowing, bawling, darting protesters, police and soldiers, and ordinary students like me trying to get home.

I hunched over my load of books and tried to run. Keeping alert to the essential weave through the crowd, I caught the eye of a National Guard soldier, just half a storefront away. His nose and mouth were covered with a mask, but in an instant, his eyes revealed that this was not Richard's Guardsman. This was a boy, not older than eighteen or nineteen—and he was panicked! My heart went out to him. I had heard that many of these guys were students, just trying to stay out of the Vietnam War.

Those eyes! Beneath his tense, reddened, puckered forehead, his eyes had narrowed to two slits filled with hatred. I steeled myself to run around him. Before I could move, he pulled at something and sent it flying directly at me—a gas canister exploded at my feet! I could not breathe and I thought I had fallen to the ground, but it was only my armload that had dropped. My throat burned—and my skin, my eyelashes. I choked and cried. Everything dripped and I wanted to vomit.

Backing up, coughing and crying, I managed to croak, "Why... *why did you do that to me?*" His brow knitted in concern over his mask. He knew, as if a slow-motion replay of the prior ten seconds had obscured everything else on the street, that he had screwed up. And then I grabbed my load, jumped over the curb and around him, and ran the final block to Parker.

As I ran, I was already telling Richard about what had happened. And I was saying that our leaders and elders had no respect for youth, even bright, well-informed, and good-hearted youth. Otherwise there would be a negotiation, not a war.

If they could explode a bomb at me—unarmed and clutching a stack of art history textbooks—why would they bother to negotiate? The destruction and bloody aftermath of People's Park proved that extreme measures were the only way: the confiscation of private property. We—and suddenly, I did mean *we*—had barely begun to change our nation. But I would be a part of that change only if I stopped running away and began to pay attention.

Late that night, I replayed my run home down Telegraph Avenue. I remembered crying more from my fear and frustration than from the noxious mist of tear gas. But then came my fiction, my fantasy, my wish for a physical courage I had always lacked. In that version, I picked up my books and purse and stood straight, my dignified, self-assured, twenty-two-year-old self staring down this uniformed teenaged hireling. I suppressed choking as tears flowed into my nose and mouth, tilting my chin up defiantly. And then, the consequences be damned, I raised my hand and gave him the finger. And I walked right on by him with tears streaming into the smile on my lips.

The Wild, Wild West

Jeanette M. Nowak

I'm the youngest of seven children, born and raised in East Los Angeles. Even though I was part of a large family, there was no sense of community or unity and no responsible adult to turn to when things got out of control, which happened almost daily. That's because the "adults" in my life were out of control themselves. As I look back on my childhood, I can only describe it as a combat zone.

My first taste of combat took place in the early 1970s when the drug culture was active and thriving, long before the "war on drugs" campaign took shape. As far as the drug scene goes, it was the wild, wild west, and there was no sheriff in town, especially not in my house.

El Monte, a city in the East LA area, was the type of place even the cops avoided. I had moved there with my mother and five of my six older siblings just after my parents had separated for the third or fourth time, leaving my drug-addicted, mentally unstable, alcoholic mother at the helm of our wayward ship.

As a child, we moved quite often. In the span of two years, in fact, we moved four times. When we moved into the house in El Monte in 1971, it was one of those four houses. I was seven at the time and, to me, it seemed like just another house in a long succession of homes. After only a few weeks, however, I realized that this was not the case at all. The house in El Monte would prove to be the most dangerous place we had ever lived.

The house was nice enough, as I recall. It had all the standard necessities, a yard, a few bedrooms, and a kitchen that seemed to be in the center of the house. The problem was not with the house at all, but rather, with our neighbors. Shortly after we moved in, we realized the Mongols, an extremely notorious and violent motor-cycle gang, were our next-door neighbors.

Stereotypical for a motorcycle gang of the 1970s, the Mongols covered themselves with tattoos, wore black leather, and kept their hair long and dirty. The backs of their jackets bore the name and symbol of their gang, an illustration of a biker riding a Harley. They drank a lot, smoked a lot of pot, and, of course, heavily consumed all sorts of other illegal drugs. They also sold and distributed them, unafraid of the police. The Mongols lived above the law; they were aggressive and highly territorial. They fought a lot and for many reasons, but mostly to defend their right to sell drugs, which was the lifeblood of the gang during its early years. Needless to say, the Mongols were not at all "neighborly."

The Mongols didn't appear to have jobs aside from their drug business, which meant they were always home, and "customers" came and went at all hours of the day and night. And, since they were always seeking to expand their clientele, shortly after we moved in, they began soliciting my teenage brothers to buy drugs. Raul and Danny were twelve and thirteen years old. When they came home and told my mom about this, she simply said, "Just ignore them and they'll leave you alone." But, being good salespeople, they remained persistent.

My two older sisters, Ronda and Lydia, fifteen and sixteen at the time, seemed to attract a lot of attention as well. Young and pretty with slender bodies and long black hair, they were constantly fight-ing off the advances of gang members while passing their house to and from school. Again, my mother's advice to my sisters was simply to "ignore them." But, as we tried to settle into our home, our entire family became targets.

Eventually my mom had to admit that her passive approach was not going to stop the Mongols. Frustrated, she decided to take matters into her own hands. You might say my mom's *Irish* came out the night she decided to confront them. I'm not sure if she actually had a plan or if she ever thought about how things might turn out, but I doubt she imagined it would all go so terribly wrong.

Hot-headed and determined to put a stop to the whole lot of them, she threw on her jeans and boots and marched over to their house looking for a fight.

I can't decide if this was brave or stupid on my mother's part, but when she arrived, their party was in full swing. It was risky just being on their property, let alone going there with a full head of steam demanding to talk to the person in charge. As she stood in front of Johnny, the leader of this gang, I imagine she too wondered what she was doing there. She was entirely outnumbered and unprepared for this encounter, and found herself surrounded by gang members as she attempted to deliver her message.

As the story goes—and as Johnny often told people whenever asked how he and his "ole lady" met—my mother walked up to him during his party and stood in front of him saying, "You sons-a-bitches better leave my kids alone!"

Johnny sat silent for a few seconds, calmly and confidently staring at this petite, redheaded woman, who had no idea what she had gotten herself into. On a *good* day any member of his gang would have no problem killing her right where she stood. Johnny could see that my mom was not intimidated by him or his gang. Amused by the sheer guts it took to confront him in his own home, he let out a hearty laugh.

After that, my mother and Johnny became inseparable. Johnny would often tell the story about how brave my mom was, and how much that instantly "turned him on." Eventually, he became a fixture in our house, sleeping over most nights. To my mother, that must have seemed like an improvement over the way things were previously, because being with him came with a certain amount of protection. My mom took good care of Johnny too, feeding him and his friends, which basically turned our house into a place for Johnny and his gang to hang out.

As a result, gang members, drug addicts, and criminals occupied our home, partying at all hours of the day and arriving with all manner of weapons—knives, machetes, and a variety of guns. In time, our house resembled Johnny's: filled with rowdy gang members, loud parties, and a variety of drugs and weapons.

Even worse, in order to continue running his business, Johnny soon moved his entire drug operation into our house. The drugs he sold came mostly in pill form and therefore needed to be chilled. So, next to our food refrigerator, he installed another fridge, one packed with drugs and padlocked with a heavy chain. Whenever the refrigerator door was unlocked, guns appeared and someone stood watch while drugs were stocked, sorted, or removed. Once, my brother Raul was made to sit in a chair holding a rifle pointed at the back door. He was told to pull the trigger if someone walked in. Luckily, that day, no one did.

The pills Johnny sold came in an assortment of colors: red, white, gray, and yellow. They were kept in large quantities inside plastic bags. On occasion, Raul sat at the kitchen table sorting pills for Johnny, preparing them for sale. "Reds, reds, reds, whites, whites, whites," he would repeat as he sorted the pills into piles and put them into plastic bags.

With a house full of drug addicts, Johnny worried about the safety of his *merchandise*, which is why he kept guns. There were so many guns, in fact, that my mom gave Johnny a wooden gun case for his birthday.

I remember the night she gave it to him. It was just our family, nobody else, and we sang "Happy Birthday" and watched Johnny blow out the candles on the cake my mom had made for him. When he blew out the candles, his reaction seemed odd. Instead of being happy, he began to cry. No one had ever done this for him, he said, not even his own family. This was his first birthday cake. It seemed so strange to me that a grown man had never had cake and ice cream for his birthday. I felt sorry for him. We may have been the closest thing to a family Johnny had ever known.

Then came a point during my mother's relationship with Johnny when he had to go to prison. I'm not sure what the exact reasons were behind his incarceration, although I imagine it had something to do with his drug business.

Just before turning himself in, Johnny gave my mom certain instructions. He told her that after he was gone, his "guys" would come and remove everything that was his from the house. "They're going to come for the drugs and the guns. You let them. Let them have it all," he said, "but whatever happens, don't let them have my machine gun." Wanting to remain loyal, my mom promised Johnny she wouldn't.

Among the many guns in the house, Johnny had acquired an Army-issue machine gun. It stood on a metal tripod and used two-inch bullets fed into its chamber from one side. Apparently, it was stolen property and had originally belonged to the Hells Angels.

As word traveled of Johnny's incarceration, members of the Hells Angels decided it was time to reclaim their property. This led them straight to our door. At first, requests for the gun were quite civil. Various members of the Hells Angels began delivering handwritten notes to my mother. The notes let my mom know, under no uncertain terms, they wanted their gun returned.

Wanting to keep her promise, my mother remained steadfast and refused to hand it over. Throughout the course of several days, a flurry of notes were sent back and forth between my mother and various members of the Hells Angels gang, all with a common message: "Give us the gun!" My mother's response was always a firm, "No!"

After several days, as the messages became more and more threatening, everyone in the house became noticeably more tense. When the messenger knocked on our door to deliver the final note, we could see a line of Hells Angels' motorcycles parked along the curb just outside our house. Holstered onto the sides of their bikes were guns and machetes. As the last note was placed into my mother's hand, she read the words, "Give us the gun OR ELSE!"

Later, my mom said that when she saw the Hells Angels lined up outside and she read the words, "Or else," it was like a bomb went off in her head. She said out loud, "What the fuck am I doing?!" She closed the door, ran to get the gun, and decided to throw it out a window facing the street where the gang members were waiting.

Perhaps she didn't feel safe merely handing the gun over to them. Given the scenario, I can't say that I blame her. But, when the Hells Angels saw the machine gun coming out of the window, they reacted as if they were about to be fired upon, and began shooting at our house.

When I heard someone shout, "Get down!" I darted under the bunk bed and found myself next to my brother, Raul. He had a crazed look in his eyes and a freakish grin, but he didn't say a word to me.

Lights flashed and I could hear the sound of breaking glass as it fell all around us. We hid under the bed, covering our heads with our hands to avoid the spray of bullets that pierced the walls right in front of our eyes. The glass fell on the bed above us and onto the floor in front of us, but not on us. We stayed under the bed until the shooting stopped and it seemed safe to come out.

The next message delivered to my mom read, "Take what you can carry and be gone by morning!" By this time, there was simply no point in arguing. We packed up what we could carry and—as the sun came up the following morning—we walked down the street and out of that neighborhood, as fast and as far as we could. We never saw Johnny again.

The Other Side of the Chasm

Katie Daley

Our ride lets us off north of Flagstaff on Route 180, a two-lane road humming with Winnebagos bound for the Grand Canyon. We stick out our thumbs confidently, figuring we'll be invited into one of them and arrive at the canyon in no time.

"Katie, man, we're almost there," chortles Lenny, my boyfriend and traveling partner. "In like Flynn."

After a few hours of standing up to the whoosh of passing RVs, the high desert air makes us giddy, and we start to enjoy not being charming enough to stop traffic. We play up how indignant we are at the lack of generosity of our fellow Americans and make up disturbing stories about their empty lives.

"Aww," Lenny wails as another Winnebago rumbles by. "Those things aren't mobile homes—they're mobile tombstones. Driven by zombies." He turns to me, his dark, shoulder-length hair blown back by the speed wind, his dark eyes sparking with a smirk. "How else could they possibly resist us?"

"Try not to take it so personally, brother," I say, patting his arm as we watch the truant RV swerve out of sight. "Didn't you see that mini TV on in there? They're too hypnotized by soap operas to take in the *real* opera happening right here on the side of the highway."

To beef up the laughter factor, Lenny coaches me on how to

hitchhike like Clint Eastwood—jacket hooked on left index finger and thrown over shoulder, right thumb casually pointing into the vastness behind us, brows knit slightly together as if we have much more important things waiting for us further down the road.

"No, Katie, not so eager. Bring your arm down, like you're hardly hitching. Now, look a little more pissed off. But not too pissed— you can't care *too* much about this. You're not *depending* on these peons—*they're* the ones depending on the chance to give you, wonderful you, a ride. Okay, here comes a car. Remember, keep that thumb loose and carefree. Turn your head, real slow, watch it pass. Aw, can you believe it? Not even glancing our way. Wait, not yet— okay, now! Spin on heels! Throw jacket to the ground! Whap! That's it! Hands on hips! Make sure those baby blues of yours are glinting in the sun. You've got it, girl, you've got it! They'll never forget this moment for the rest of their lives."

We play like this till dusk folds into darkness and we retreat into the pine forest behind us, where we spread our sleeping bags over pine needles, the softest mattress we've had since we left Cleveland. Lying on our backs, we send smoke rings up between the tree branches and murmur a few words to each other between long drifts of comfortable silence.

As Lenny dozes off and an occasional passing car plows its headlights into the night around us, I pull out my flashlight and paperback copy of *The Electric Kool-Aid Acid Test* by Tom Wolfe, which I've been reading since Colorado. I'm at the part where the face-painted, costume-wearing Merry Pranksters ride their psychedelic school bus to the Cow Palace to see the Beatles in 1965. Even though I'm disappointed that this acid trip, of all their LSD-sparked journeys, turns out to be their most disturbing, I can relate.

I love the Beatles and figure their sunny harmonies would normally bring on blissful hallucinations, but my one experience with big concert halls like the Cow Palace disturbed me, too. I went to see Neil Young at Public Hall in Cleveland, but he and his band were so far away I could fit them between my thumb and forefinger as we peered down at them, and the music sounded like it was coming from the bottom of a can of Budweiser. I felt betrayed by the fact that I'd saved up a month's allowance to watch my soul mentor play puny versions of the songs that had broken open my life.

It never occurred to me to stand up and walk out on Neil Young, so I'm fascinated by the Merry Pranksters' decision to leave the hall halfway through the Beatles show. They were getting bad vibrations from the thousands of screaming "teeny freaks" who swayed obediently according to each tilt of the Beatles' heads. And because the Fab Four weren't using their astounding crowd control skills for any apparently meaningful purpose, the whole scene—the teeny freaks *and* the Beatles—began to look like "a state of sheer poison mad cancer" to the tripping Pranksters. At one point, a throng of fans rushed the stage, trampling other fans and setting off a wildfire of fainting. The Beatles had to wait backstage till the chaos was over and the show could go on, but the Pranksters walked out on history. Even though they'd been building their lives up to this shiny apple of an event for months, they'd seen that it was rotten at the core, and they said no. I admire people who move on when they realize they're wasting their time, being had, or that something—especially something they've been counting on to lift them up—isn't right. I wish the same kind of cocksureness for my own life. In particular, right now, I wish I'd walked out on our breast-fondling trucker a few days ago.

He'd picked us up outside Albuquerque and at first seemed kind and brotherly enough. But then he pulled onto the shoulder, asked Lenny to get out to check the cab tires, and once Lenny was out of sight, reached over and brushed his fingers across my left breast. I looked away, trying to convince myself it was an accident, but as he yelled to Lenny to check the trailer tires further back, he quickly tugged on my breast as if it were a plum he was trying to pluck off a branch.

I wanted to snatch our packs, jump out of the cab, and shout, "Hands off, man! This is *my* tit, not yours!" But I just sat there, my eyes darting back and forth, trying to find a way to believe that this guy, this "brother" who'd navigated his wide load over to the side of the road to pick us up, had not just grabbed my breast.

Later, as we accelerated down the highway again, me still speechless and Lenny still oblivious, the guy offered to put us up for the night in his motel room. I was appalled, and Lenny was ecstatic. When we pulled into a truck stop to eat lunch, I took him aside to tell him what had happened. But instead of being shocked and pissed off, he looked thoughtful and said, "I've got a gut feeling about this guy. He's harmless. Let me talk to him."

I protested, but I let Lenny have his man-to-man chat. As usual, I was listening more to someone else's gut feeling than to my own. I was paying more attention to what Lenny wanted—a free place to stay—than to my own daydream of being fierce enough to tell the guy off and leave him in the dust.

The trucker showed up from his talk with Lenny sheepish and regretful. After telling him what he did "really sucked," I accepted his apology, but only because I didn't want him to think I was a bitch.

We ended up sleeping in his motel room that night, but when he slipped out the door at dawn without having laid another hand on me, I felt no relief. I felt like one of the teeny freaks in *The Electric Kool-Aid Acid Test*, passed out on the floor of the Cow Palace, trampled by the mindless stampede of my own politeness and my failure to take from life what I really wanted.

Now, under Arizona's pine needles and stars, I close the book and scooch further down into my sleeping bag. As I sleep, I dream that the Beatles pick Lenny and me up in a yellow school bus and take us all the way to California. It feels much more magical than a ride, though—we're in this together, the Beatles and us buoyed up into the same prevailing winds of adventure and the giddy understanding that sometimes, it's much better to travel than it is to arrive.

When I wake, I'm floating in bird chirps and early morning, high desert sunlight. I feel happy, lucky. I know all is not right with the world, but I feel that I'm right with it, even the parts that aren't right with themselves.

After I tell Lenny about the dream, I make a proposal. "Lenny," I say, lighting up my first cigarette of the day, "let's forget about the Grand Canyon. Nobody's stopping for us. Besides, even if we did get a ride, it'll just be crowded with all the jerks in Winnebagos that didn't pick us up yesterday. Let's head for California instead."

Lenny studies me, and I swear I can see some of the light draining from his face. Part of me feels the same way. Changing directions is no small deal when you're standing on the middle of the Colorado plateau, the morning rimmed with moonlike mountains, the high desert air making your life feel vast and possible. When the legendary Grand Canyon is only seventy-five miles away and you can feel it waiting for you, while to the West, the Pacific Ocean and the end of the road stand bland and eternal. Why go to California now, today, when it will always be there? Why rush away from one of the wonders of the world when you're only an hour or two from stepping into it? Especially when you're a tenderoni hoodlum from Queens like Lenny, who just yesterday wept at seeing his first rainbow ever?

But it's getting harder for even Lenny to imagine the magnificence of the Grand Canyon. Didn't we watch an endless caravan of families headed that way the day before? Didn't they furrow their eyebrows at each other as they passed us? Didn't their children point at us like we were antelope in clown suits? No matter how grand it is, the Canyon can't possibly be huge enough to still all those RV TV hookups, all those game show hosts escorting losers off the stage. For sure, the canned laughter from sitcoms will be leaking into the ancient silence like a canister of nuclear waste will someday leak into the old lizard brain of Nevada.

Even so, Lenny resists. "What's the difference, Katie? If we cross the road now and hitch the other way, the same assholes who wouldn't pick us up yesterday on their way in won't pick us up on their way out."

"No, Lenny, I'm telling you, the Beatles are gonna pick us up in that yellow school bus and take us all the way to California. We're set!"

Part of me is joking, but another part is clarified by some kind of mystical intuition. My mind feels cleansed from the dream, and I'm lit up with a boldness I don't usually have.

Lenny chuckles. "Yeah, sure. So if we've got a guaranteed ride all the way to California, what's the hurry? Come on, Katie—we're so close to the Canyon I can taste it."

So we strike a compromise. We'll hitch towards the Canyon for two more hours, and if we don't get a ride, we'll head the other way.

Two hours later, we cross the road, stick out our thumbs, and get a ride within ten minutes straight to I-40. I'm elated as we saunter down the on-ramp and set up shop on the highway shoulder. I've just been released from the obligation to find sharp pangs of beauty in the chasms below me while standing among throngs of ooing, ahhing, unbruised Americans. I'm on the wide-open road again, and I'm brimming with it.

"Okay, Lenny, you ready to hang out with the Fab Four for a couple days?" I start singing "She Loves You" and pump my hitching thumb in the air to the rhythm of *yeah, yeah, yeah.*

He smirks, amused but not convinced by my belief in the yellow bus of my dream.

When you stick out your thumb on a road with traffic, you don't have a solid sense of the day like folks who get up and go to work or school or down to the local bar. You have no idea who you'll be talking to or what you'll see. You don't know where or even if you'll sleep that night. The knife blade of mystery that life really is, underneath all the routines, is standing right there with you on the side of the road, glinting everywhere you turn. So it strikes you as especially amazing and right when you have a strong premonition. And when it steps up to become part of your day, it feels more vivid than pretty much anything that happens at home.

So, when the yellow school bus hauls itself up over the crest of the hill and comes into sight, I'm not surprised. Still, I'm only one quarter serious when I say, "Look, Lenny—it's our ride to California with Sergeant Pepper's Lonely Heart's Club Band!" Seeing the bus makes me think of schoolchildren on a field trip, or a bible class off to three days in the desert—not a ride to the West Coast.

Lenny's still rolling his eyes at me when the bus pulls over onto the shoulder a couple hundred yards away from us.

"See?" I murmur in a deliberately snide tone. What'd I tell you?" I begin singing, "Here comes the sun, little darling..." But I'm thinking, *flat tire, engine trouble.*

"Katie, shhhh—stop singing! Is that them honking?"

We listen. Nothing. Then, *wonk! wonk! wonk!*

"That's it!" Lenny exclaims, grabbing his pack and putting it on. "They're honking for us!"

He's several steps into his sprint towards the bus before I shoulder my own pack and fall in behind him. Why are we running? I wonder as I huff up the hill. They're only honking because they need some kind of help. They're not gonna give us a ride. I don't know this yet, but my habit of ignoring my intuition is in the first classic phase of death and dying: denial.

When we get to the bus, the door is already open. "Mornin'!" the driver calls over the rumble of the engine. "Where you guys headed?" He has kinky red hair that straggles down past his shoulders, a single gold hoop gleaming on his earlobe, and is wearing a long string of beads around his neck. He isn't George, Paul, John, or Ringo, but he does have Merry Prankster potential.

"Are you stopping for us?" I ask at the same time that Lenny drawls out gleefully, "Cal-i-for-ni-a!"

"Well, I'm not stopping for road kill. Hop in. We're headed for California, too. Welcome aboard."

A Berkeley Spring, 1969

Jill Taft-Kaufman

Nothing can be understood about that spring and the period leading up to it without first remembering the war and the draft. I appreciated the mordant humor of the bumper stickers you saw on seemingly every other VW in Berkeley that year: "Join the army: Travel to exotic places, meet new people—and kill them!" Bravado and disdain of "the man" felt palpable as I walked to my Chaucer class.

It was a beautiful May morning. A group of students playing Frisbee near the food pushcarts timed their jumps and throws to chants of, "Hell, no, we won't go!" Dogs ran and shook themselves in the nearby fountain. The entire landscape was awash with light, color, and sound. Rhythmic vibrations of Country Joe strumming and singing, the "Feel Like I'm Fixin' to Die Rag" in lower Sproul Plaza were a seductive alternative to where I was headed, into the dimly lit English Department's Wheeler Hall. There I would sit with three hundred others, listening to how and why Chaucer's work from the late fourteenth century about a group of pilgrims on a journey telling stories was significant.

Few things seemed as significant to us as our own narrative: our country had become a killing machine, and many of us were being asked to lay our bodies down to feed this machine or to stop it. "And it's one, two, three, what are we fighting for..." Country Joe twanged. We had pangs for the killing we were doing; we had fear

157

for the dying that might also soon involve us. The war had become personal. That was our story.

As a female, I occupied a privileged position. I was filled with worry and sadness, but ultimately, the war would not come home to my doorstep. My brother and father were too old. I was the wrong sex. "Come on all you big strong men, Uncle Sam needs your help again." My male friends were planning escape means and routes from the deadly invitation to Southeast Asia. Even my friend, Hugh, who was known among our friends as "the red ant" for his hair color, freckles, goofy sense of humor, and the fact that he had been conspicuous at the last Halloween party as an ant, with his date dressed as a can of Raid, was now as industrious as that small insect. He ran ten miles each day so that when he got his draft notice he could arrive for the medical exam having shed enough pounds from his slight frame to be rejected.

Down the block from where I dawdled in the perfumed spring air of Sproul Plaza that late morning, stood the 1950s pink stucco apartment building on Blake Street where I lived. Across from the building, on Telegraph Avenue, was a rapidly growing patch of land that was becoming a visual foil to the war: People's Park. The brown, scrubby, empty lot that used to be there was turning green and multicolored, flourishing under the hands of students, community folk, street people, and anyone who wanted to add their symbolic and literal contribution to what it meant to create rather than destroy. Flowers, greenery, artwork, and people dotted the small area—a kind of planting for peace. Grass of both sorts abounded. Musicians, leafleteers, food hawkers, jugglers, and spontaneous gardeners crouched on the ground, lounged on makeshift seats, and lay breathing deeply. The air was palpable with the distinctiveness of a Berkeley spring—freshness, Cannabis, falafel, and flowers. Such loveliness spilled freely out to anyone who passed. Woody was right: "This land is your land; this land is my land."

To university officials, sitting high up in buildings of cement, however, such appropriation of university property needed to be

halted. Their initial casual ignoring of events in the park was changing into hardness. Ronald Reagan encouraged them to put a stop
to flagrant seizing of the property of the state of California and to
assert university ownership. The administration now determined
this land should be a parking lot.

For a while, the tension between the two sides, students and
community versus the administration and power-filled interests,
remained implicit rather than overt. Then, one day, passersby and
park users were stunned to find an eight-foot, chain-link wire fence
hastily constructed to keep them out of what had become their
park. My own anxiety about the intensity surrounding the park
was gradually building. Growing up in Long Beach and having just
visited my home a few weeks earlier for spring break, I hadn't yet set
aside some of the lessons of my childhood. Long Beach and I had
dreamily rehearsed the 1950s even as the '60s careened toward its
end. In my junior high school in the early '60s, order, control, and
limits had shaped our lives. I remembered the school administration warning us that six people constituted a gang. Life must have
demarcations. *No groups of six.* No laughing matter.

Here, in my emerging life as an adult, I was often torn. I wanted
to embrace the events of the day and also honor the reason I was
at Berkeley, to explore and discover all the learning that this "jewel
in the crown" of the University of California system had to offer.
My education over the park was accelerating. There had been skir-
mishes near it. An innocent young bystander had been killed by
police in these streets of Berkeley. Another, blinded. Law and order,
fences, and weapons. Student protest had turned lethal. Campus
cops, who would soon be joined by 2,700 National Guardsmen
ordered in by Ronald Reagan, were now aided by the Alameda
Sheriff's Department.

The Alameda cops were in a class by themselves; they were,
indeed, the "Blue Meanies." They did not resemble bandy-legged
Officer Ryan in Long Beach at the Dollar Market Grocery, who would
wink at my mother and me while we had sodas at the fountain in

the store when I was a little girl. Why were these helmeted figures in full riot gear now near Sather Gate, striking nightsticks against their palms as they stared at us? Why were the eyes I was facing above the shields on their helmets filled with hate on this beautiful day? "There's something happening here; what it is ain't exactly clear."

"Be it of were, or pees, or hate, or love / Al is this reuled by the sighte above," the professor was intoning in the dimness as I settled into Wheeler Hall for a lecture on "The Knight's Tale." I tried to decipher the cadences of Old English, resolve the mystery of who was wearing the musk oil near me, and push down the discomfort in my stomach from the sneering faces outside. I was not in the mood for Middle English. My mind jumped. The day was promising to burst all around me! Can we help you find "the peace and the star, oh my friend…"

"And God save al this faire compaignye! Amen," the professor ended his talk with an attempt at playful ambiguity. I looked at my watch. Class had lumbered to a close. We all picked up our books, thick hardbound copies of *The Works of Chaucer* with a pilgrim astride a horse etched on the cover. We slowly filed out of the heavy doors of the lecture hall that led into the dark, wood-paneled outer lobby of the building. People were discussing the lecture, the upcoming assignment, lunch, People's Park, the Guard, the Blue Meanies.

I exited out into the sunlight, squinting as I went, and started to walk down the steps of Wheeler. Below, Sather Gate winked in the sunlight. I was looking forward to going home to see if my roommate wanted to fix lunch together before afternoon classes. But something was making a sound overhead as I took step after step. Something that whirred and moved the air around us…something that resembled…that *was* a helicopter up above us, whirring menacingly close, with a blaring loud speaker and a distorted voice coming out of it yelling: "DISPERSE! DISPERSE IMMEDIATELY!"

I started to walk fast. I came abruptly down the step into the hate-filled face of a cop. I took several quick steps backward. His bulky body advanced on me, and I began to run. The bulky body followed, and then I couldn't see it clearly anymore. I couldn't breathe anymore. I couldn't control the mucous in my nose or the stinging and tears in my eyes. My legs were trying to run away, but where was I going? I couldn't see. I couldn't get a breath. My lungs were too heavy. I couldn't stop crying. I was coughing. I was falling. I was crawling while I cried, sneezing when I could stumble up and run. I was running. The cops, wearing gas masks, chased me, chased all of us, hammering out at those who didn't run fast enough, flailing and waving their nightsticks, beating the air, bodies, and ground as they cudgeled where they thought you had dropped to the pavement to crawl away.

But you can't run or crawl away from tear gas. It covers everything. It spreads. It was coming down from the sky above. A thick fog covered the Plaza. Or was I even still in the Plaza? I was trying to run from it, to my home, toward the park, toward safety. Did I still have my Chaucer book? I didn't want to drop it. Was I still holding it? I couldn't see my arms. I couldn't see anything. My eyes were filled with tears that just kept coming. My brain filled with confusion. Run toward home. Run toward home. I couldn't run out of it. The tear gas chased me down Telegraph. It covered the park. It dispersed the people. It hid the plants. It diffused the spring day. It blocked out the sun. It brought the war home to Berkeley.

Later, when the smoke had cleared, we learned that the Guard had been instructed to throw canisters of gas upon "any large group on campus that looked suspicious." What could be more suspicious, we mused afterwards, than three hundred students, an "effete corps of snobs who characterize themselves as intellectuals," to use the words of Spiro Agnew, exiting the English Department Building clutching Chaucer. We fell into the arms of the Alameda Sheriff's Department waiting for us. People's Park was met with full institutional violence urged on by the governor. "If it takes a bloodbath, let's get it over with, no more appeasement!" Reagan decreed.

Deaths at Kent State and Jackson State followed the subsequent spring. "Sometimes I feel like a motherless child, a long way from home." These deaths brought home the deadly consequences of protest on American college campuses in a country founded on revolution that had moved far from its professed ideals.

Sometimes, as I think about who I am today, in another century, I wonder why, of all the moments I experienced during my years at Berkeley, this particular incident lingers so boldly. Other sights, sounds, textures, and events layer themselves resonantly as well. Perhaps this memory looms so large because it forced me viscerally into confronting a major irony, not in a text in the English Department, but in the world around me.

I was gassed, not because of my civil disobedience, although my activities in that regard gained momentum from that day forward. Instead, the canisters were thrown at us while we were in the midst of doing what we were supposed to: getting an education. The war came to us three hundred students of English literature without the deadliness of "friendly fire" in real war, but those wounded and killed minding their own business on Telegraph were not as fortunate. The incident played up the dysfunctions in our society that turned a university campus into a battleground. It vivified more than any sociology class could for this middle-class white girl from Long Beach a powerful lesson that many people already knew, a lesson for the future.

These days, I am dismayed over the déjà vu of struggles that were not won, successes that need to be refought, wars elsewhere that still squander our national treasure, and backlashes that consume our time and energy to fight them. I wonder whether people in this country have the willingness to take to the streets as they did throughout the protests of the late '60s and early '70s. While we are held thrall by devices of distraction and insularity, I am heartened by examples from people all over the rest of the world and pockets in this country where those who are fed up with economic inequities and unjust distribution of resources collectively protest, strike, and lay their bodies on the line against institutional injustice and repression.

My tumultuous education at Berkeley in the days of noise, color, and movement stamped me with a vibrant sense that anything and everything could happen. That it should happen. That we could realize ourselves as individuals and also collectively: passion and political consciousness simultaneously jostling towards a progress of humanity. Peter Weiss's character based upon Jean-Paul Marat expressed it succinctly in *Marat/Sade*: One's goal should be "to pull yourself up by your own hair / to turn yourself inside out / and see the whole world with fresh eyes."

We turned ourselves into shapes we hadn't yet assumed; we questioned, prodded, provoked. We didn't settle. We heard and felt speeches, emotions, bodies beside us—laughing, crying, and shouting with anger and joy. We attempted to turn ourselves and our world inside out.

We had powerful forces against us. Yet the exhilaration of feeling that we might have transformed the calcified thought and destructive actions of those in power stays with me. In the last four decades since I've left Berkeley, I have tried to keep the spirit of my experience from that ineffable period with me. To do so, I seek out people who are still passionate for justice.

As a professor of Communication and Dramatic Arts at Central Michigan University, I have specialized in adapting, compiling, and directing material not originally written for the stage. Political and social issues have been at the heart of the texts that attract me. My numerous scripts and productions over the years have featured an implicit aesthetic dialectic with audiences. Performers have conveyed poetry of political resistance in Latin America, narratives of homeless people in this country, oral histories of women facing unwanted pregnancies during the illegal abortion era, poetry inspiring participatory democracy at the voting booth, testimonies documenting violence against women, and stories from soldiers in the Vietnam War.

Working within educational theatre, exposing students and audiences to ideas of political significance, challenges me to emulate Brecht as well as Tony Kushner; both stressed that good political theatre has to be, at heart, good theatre. It is, in fact, crucial that provocative ideas calling for critical reflection be entertaining. When my student ensembles and I are in the process of developing creative configurations for audiences to contemplate, I feel as though I might still pull myself and them up by the hair and collectively build visions for transforming the world.

The Revolution and Egg Salad Sandwiches

Nancy Kilgore

Columbia University in the City of New York, spring, 1968.

In my Frye boots and Mexican dress, I strolled across the campus with two of my friends, "Bush" and "Norman." This use of last names, reminiscent of prep schools or football teams, was a guy thing that didn't include me, and I always chafed when I heard it. But it wouldn't be until a few years later, when feminism surfaced and I joined a consciousness-raising group, that I could articulate the feelings it triggered: once again, excluded from the boy's club.

Today that feeling was merely a twinge in the back of my mind, though, because we had a bond that went beyond gender. We were young people who knew that the war in Vietnam was wrong, and we had the brashness to believe we could stop it. We would become part of something much larger than our university or ourselves. Today we would become part of history.

The protests and rallies had been going on for weeks. We'd heard impassioned speeches by student leaders and radicalized Vietnam vets, we'd listened to Malcolm X, we'd talked and debated and agonized over our own roles, and now the three of us had made our decision. This was the night of "the bust," and we were going to join the protest. The occupation.

What did it mean to occupy a building? My stomach fluttered, and, to counteract the fear, I entertained the boys with an imitation of the old lady who stood on 114th Street, my street, and extemporized about current events. "Did you hear about that Michael Crudd?" I croaked, mimicking her voice, and we laughed uproariously. How incredible that anyone wouldn't know the correct name of famous Mark Rudd, instigator and leader of our "revolution."

As we made our way to our building, the campus was vivid in spring bloom, everything around us imbued with special meaning—the grassy terraces rimmed by distant buildings, the stone-paved plazas, the expansive tiers of stairs leading up to the grandiloquent Low Library. Presiding over all, the nine-foot statue of Athena, *Alma Mater*, resting on her throne. With her scepter raised in one arm, the lofty pillars of the library behind her, *Alma Mater* seemed the embodiment of the entrenched power that at this moment was so abhorrent to us. As we climbed the steps and passed beside her, Norman, jaunty and confident, flipped her the bird.

We had arrived at college with a respect for authority fostered in us as children, but now everything had changed. That spring, in rapid-fire motion, Martin Luther King Jr. was shot and killed, the war in Vietnam escalated, villages were massacred, and our government became a symbol of oppression. We were angry. We wanted to end the war, and we wanted to end racism.

We advanced across the ponderous landscape, caught between a familiar impulse toward lightheartedness—this was, after all, the place where we hung out every day, talking, laughing, engaging the issues of the world—and the knowledge that what we were doing was scary business. There were rumors that the TPF, the Tactical Police Force, whose name alone carried images from science fiction, would come and arrest us. But what would happen? And how?

And where was Knox? Knox, the cheeky and charming self-styled revolutionary, better known to me as Greg, was my boyfriend. Knox, who stood up boldly at the rallies exhorting us to *fight the good fight! Join the resistance! Don't trust anyone over thirty!* We would form a cadre, I fantasized. I would be the Tanya to his Che Guevara. But today, at the moment of truth, Knox was nowhere to be found. This demonstration was a big step into the unknown for me: I would be arrested. I would go to jail. Beneath my nonchalance, I was scared. But where was the love of my life?

"He'll be here later," Bush assured me.

The building we were heading for, Schermerhorn, was a massive edifice of stone and wood with high ceilings and an air of solemnity. But today the mood was anything but solemn, and when we arrived, the scene was chaotic. I had always been the dutiful student, arriving at class on time, handing in my papers, taking exams, but now there were no teachers or authorities, just us young people, huddling in groups, camping out with sleeping bags on the floor, rushing back and forth with swagger or bewilderment, making plans, announcing rumors. We were *occupying* the building.

But what were we supposed to do? What were the rules? There were no rules. We invented them as we went along. The student leaders invented them, the leaders being anyone who had the guts to stand up and present an idea, a plan. Our de facto leader Mark Rudd and his group occupied the center of university power, the president's office in Low Library, where their photograph, later published in *Life* magazine, would become an icon of the protest movement. But here in Schermerhorn, although there were lots of speeches, lots of ideas, and lots of plans, there were no leaders.

I wandered around the building, searching for familiar faces, strolling over to look out the windows where the counter-protesters, the ROTC boys, formed barricades to prevent deliveries of food and shouted hateful slogans. I drifted back to my seat on the marble staircase.

"The suits!" a boy shouted, running from the window. "The suits are coming!" A clutch of fear ran through the crowd. Ah, adolescence. How easy it was to know the good people from the bad. The bad ones wore suits. The suits, it turned out, wanted to persuade us to get out of there before the police came. But of course we couldn't do that. We had a cause. And besides, we couldn't trust people in suits.

"To the roof!" The call resounded. Bush and Norman were going to the roof. Did I want to come? What for? I asked. To watch for the pigs. And it's really cool up there, they said. Have you never been? I had not. Intrigued, I followed them.

And it *was* cool on the roof. The view over the campus, with its plazas and patterns, its greens and elegant buildings, was like the view from an airplane, with the New York skyline shimmering in the twilight and a sliver of red cloud across the horizon. The people on the ground, protesters, counter-protesters, professors trying to reconcile the two, onlookers, and university officials, were ants scurrying to and fro on the face of the earth. We were all just tiny creatures in a larger universe that would go on, whatever we did.

Bush and Norman went directly to the edge of the building and sat with their feet dangling over. "Are you nuts?" I said. "That's four stories high!" They laughed and pooh-poohed my concern, but I hovered at a safe distance behind, and when my anxiety intensified, I went back down the stairs.

And now I was hungry.

In spite of the barricade, food had been smuggled in, and a group was gathered around a table set up in the hall. One girl, tall and slim, with short dark hair, stood in front of a giant bowl filled with dozens of hard-boiled eggs. "Can I help?" I asked.

"No, this is a snap," she said, and proceeded to take two knives, hold them inside the bowl and, with quick motions, cut up all those eggs in a few minutes. Wow. I'd never thought to chop eggs like that. As she chopped, she gave orders to the others: put the sandwich bread there, get the drinks from the cooler, set out the paper plates. She had flair and buoyancy, she was super-efficient, and she was doing something important for the revolution. This girl, I thought, she doesn't worry about what people think. She isn't shy and self-conscious, doesn't second-guess herself like I do. This is the real Tanya. If I could have that kind of confidence, I, too, could take charge, be a leader of the revolution.

After we ate, there was more milling around, more talking, more announcements: "They're coming at six!" We scurried to our positions and sat in lines along the hallways like we had for the air raid drills in elementary school. We were instructed in nonviolent resistance: *Go limp. Just let them drag you. Whatever you do, don't get up.*

They didn't come at six.

"They're coming at seven thirty!"

They didn't come at seven thirty.

Our conversations jigged back and forth between stories about jail to the silly jokes of punchy kids half-scared, half-exhilarated.

Knox still hadn't showed. Knox never did show up, and perhaps this was the beginning of his unmasking, the ending of my fantasy. But by this time, I didn't miss him. Each moment was loaded, full of elation and anxiety as I sat with my comrades and sang "We Shall Overcome."

And then it happened. In the middle of the night, when we had all just drifted off to sleep, the cry came, "They're here!"

Outside the window the sight was more chilling than any I had imagined: A line of men in helmets and riot gear and lit by a string of eerie spotlights advanced toward us, an army in the night.

As we sang "We Shall Not Be Moved," the TPF knocked in the doors.

"Get up!" they ordered. "You're under arrest!"

No one got up.

Again they ordered us up. No one moved.

They began to drag the boys, who were closest to the doors, throwing them outside like sacks of potatoes. They worked their way down the hall, and when they got to my friend, whose name was also Nancy, the officer, middle-aged and puffy, bent over and looked at her with a big sigh. Nancy was a beautiful, angelic-looking blonde. "Aw, come on, sweetheart, just get up," he pleaded.

Nancy, stone-faced, didn't budge. He dragged her out the door. I was next. I went limp and found it painless. They were gentle with us girls. When we got outside, we stood up and were herded into paddy wagons.

Watching Manhattan go by through the window grills of a paddy wagon, twenty of us packed onto benches meant for ten, felt surreal. This was our city, these were streets we roamed and explored freely, and now we were prisoners. No longer the privileged college students, now we were the faces we had seen on the other side of those paddy wagons, the faces of the disenfranchised.

As we were escorted into the "Tombs," Manhattan's central booking facility, we stood waiting while a line of prostitutes, jaded women in high heels, short skirts, and lots of makeup, was led in beside us. As they passed, they looked at us scruffy students with a mixture of humor and commiseration. The police then took us into a room where we were charged, and as we stood in a line facing the policemen, we were shocked to see that one of the boys had a line of blood running down his face. At the same time another boy muttered a sarcastic comment about police violence, and one of the officers went red in the face, raised his club and charged at him. "What did you say?" he shouted. "Who you calling violent?" We froze, exchanging furtive glances and saving this incident to recount later.

We were herded into cells, all seven hundred of us, the largest population the Tombs had ever held, twenty-five of us girls in a two-woman cell. A matron pulled us out one by one and over to the next cell where she stuck a gloved finger up our vaginas and rectums, examining for drugs. Sophisticated as we were in political discourse, we didn't have the words or even the concepts to talk about this feeling of violation. We stayed there all night, sleeping in shifts, not knowing how long we'd be there, running on adrenaline, fear, and a new solidarity, the solidarity of the oppressed.

The next morning we were arraigned and released. The Tombs just didn't have the capacity for all of us. Only later did we learn about the police who, after the bust on campus, went on a rampage, chasing down and beating bystanders with their Billy clubs. The bad people, we now understood, wore police uniforms.

I went back to my student life, shaken and sobered, but the

University remained in upheaval and the country unsettled for some time to come.

I didn't stay with Knox and never became another Tanya, though I did participate in a few more protest marches. But after that and for the rest of my life, when I make egg salad sandwiches, I put the hard-boiled eggs in a bowl, chop them with two knives, and remember that night at Columbia.

Under Siege

Joan Annsfire

How we battled on
that first year; big-city girls away from home
we dodged salt pellets, knee-knockers
and clouds of pepper gas;
as the tanks rolled down High Street,
we were high on freedom,
had held our own in meaner streets;
challenged but undaunted
behind the lines of bayonets,
we were currents, strong and wild;
charged by the electricity of danger,
their weapons unable to hold us back
from a world changing faster
than we ever could have believed
possible.

How we came home
to the funky apartment with
the rickety, old porch swing,
our stodgy roommates,
too timid or cautious
to try their hands at revolution,
busy playing other games

like seduce the professor, become a great artist
or just lay as low as possible
until the strike closed the university
leaving us only
the school of the streets.

How we got stoned
on grass, hash, and acid;
once, tripping together,
I saw eagles with huge talons
trying to take you from me,
but I didn't need birds of prey
because you disappeared anyway,
to the house of your latest boyfriend
as I, your abandoned comrade-in-arms,
stumbled through my acid-induced haze
alone.

How I holed up
in my room as the cold crept in
from every leaky window pane,
reliving the days of love and war,
remembering the way your pointed teeth
punctuated your sly smile,
the casual toss of your head,
and later, the silences
that grew as long as the shadows
of late autumn unfolding.

How I cried
in the snow that winter;
when the inevitable
rotation of the earth
was the only revolution in sight,

my hopes folded
and were carried away like the tents
of nomads moving on
to more promising territory.

How I was laid low,
bent over under the weight of tradition,
heavier than the force of gravity;
platitudes carved in stone
came down from every mountaintop
transporting you to a place
far beyond my reach,
laying waste my furtive dreams
and eviscerating my fragile universe
of delicate and bright desire.

Speaking at the Last SDS Convention

Frances Maher

John navigated Sarah's stroller around a slew of abandoned bottles and garbage bags, looking for the meeting. The tenements near the South Wabash area were nothing like the Chicago masterpieces of my architect father's beloved Frank Lloyd Wright. No Chicago School skyscrapers here. No beautiful lakeside Art Institute, no Palmer House. We were headed to the Chicago Coliseum at the bottom of South Wabash Avenue, which looked like a run-down storage warehouse, the kind of place you see from the highway—and avoid if you can. Sarah giggled at her jiggly ride and I thought, she's only five months old, she's with us, she loves her stroller, that's all she needs to feel secure. But I wasn't used to this kind of neighborhood, though it wasn't so very different from our own three-decker apartment in Somerville, Massachusetts. I walked close to John.

We found a metal door in the vast wall with a hand-lettered sign saying "SDS," where some hippie-looking people were handing out leaflets. After leaving the sunshine, we found ourselves in a vast, murky boxing arena. The concrete walls and floor were dirty, cold, and damp. People were milling around, sparse and looking lost, or hunched in small groups. Just a little freaked out, I coughed and shivered again. I understood that we had to leave behind many comforts for the sake of the movement, but even the dingiest college auditoriums had a few windows. I made my way to the boxing ring, a high platform in the middle of it all where I was about to make the first public speech of my life.

We had arrived at the 1969 Annual Convention of Students for a Democratic Society, the main student organization against the Vietnam War. This convention was going to decide which of two main factions, the Worker Student Alliance (WSA) or the Revolutionary Youth Movement (RYM), was going to take it over. WSA, our group, was sponsored by the Progressive Labor Party. According to our leaflets we were a "revolutionary Communist organization" committed to creating a socialist society through a workers' revolution.

RYM's version of revolution called for "Offing the Pigs" and attacking the state through acts of sabotage such as robbing banks and blowing up railroad tracks. For some reason, they thought this behavior would appeal to youth fed up with the system, their "vanguard." They scorned WSA's class analysis.

When I reached the platform, I noticed a brigade of Black Panthers were standing at military attention, their German Shepherds flanking them. Now I saw with a jolt that they had guns kind of casually hanging off their belts and that they were ringing the whole arena. These Panthers were RYM bodyguards and weren't our allies! I winced. But the WSA had bodyguards too—Jared Israel, the head of WSA and PL in Boston, was flanked by two large burly men who looked armed. The stakes were high, as each group vied for control over a national office, a mailing list, and a newsletter that had mobilized thousands of students across the country. In the last few months, the members of the two sides had gone from distrusting to hating each other. Any small encounter could start a fight. Right now, down in the dark there somewhere, John was pushing Sarah in her stroller. He had told me he would be keeping her moving so she wouldn't cry. Shouldn't I be worried? I could imagine her peacefully sucking away on her bottle—what a relaxed baby she was! I decided to relax, too. I could tell Sarah later that she was present at an important moment for the movement.

And me? I was twenty-six years old, with a five-month-old baby and a thirty-one-year-old husband who had been a movement organizer for four years. What was I thinking, a young woman only ten years ago a debutante, now a Communist revolutionary in such a place? What happened?

I had to remind myself that as a sophomore at Radcliffe in 1961, I had gotten bored with my preppy boyfriend Tommy. The tailgate parties at Harvard football games were freezing cold, in spite of the sickly-sweet, bourbon-loaded White Russians. All they talked about was hockey and football and their exclusive men's clubs. The Hasty Pudding Shows in the spring featured silly boys getting drunk, while the Radcliffe girls did all the work and got none of the credit.

For the first two years, I'd felt secure having a boyfriend but I didn't like being *only* someone's girlfriend. Radcliffe girls were supposed to be smart. I went there to study history and find a serious calling, but didn't find the Harvard I'd imagined; I wanted to date sophisticated intellectuals from the literary magazines, or at least the *Harvard Crimson*.

So I joined the bohemian life of artists and writers around Harvard Square through Freddy Lawrence, who became my next boyfriend. We spent Saturday afternoons in his artist friend Svetlana Rockwell's apartment, scorning the crowds making their way across the Charles River to the football games. In Provincetown in the summer of 1963, I turned twenty-one and smoked marijuana for the first time on the dunes. For a while, Freddy even had an apartment in the Village. The bathtub doubled as the bottom of the kitchen table and we would take the table top off to take a bath. I thought about becoming an editor, or even a writer, and dreamed a whole world of possibilities about how to live my life.

But poor Freddy at twenty-six had no real plan for his own life. So, full of pity and sadness, I moved on. Just before graduation in 1964, I met John at a fancy dress ball in Boston. I already knew who John was—one of those famously cool graduate students that hung out at the University Restaurant on Massachusetts Avenue. He and his brother Albert were reputed to be very radical. By that time I had begun to notice the sit-ins and marches for civil rights in the South; some of my graduating friends had even joined a voter registration project called "Mississippi Summer," where people I had known and admired were putting their futures on the line for a public cause. But I still felt like the spectator I'd been at those tailgate parties, the Provincetown dunes and Village cafes. You can't go to Mississippi and just be a spectator, so I went to Norway with my parents instead.

⟨❧⟩

I looked around the gathering and wondered if anyone from Mississippi Summer was here. What had happened to those simpler times when the whole movement was together? Well, I was not a spectator anymore! By now, I'd been in the Movement for four whole years. I couldn't see John and Sarah anywhere. I trusted him, though. We were in this together. I started thinking again about those last few years.

⟨❧⟩

In 1965 I moved in with John without telling my parents, and worked at the Dudley Street Action Center in Boston, a welfare reform project sponsored by SDS. White college graduates were ringing doorbells, talking to black women and playing with their children. Some apartments were disorganized and dirty, and some were carefully tidy. The furniture was worn, and the TVs were always blaring. The children giggled and whined. I was in awe of these women, especially the grandmothers, who were often raising grandchildren and keeping the family together. An organization called MAW, or Mothers for Adequate Welfare, was born, and I turned against peanut butter sandwiches for life.

John and I got married to show Daddy I wasn't becoming "damaged goods"—my parents never learned about Freddy. A few months before the wedding, Daddy had yelled, "You're living with a man?" and asked John his intentions. When John proposed, I was relieved and happy.

I became a high school history teacher. At Dudley Street I had been confused, ensconced inside a privileged life and trying to live, for the first time, a useful one, but teaching gave me a new clarity. American History was a story I could tell about different groups of people creating a country together. I always spent six weeks on the American Revolution, reveling over every detail of the colonists' growing radicalism against the British. My own ancestors were the underdogs, fighting against tyranny, casting their lot on the side of democracy, and winning. When my country betrayed these ideals in Vietnam, the war became my cause. The North Vietnamese, using our Declaration of Independence, stood for freedom fighters everywhere, and I could join them. In 1968 I created a high school curriculum on Vietnam with three colleagues and brazenly taught it to my students.

Now 1968 had come and gone. The Chicago riots. Malcolm X, Martin Luther King, Bobby Kennedy—all shot. The assassination of JFK had felt surreal. These men were the leaders of my generation—we read their speeches and followed their lives.

Why wasn't our own elected government listening to us, tackling racism and poverty, and ending the war? Instead, Lyndon Johnson bombed North Vietnam, and we predicted that Nixon was going to be worse.

People from the Progressive Labor Party knew why all this was happening, and harangued us. "Don't you see that capitalism is the enemy? American Imperialism oppresses struggling peoples all over the world!" The United States had supported dictators in Cuba, Guatemala, the Dominican Republic—Vietnam was just the latest. And at home, look around—the civil rights movement is just part of all oppressed peoples' ongoing struggle for equality.

We read *The Communist Manifesto*, Lenin, and Chairman Mao in PL-sponsored study groups for non-members. In *What Is to Be Done* we learned about the idea of a vanguard party—intellectuals and former members of the bourgeoisie would inspire and lead the working class. This made sense to us. I was impressed with PL members who left college for good and went to work in factories. Boston PL leaders persuaded us to sell their newspaper *Challenge* at demonstrations and factory gates. If only they knew about our vision, they would join us...but they chased us away.

John and I sadly broke up with the many old movement friends who were unwilling to see the need for a working class revolution. Somehow, being right was more important than being effective or persuasive. Finally, in January 1969, a month before Sarah was born, John himself joined PL.

❧

I looked out at the arena again, trying to find John and Sarah in the gloom, thinking that my whole life had been leading to this moment. Here I was at the focal center of a history-making event, representing a national movement for permanent social change through a popular revolution, though I fervently and secretly hoped that the revolution would be peaceful. After all, I had a little girl to raise.

But to be honest, there were some problems with my story. I peeked down at my handcrafted gold wedding ring from the fancy Harvard Square jewelry store. We were still seeing our parents regularly. We argued about politics, but they gave us money—quite a bit of money—and welcomed our visits. I was a perfectly respectable high school teacher and a virtuous married woman. John had had an MIT teaching assistantship one semester we could boast about. We kept our political activities—our movement friendships, our study groups, our demonstrations—away from our families. Were we living double lives, or were we just covering our bets?

I jerked myself back to the scene again. This morning, Cathy Wilkerson from RYM and I from WSA, were supposed to debate the issue of male chauvinism in the movement. Some women in the SDS were complaining about being excluded from the leadership. Why did WSA choose *me* of all people to speak? John said, "They gave it to Jared to decide. After all, Jared is the top honcho in Boston and Boston is the center of WSA."

What about the other WSA women in Boston? Jared explained, "No one else wants to do it. Look, you're a teacher, you can talk, right? We'll help you with the speech." Which he did, by helpfully explaining PL's line again. "You must say that male chauvinism is simply a vicious tool to divide the working class."

I knew I had a lot to learn.

I wore a white blouse and a modest khaki skirt—my miniskirts, fishnet stockings, and long earrings a thing of the past. Cathy wore a loose man's shirt and jeans, sunglasses and a bandanna. The announcer introduced me as "Friedl Myer," mispronouncing my name and Cathy as "Jane Smith." Huh?! Oh, I get it—she's in disguise and about to go underground! I felt both contemptuous and impressed. I cleared my throat and spoke my careful sentences loudly. "Like racism, male chauvinism is a tool of the bourgeoisie to divide the working class."

Wild cheers from half of the several hundred listeners: "Down with capitalism and male chauvinism!" Boos and catcalls from the other half. "Men and women must overcome their differences so that we can defeat the common enemy." More cheers, more boos. I trembled with excitement. This was fun! It was like conducting the Glee Club or something. It hardly mattered what I said. When Cathy spoke, the people who had cheered me booed, and vice versa. She declaimed the RYM line, that male privilege was as important as white privilege and that sexism was innate to men. The whole thing ended, as far as I could see, in a draw.

WSA members congratulated me for a job well done, but I felt ashamed. My voice had sounded high and tinny, not loud and bold, and I felt like a performer in someone else's play. Wasn't I an activist and an organizer in my own right? I was even going to work in a factory this coming summer, a sure sign that I was serious about my commitment to organizing the working class for the revolution.

John and Sarah and I returned to our large sleeping bag in an overcrowded movement apartment in Chicago, with roaches crawling on the kitchen counter, and then visited John's family in Houston, complete with swimming pool, maid service, and doting grandparents for Sarah.

We didn't yet know that that we would bring a whole colony of roaches back with us to overpopulate our third-floor apartment on the Cambridge-Somerville line, or that SDS would split apart and disintegrate that summer. We had no idea that we had been present at the beginning of the end of the student movement. We didn't know that we would transmute our fierce revolutionary goals into lifelong commitments: ending American imperialism abroad, fostering economic justice at home. I became a Women's Studies professor; John, later, a community organizer. My second husband was a Labor Studies professor and is now a writer about these self-same issues. Carry it on!

On Being a Marxist Nun from Kansas

Kathleen A. O'Shea

I entered the convent in the 1960s. Anxious to work in the fields of the Lord, I set out for Chile. At eighteen I was afraid to tell my parents I'd volunteered for a foreign "mission," though they were proud enough of my brother in Vietnam. So I told them I was "chosen"— which is what the letter from our Mother General in Rome stated. It said, "You have been chosen." I knew my mother would be pleased about that. And so she was.

I was in Chile from 1965 to 1973—through two presidents and a military coup—historic times. But when I arrived I was apolitical. My life was about God, not politics. By fortune or fate, I arrived at the same time as Paolo Freire, the renowned Brazilian educator, and learned he was in exile there for his radical thinking and teaching. *Exile* and *radical* being two words I'd never used before.

We had a progressive Mother Superior who announced one evening that anyone who wanted to take a seminar with this brilliant man at the Catholic University could do so. It wasn't mandatory, but at the time I wanted to go everywhere and do everything. Our convent and school were on the outskirts of Santiago in the piedmont of the towering Andes. Catholic University was downtown where I'd already seen antiquated oxcarts and horses swaying in and out of the more modern buses and cars.

When I arrived at class that first evening, I met Freire. I remember his short stature and his beard and feeling energy exude from him as I'd never felt before. He had not yet written *Pedagogy of the Oppressed* and he was still formulating his thinking, using nuns and priests as sounding boards. Our community was already going out on literacy campaigns—which meant we were teaching people to read and write in small villages throughout Chile. We were a perfect fit.

Over the years, people, students, family, and others have asked me, in reference to those times, "What was your most political moment? The moment that changed you forever?"

You might think it was when I arrived at the school our community owned and operated (called a rich school because we taught in English and the students paid tuition). There, the second graders I taught had maids in their forties and fifties who carried their books to the classroom for them every morning and arrived at the classroom door to pick them up every afternoon.

After the first week I put a stop to that and told the "maids" (even though I spoke no Spanish, and they no English, we understood each other) that the little girls would have to carry their own books upstairs, and they would have to wait for them downstairs in the patio. This was not a political thing; it just made sense. I had sixty-five second graders and sixty-five maids-in-waiting—the sheer numbers were mind-boggling to me. And I thought no one as old as my mother should be carrying anything for young healthy children. About a week later I was called to the principal's office and told I had made quite an impression already. The parents were in an uproar; the children were crying; the maids were frustrated, and this (the book carrying) was the way it was always done.

Or perhaps it should have been political that Sunday afternoon our Mother Superior called us (the nuns) together and told us the US Marines would be arriving that afternoon to teach us how to make and throw Molotov cocktails. These maneuvers would take place in the open field behind the school in the shadows of the magnificent Andes. Though I would not have said so at the time, this was a bit mind-boggling. Were these the same US Marines fighting alongside my brother in Vietnam? By way of explanation we were told there was a chance we might have to defend ourselves from the Communists. As nuns, should there be a takeover, we might be in danger. The Communists were nonbelievers and would want to get rid of believers. At some level this made sense.

And so it was while my brother was fighting the Viet Cong I convinced myself I might soon have my own war going on. The good part was that I'd finally be able to defend the faith and give my life for God. So we, the nuns, and a small troop of US Marines made and tossed bombs all afternoon, which must have frightened the fenced-in sow and her eight piglets to death. Afterwards we ate homemade chocolate chip cookies and drank Coca-Cola (already a huge industry in Chile) into the evening hours. It was a good day, but I never thought it political, and the Communists never arrived.

Or it could have been political that weekend a couple of years down the line when I was invited to a *Fundo* (hacienda) to attend a First Communion of the brother of one of my second graders. I invited another nun to go with me, and we stayed all weekend. Our rooms were along the corridor of an inside patio, and when I stepped out of our plush accommodations on Saturday morning to take a breath of fresh air, the first thing I noticed was the little boy, Hernan, the guest of honor, who was to receive the body and blood of Christ that very day. He was dressed all in white, a little white suit and tie and black shoes, handsome for his age. With him was Aida, the family nanny who had been his mother's nanny when she was a child and who had come to live with her after she married to take care of her children. Aida was a lovely woman; she would have been in her seventies by then, I imagine. And precisely at the moment I looked over at the two of them, little Hernan snapped his fingers and pointed down to his shoe, and Aida obediently knelt to tie it.

I was both ashamed and enraged. I felt my face burn with a blush, and I wanted to run across the patio and slap little Hernan and shake him and force him to apologize to Aida. This did not seem political to me; it just made sense. I came from a large Catholic family where no child ever ordered an adult to do anything.

Perhaps I should have thought it political when I'd been at the school for a while, and some of the high school students who knew me from their religion classes started bringing their university boyfriends over to my classroom on Saturdays where I was usually grading papers. They said they wanted me to meet them. As time went on, they (the boyfriends) initiated discussions where they used words like capitalism, socialism, and Marxism and talked about people like Karl Marx, Fidel Castro, and Salvador Allende. These boyfriends were enthusiastic about our talks and were constantly throwing questions at me regarding my opinions on all of this. Frequently, in English, they would say "you capitalists" in a tone of voice that seemed like a put down, though at the time, I couldn't understand why they included me. I didn't know what a capitalist was—and I wondered if anyone in my family at home in Kansas would know.

But I loved these interchanges because they made me think about things I'd never considered. I was somewhat intimidated by these college guys who were about my age. I liked what they were teaching me; yet, at the same time, I was afraid of their knowledge. They wrote and diagrammed things all over my second-grade blackboard as if we were in a political science class. I was fascinated. The drawings emphasized various points they wanted to make as they introduced me to Marxism. I didn't think any of this was political, only that it was very interesting and I was learning a lot; they brought me many books and papers to read.

Miguel Angel, a very impassioned and handsome young man who played the guitar and wrote protest songs he often sang for me, brought me speeches Fidel Castro had made to the Cuban people. I remember him giving them to me, a stack of papers mussed up but in exact order, insisting I read them and let him know what I thought. With unbelievable intensity in his beautiful dark eyes and anger in his voice, he asked, "What do you think of a man who wants every child in his country to have shoes? Can you think this man is bad?"

His voice was accusatory, and he spoke as if I had an opinion about it and as if I represented some political philosophy that didn't like it. I was ashamed to tell him I had no opinions about it at all about it. I'd been taught to fear Fidel Castro and had never questioned that stance. But the way he approached me, it seemed to me I should have had an opinion. So I told him I'd read the papers and let him know.

There so many examples of what should have been my most political moment. But the real one was quite unexpected.

The summer of 1967 I spent some time in a tiny village in the South of Chile working at a Maryknoll mission, giving the Maryknoll Sisters a chance to make their annual retreat and go to Santiago for rest and recreation. It gave us a chance to experience life outside of Santiago. I did it for two reasons: first because I was still looking for the "poor" I'd come to Chile to be with and second because I thought it would help me learn Spanish.

A bus loaded with people and animals left me in a dusty plaza where tumbleweeds were blowing across the road around three o'clock one afternoon. The air was hot. There were no people. I thought I'd walked onto a set of a John Wayne movie. The entire village could be seen in one glance. It was not a town, but a gathering, perhaps, like the pictures of missions I'd seen in *Maryknoll Magazine* as a child. The whole place appeared to be abandoned. In the center was the church. I entered the building next to the church where I assumed the priests lived. On the table was a handwritten note: "Sister, Gone to Chillán. Will be back in a week. Don't drink water. Well is poisoned. Fr. S."

That was the beginning.

On one of the days we returned from our travels to various villages, Father S. said, "Sister, come with me. I want you to meet the head of our Communist Party." I was shocked, nervous, afraid—totally baffled that a place such as that little village could have a Communist Party. Today I know that Father S. must have enjoyed my reaction.

He took me out to the bean field behind the church where a number of peasants were tilling and planting, and in a friendly voice called a little man named Juan. Seeing me in full religious habit, Juan approached me and removed his wide-brimmed, colorless hat that protected him from the strong sun. Bareheaded as he was, he genuflected in front of me, took my hand and kissed it. He was dark and wizened from long days in the sun, probably in his sixties. He wore no shoes and had on tattered clothes that seemed to blend into his body. At nineteen I was humiliated and speechless. I knew this man shouldn't be bowing to me; at the very least my mother would not approve. I knew he was a wise man, one I needed to learn from—one, perhaps, *I* needed to bow to—but I didn't know how to process or speak to that.

At first I didn't understand that Juan was the Communist Party leader. For whatever reason, I thought he might be a person Father would ask to introduce me to some other person. But before I had a chance to ask, Father S., who had embraced Juan like a long-lost brother, said with great pride, "Juan is also the president of our parish council."

Juan beamed and bowed his head. I stood there dumbfounded. What could I say? Nothing. The head of the Communist Party and the president of the parish council of the Catholic Church all bound up in this little, smiling, humble man before me. We hadn't even spoken, but I knew I liked and respected him. A lifetime of learning fell apart that moment.

Father S. and I didn't speak about the encounter. I didn't know what to say. But the next day, I went back to the field on my own to talk to Juan. He came over as soon as he saw me and repeated his rituals of the day before. So, standing there under the hot sun and in my broken Spanish mingled with many gestures, I asked him if he believed in God.

Immediately his face lit up, and he said, "Sí, sí, Madre."

So then I asked him, "What does God do for you?"

He responded by smiling and pointing and using single words in Spanish. "The sun, the rain, the crops, the wife, the children."

I watched and listened. He was so proud of those things. Then I said, "And you are Communist too, right?"

To this, his face lit up in the same way it had for my first question, and again he said, "Sí, sí, Madre."

"So what does communism do for you?" I asked.

Immediately he raised his finger as if a light bulb had just been turned on in his head. Again with great pride he pointed to a little hut across the field in the distance and said, "For my family, they gave me a house."

That conversation with Juan remains my most political moment in Chile and the one that changed my life forever. The world I inhabited was no longer black and white. Beyond everything I'd ever been taught, I realized there were many shades of gray. I not only understood what Juan told me; I knew he was right. Both philosophies had a place in his life, and, for Juan, there was no conflict between the two.

❧

I am currently Co-Director of Bethany House, a Catholic Worker homeless shelter for women and children in Rochester, New York. Besides temporary housing, we have a food pantry that allows us to give out free food and a clothing room where we give out free clothes. Everything we have to give away is donated.

When a person arrives with a donation, whether it be food, clothing, furniture, money, or toys, we do not ask for their personal philosophies. It makes no difference who they are or what they believe—we are grateful for their assistance.

In the same vein, when a woman comes to the door and asks for diapers or baby food, or when someone calls and says they are a family of five and have no food, or when the police bring a woman in the middle of the night who had to be removed from a domestic violence situation, we never ask what they believe or if they have any religious beliefs at all. We offer them hospitality in every way we can.

This is a way of life Juan would understand.

The September Wind

Sara Etgen-Baker

My father's rickety old truck meandered through miles of unfamiliar country towns with strange names, past cotton fields with bolls burst open and ripe for picking, past amber meadows with leafy corn stalks ready for harvesting. The September wind blew through the truck's open windows, stirring my hair and whispering of change. My childhood, like summer, was fading and yelled, "Don't go! Don't go!" But the road to college lay ahead—there was no turning back. So, I closed my eyes and listened to the wind, waiting until it enveloped me.

When I opened my eyes, the September wind—like warm and gentle hands—caught the golden leaves as they fell off the trees. And for just a moment, I thought I heard the leaves sharing secrets with the wind. "The September wind," my grandmother once told me, "oft' times tells the tales of unspoken secrets and hidden truths." In that instant, the September wind caressed my face. Then tears, deep gut-wrenching tears, cascaded down my face.

"When you cry your tears are the words your mouth can't say nor your heart can bear. Trust me," murmured the wind, "for I understand broken dreams and silent screams. Share your unspoken secrets and heartache with me."

Now I closed my eyes and thought back to that summer day when my dreams were shattered.

"Southern Methodist University!" I gasped as I opened the

acceptance letter. I ran inside waving the letter and whooping loudly. "Mother! I've been accepted at SMU!"

"What do you mean?" Her mouth flew open. "I didn't know you'd applied for college."

"Well…uh…well…" I stammered and lowered my head. "I didn't tell you."

She pulled down her glasses, peering over the rims. "Well, you should have told me!" She lifted one eyebrow. "You can't go to SMU."

My eyes widened as I stared at her in disbelief. "And just *why not*?"

"It's simple." She paused, gathering her thoughts. "Only boys need to go to college."

"Whatever do you mean?"

"Girls don't need college, but boys do, because one day they'll be the breadwinners. Besides, your brother has his sights set on SMU, so we'll be helping him with college expenses, not you."

My mouth flew open. "I can't believe this." My voice dropped. "I don't understand; you know I'm smart and make good grades. I need to go to college so I can be an independent woman!"

"Well, you may go to college—just not SMU. It's too expensive! Be practical and choose an affordable small university where you can work and put yourself through college."

My normally calm and pleasant demeanor changed; I looked past her and snapped, "You've sentenced me to a life of mediocrity." I crumpled the acceptance letter into a tiny ball and threw it at her feet. "That's not fair! How could you? How could you?"

"Fair or not, that's the way the world is!" She folded her arms across her chest. "Now, there'll be no more discussion."

I spun away in a huff and stomped out of the room. Although her words tore me apart and dashed my dreams of independence, I eventually complied like the silent, agreeable, good girl I was expected to be. I selected a rural state university and found a part-time job shelving books at the university library. Secretly, I harbored a deep resentment toward my mother and the prevailing culture that had no qualms valuing males over females. But by September, my resentment, like a cotton boll in the open fields, had ripened and was now about to burst.

❦

When I opened my eyes, the college campus came into view. Just as my father turned into the dormitory parking lot, we passed a group of barefooted students—long-haired, bearded men dressed in bell-bottoms and long-haired women dressed like peasants wearing psychedelic colors. I tried not to stare at them even though they frightened and mystified me. One of the men looked straight at me, held up his right hand, extended his first two fingers into a V-shape, and mouthed the word *peace.*

Mother wrinkled her nose and shook her head. "Look at those dirty hippies," she grumbled. "Hippies say that they want to save the world, but all they do is smoke pot and play Frisbee! Who'd want to be a hippie? Promise me you won't become a hippie!"

I flung open the truck door and grabbed my suitcases. "Mother!" I grimaced, took a deep breath, slammed the truck door, and snapped, "I came here to earn a degree—not become a hippie!" Secretly, though, I thought, *Maybe I will become a hippie.*

Through the open window she handed me twenty dollars. "This is all the extra money we can spare. So, use it wisely. Remember to be a good girl—don't become a hippie! We'll pick you up in December." With that proclamation, I watched my parents drive off until they disappeared from my view.

After checking into the dorm, I weaved my way through the labyrinth of hallways and eventually found my room. My hands trembled as I turned the key and opened the door. I stood at the entryway shocked to find my room looked like a hospital room, desolate and barren, with its white cinder block walls, white curtains, white sheets, and gray tile floors. Then my resentment churned in my stomach, for my dorm room here looked nothing like the ones at SMU. Suddenly, I felt nauseated, bitter, and all alone.

"Attention freshmen women!" The voice blared over the dormitory intercom. "You *must* attend orientation in the lobby in five minutes." I threw my suitcases on the bed and scurried down the hall, only to find that orientation had already begun.

A stout, elderly woman marched toward me. Her bony hands, white as a winter's day, reached out and handed me a packet of information. "You're late!" she growled like a junkyard dog. "I'm Mrs. Evans—your dorm mother. Turn to page three!" Then she read: "Your dorm mother ensures you keep curfew hours, records who has permission to leave overnight or on weekends, reports the names of residents who miss curfew and bed check to the Dean of Women, and contacts parents when residents violate curfew."

She took a long sip of her coffee and continued. "On page four you'll notice that outside doors are locked at curfew. Curfew is nine p.m. on weeknights; eleven p.m. on Saturdays; and six p.m. on Sundays."

My stomach tightened. I swallowed hard and almost choked. I knew I was in trouble, because I was working four nights a week until 10 p.m.—an hour past curfew. I raised my hand. "What should I do if…"

The girl next to me nudged me in the side and spoke in clipped sentences. "Keep quiet." She looked straight at me. "Follow me after this meeting. My name's Shannon."

After the meeting I followed Shannon to her room. Within minutes her twelve-by-fifteen-foot room was filled with angry, verbal coeds.

"These rules are a trip," asserted the girl sitting next to me.

"I hear that!" exclaimed Shannon. "You know the men on campus don't have curfew or bed check." She raised her voice a notch. "They even get special keys that unlock their dorm's front door! They can come and go as they please."

"For real?" I shook my head in disbelief. "That's not fair! Why is that?" I rambled, searching for an answer to my own predicament.

"I have a job that'll keep me away from the dorm way past curfew. I need that job and the money." I paused. "What am I gonna do?"

"Search me!" said another coed. "I haven't got a clue."

"I have an idea," offered a slender young woman. "My room's at the back of the building. So, just tap on my window, and I'll sneak any of you into the dorm through the back door."

"Don't you get it?" Shannon's face reddened as she raised her voice. "We shouldn't have to sneak into our dorm. These curfew rules are archaic, sexist, and unfair!" Clenching her fists, she shouted, "We need to fight the oppressive establishment!"

Several girls nodded their heads in unison and harmoniously voiced, "We can dig it!"

"But what can we do?" I whined. "Rules *are* rules."

"How about a petition?" suggested a frail, mousy-looking girl sitting in the corner.

"Far out!" another unified response.

"Let's start right now," Shannon insisted. Within minutes we'd drafted a petition that read:

ELIMINATE CURFEW/BED CHECKS AT WOMEN'S DORMS
Female residents have curfew and bed checks. Males don't. Males receive special keys that open the front door of their dorms. Females don't receive these special keys. Female residents should have the same rights and privileges as males. We, the undersigned, demand the elimination of curfew and bed checks for women and demand special front door keys.

Before leaving Shannon's room, we each took a handwritten copy of the petition, vowing to get at least twenty-five signatures on our individual petitions before reconvening on the following Sunday.

❧

"Wow! Look how many signatures we have!" I gasped, tossing the papers up in the air. "Let's count 'em."

Flipping through the pages, Shannon counted the signatures.

Then she jumped up and down squealing, "Ladies, we have over three hundred signatures!"

"What do we do now?" voiced our mousy-looking accomplice.

"We need to take our petitions to someone who will hear our concerns." I cleared my throat. "How about the Dean of Women?"

"Spiffy idea!"

"Right on!"

❧

Two days later Shannon and I found ourselves sitting in front of Dean Wilson.

"Tell me"—he lowered his reading glasses and peered down his nose—"what brings such pretty young girls to my office today?"

"Well, sir…" My voice cracked. I handed him the stack of papers. "We wanted to talk with you about this petition from the members of WFC."

"The WFC?" His eyes narrowed. "What's the WFC?"

"Women for Change," explained Shannon.

"You pretty girls aren't radical hippie feminists are you?"

"We prefer to think of ourselves as student activists," I suggested. "We believe we have a legitimate concern. We want to be treated fairly and equally, like the male students, with the same privileges to come and go."

He glanced over the petitions. "I appreciate your bringing your concerns to my attention." Then he paced around his office, stopping to stand at the window with his back to us. "The university reserves the right to operate *in loco parentis*—to protect its students. Girls need to be in their dorms by 10 p.m. and should be monitored on weekends—to protect them."

"Protect us from what?" I challenged.

"From harm!"

"But why does the university feel the need to protect female students but not male students?" Shannon asked.

He faced us. "Because females are the fairer sex and need to be protected."

"But sir, don't you see the policy is unfair? You're using a double standard!"

Dean Wilson's face turned red like a volcano about to erupt. Then he squinted his eyes and tightened his lips, echoing my mother's dismissive words. "Fair or not, that's the way life is." He folded his arms across his chest. "They'll be no more discussion."

He strode across the room, opened his office door, and said, "I'll take your petition under advisement. Now, if you'll excuse me, I have another meeting I must attend."

"You haven't seen the last of us!" threatened Shannon.

Suddenly, I wanted to challenge this man and the established belief that males inherently had more rights than females. "Don't count us out so fast!" I added as Shannon and I stood up and left.

❧

"That meeting was a bummer!" Shannon exclaimed as we walked back to the dorm together.

"And can you believe the Dean of Women is a man? Something's just not right about that!" I stopped and turned to Shannon. "But what did you mean when you said, 'You haven't seen the last of us'?"

"We need to make a stronger statement—like a sit-in." Her cheeks flushed with passion, and her eyes sparkled with an irresistible ferocity. "Are you in?"

Shannon's question begged me to listen to my inner voice. "That's a huge question." I stared at her, trembling on the inside with fear and courage. The fearful part of me wanted to hold onto the inequities and injustice and remain bitter, angry, and resentful. The weaker part of me wanted to shove it all away, pretend it didn't exist, and submit to being a good girl. Yet another bolder, braver part of me wanted to put behind me everything familiar and secure.

I stood on the edge of the precipice—the September winds swirling around my feet. In front of me was a massive drop-off, and I had no idea of what lay below. With nothing to hold on to I wondered, *Will I fall into the vast abyss waiting below?* Or will I, like the leaves caught in the September wind, float to the ground beneath me? But the September wind stirred my hair, reassuring me as it blew across my face. "Take the leap. I'll catch you." So, I leapt and said, "Yes, I'm in."

I awoke early the morning of our first sit-in—slipping into the bell-bottom jeans and tie-dyed T-shirt I had purchased with the twenty dollars my mother had given me. I felt powerful as I picked up my sign that read "In Loco Parentis Unfair to Females." WFC members and supporters, over two hundred strong, gathered at the Commons in front of the Administration Building. We waved our signs and chanted phrases from Helen Reddy's song: "We are woman; hear us roar in numbers too big to ignore." "We are strong; we are invincible."

With a little nudge from the news media and the local chapter of the ACLU, our sit-ins gained some regional notoriety. By semester's end, curfew for women was abolished, and we received those precious front door keys. During the second semester a headline in the university newspaper reported that Dean Wilson had been *promoted* to Dean of Student Activities. His successor, a female, was sympathetic to women's issues and fostered a more open attitude between the status quo and emerging women's issues.

I remember those early college days with such extraordinary vividness. Like the leaves floating on the September winds, I learned to leap past the fear of the changing season within me and to trust the vibrations of a deeper, more authentic self. As a result, my remaining college years were even more vivid and intense—almost surreal. Yet, there was nothing surreal about the '70s. It was a decade of bitter truth, turbulence, change, and creativity. And like other courageous young college women in the '70s, I started on an historic journey—never looking back—challenging the status quo, embracing feminism, and appreciating my own mystery.

Altamont

Amber Lea Starfire

We'd slipped from our homes while the crisp December sky still glittered with stars, eight of us squeezing into Jim's beat-up old Chevy, the girls sitting on the boys' laps, for the two-hour ride from Redwood City. At fourteen, I am the youngest. My boyfriend Dac's bony legs feel fragile beneath my own, and for the last half hour I have been holding myself up between the seatback and the door frame in a vain attempt to make myself lighter.

The sky blushes subtle shades of peach and coral in a backdrop of gray when we finally arrive at Altamont for the West Coast's version of Woodstock. And because it is ours, we know it will be better than Woodstock; it will be the best free outdoor concert and hippie love-fest in history. All the biggest bands will be performing: the Rolling Stones, Santana, Jefferson Airplane, the Flying Burrito Brothers, Crosby, Stills, Nash and Young, and the Grateful Dead. And we, a gaggle of adrenalized, pimply-faced teens, will be a part of this history.

Ours is one in a long line of cars crawling up the hill like ants with bright eyes following each other, headlight to taillight. Finally, we reach the parking lot, a field of mowed dry grass, already chewed to dust by the cars. Chattering excitedly and in a hurry to find good seats, we bundle up in our jackets and pull blankets and bags of junk food from the trunk. In spite of the early hour, tributaries of people are trickling in from every direction, merging onto the road leading into the arena, a river of youth flowing toward the concert site.

We merge with the swelling crowd. The sky shifts to pale, dusky blue and gold, a positive promise of sunshine. The air smells of gasoline, dry grass and dust, fog, patchouli oil, and pot. Everyone is in a good mood, greeting one another with peace signs and laughter. Smiling, lanky, long-haired boys wearing fringed leather vests or jackets and patchwork bell-bottoms appear before me, hands outstretched in offering. In their palms are white pills stamped with tiny crosses, sugar cubes, or tiny pieces of paper with clear drops of LSD in their centers, gel caps filled with barbiturates, small bags of amphetamine, synthetic mescaline, and peyote. Free for the taking. I want to ride the promise of this day, the promise of peace and love and goodwill to the better world I believe is its destination. I swallow everything handed to me. I am not thinking about what the combination of all these drugs might do to me. I am mindless, floating in the energy of the moment. Not thinking, at all.

Spreading our blankets on the grass, our group stakes out a perfect spot with a clear view of the right side of the stage and watches the river of people as it swells, bursts the narrow road, and overflows into the arena. Roadies bustle about the stage setting up speakers and microphones, running sound checks. The air buzzes with voices, excitement, song. The beats of drums and tambourines collide with each other. Police helicopters chop in ovals above us, coming closer, receding, closer, receding. As the drugs filter into my system, the world begins to tilt, moving around with the sound, round and round, up and down, as though I am riding an immense carousel. Not an unpleasant feeling. But the helicopters make me feel surveilled, and a small seed of paranoia plants itself in my chest.

That is when a large, yellow school bus rumbles up next to us and stops. We watch, curious, as a burly, tattooed, leather-clad man steps out, followed by a German shepherd attached to a leash. The man brandishes a baseball bat. I notice, belatedly, the "Hells Angels" script across the back of his jacket and emblazoned on the side of the bus. He strikes the bus with a sharp metallic *crack!*

We sit up straight, surprised, wary.

"Move! We're sitting here!" he growls. The dog is silent but stares at us with hungry intensity.

Without a word to each other, we pick up our blankets and move down the hill, away from the Hells Angels' bus in search of another place to sit in the crowded sea of blankets and people. We step over children, trying not to step on blankets. It's impossible, there's no space. But the concertgoers are in a cooperative, happy mood and they scoot together, making room for us to lay out our blankets. Gratefully, we settle again. We can still see the stage, but we're lower down and the view's not as good. When people get up to dance, as they are now even though the bands haven't started playing, they block the view.

A bad feeling has taken root in the pit of my stomach—the police helicopters and the unexpected violence of the Hells Angels. I feel like a child, unjustly scolded for something I haven't done. We are supposed to be about peace and love and higher consciousness. Confusion and hurt swirls around in me while the cold earth seeps up through the blanket, and I begin to shiver. The earth tilts further and threatens to swallow me.

A line of people snakes by, a man holding a toddler aloft chanting, "Broken toe, broken toe," forging a path to the medical tent. Vaguely, I register clapping, cheers, music flooding the air, the commotion of people dancing and twirling around me. Confusion, swirling, whirling, melting. The sky is too bright. There is no sky, only feet all around me. Colors, voices, sounds, chaos, pandemonium. Darkness.

※

I awaken abruptly, my mind crystal clear and not befuddled by drugs. I seem to be floating a few feet above the ground. A band—I don't know which one—is performing onstage, and I can hear the music distinctly for the first time since the earth began to tilt. At the front of the stage, chromed motorcycles reflect the stage lights. Half-naked, painted people pressed torso-to-torso, shoulder-to-shoulder, are bouncing and undulating to the beat of the music, their hands in the air like the tentacles of sea anemones bending and swaying with the tide.

Below me, on a brown woolen army blanket, a young girl lies curled around herself in tight fetal position, her fists clenched and tucked beneath her chin. She wears a red flannel shirt and wide bell-bottom jeans. On her head, a floppy leather hat sits askew, pressed between her head and the blanket. Strands of brown hair splay across her cheeks. Around her, others sit or sway on their own small islands of cloth, and no one pays her any attention. The girl looks so young, so pale, so alone—so vulnerable in bloodless sleep. Pity wells up in my heart. I want to hold her, comfort her, rock her in my arms like the child she is.

Then I realize, with detached surprise, that she is me. How can I be that girl? How can I be here, looking down at myself? I have somehow moved outside my body. I've read about this happening to people in near-death experiences. Have I died? I peer at the girl on the ground. She could be dead. I'm not sure.

But I am floating upward, away from her. The stage, the arena, and the surrounding hills appear beneath me as one. I am struck by how much the landscape, covered as it is by writhing movement, appears like the curve of a woman's vulva, the low hills like thighs. The music, the movement, the energy of all these people is tribal, sexual, primal. The comparison comes to me as revelation, but I don't understand its significance.

I drift upward, farther away from the scene, like a balloon unte-thered. I wonder, vaguely, what will become of my body. I feel that I should be afraid, but I'm not. Instead, I sense a protective presence beside me, as though someone is holding my hand, reassuring me that everything will be okay. *Hush now, stay with me, trust me,* the presence seems to whisper. Clarity and peace wash over me like a warm summer rain, sweeping away my questions, leaving only acceptance in their wake.

I turn toward my unseen guide and allow it to lead me away from earth to witness the birth of new stars and oceans surging over new worlds.

I see Dac far below, rocking the girl's upper body, pushing her shoulders back and forth. The movement pulls at me, dragging me back and downward. I'm tethered after all by a slender cord, and I resist. I don't feel ready to go back. Not yet.

Now he is calling my name. "Linda, wake up...C'mon, wake up." A tone of exasperation. A sucking sound. A sensation of being pressed together, squeezed into a vacuum tube, and I am abruptly drawn into a tiny confining space. There's a loud *pop!* and I am once again behind my eyelids. I slit them open, peer upward into Dac's face, his mouth twisted into a tight expression of disgust.

"Whaa..." I manage to murmur.

He's pulling on my arm. "Get up. They're going to leave us."

I uncurl, stiff, disoriented, and confused as an old woman awakened rudely from her afternoon nap.

His eyes slide sideways and refuse to meet mine. "Come on, we have to get going."

He tugs my arms until I'm on my feet. Swaying to gain balance, I peer around through too-heavy eyelids. The ground around me is littered with garbage. My head hurts and my legs wobble, as though unused to the weight of my body. I lurch forward. Dac grabs my arm, keeping me on my feet, and pulls me toward our friends, their backs moving away from us. Everyone, in fact, is moving away. I think I'm going to be sick, and bend over to retch, but nothing happens, and Dac is once again tugging me forward.

In spite of his efforts, we lose sight of Jim and the others, and we can't remember where the car is parked. We trudge in one direction then another. Dusk settles over us like a gray shroud and soon it becomes too dark to see. We are exhausted, cold, and—we finally admit—lost. Dac is angry with me. "It's your fault," he says.

We head downhill, crossing dead fields toward the highway and the hopeful lights of civilization. At the foot of the hill, there's a gas station with a phone booth. Neither of us have money, so I call my mother collect.

"Where are you?" Her tone of voice tells me I am a nuisance.

"I don't know." I can taste the salt of my tears, the fear and shame burning hot in my chest. "At a gas station near Altamont…um…a Shell…" I look around for a street sign, try to remember the name of the highway. "Just off 580."

"You're *where*?"

"Altamont…I'm sorry," I say, wishing I could shrink away to nothing. It would be a relief to be nothing. To just close my eyes and float away again.

⁂

Hungry, thirsty, and tired, Dac and I wait by the phone booth, both of us still ignorant of the history-making violence that had earlier slashed through the concert crowd. We know nothing of the fighting, the shooting and knifing, which marked the beginning of the end of utopian hippie dreams. We only know the violence in ourselves, and the pain between us.

Dac won't speak to me. My head hurts. I feel half-dead, stupid, guilty. Everything is my fault. I am an idiot. If I hadn't taken all those drugs, if I hadn't insisted that the car was *this way*, when Dac said *that way*, we might not be in this situation.

When my mother finally arrives, she begins yelling before we are in the car.

"I had to drive an hour and a half in the dark to get you. How could you be so thoughtless! The traffic was *horrible*. I had to ask a neighbor to babysit your little brother. Where are your friends? You could have hitchhiked home…"

Her shrill voice is a lance piercing my eyes, and I shield them with my hand. "Please, stop yelling," I say, but I am despondent and sullen and she doesn't hear me. I need her to say she'd been worried about me. I need her to hold me in her arms and tell me she is happy I called her, relieved that I'm okay.

I don't hear the fear behind her screeching, cannot consider what it must be like for her to find her fourteen-year-old daughter, bedraggled, incoherent, and filthy from lying on the ground, with bits of dry grass stuck to her hair and clothing. Instead, I think, *I could have died. Should have died. No one cares.* I have fallen from Heaven into a deep pool of self-pity; a dark ache washes through me. Slouching back into my seat, I cover my eyes and ears against my mother, against the lights flashing by, against the reality in which I live.

I long to return to that moment when I floated among the stars, to feel again the sensation of pure being and the crystal clarity that went with it. I wish I could remember all that I saw, for I feel oddly privileged. But my mind seems filled with thick, gray cotton, and the vision is already slipping away.

I don't know what it means or why I didn't die, but the whispering voice of my unseen guide and the half-remembered visions of stars and oceans—previously unimagined possibilities—will always remain with me.

Going Up the Country

Margot Maddison-MacFadyen
With thanks to Canned Heat for their '60s song.

I'm going, I'm going
where the water tastes like wine.

Because I am from there
and she strengthened my bones as I grew,
I love the mountain.

Hollyburn—

her darkly-firred slopes
the colour of a spawning sockeye's head

her precipitous ravines
plummeting to ribbons of froth

her quiet cryptic places above
where no streetlights intrude

but nine-starred Pleiades
once faint and far off
smiles, a benefactress
in the night.

* * *

And the memory of Ambleside
nestled where Hollyburn's feet
dip into the ocean
at the mouth of the Capilano

her headwaters high above
in those hidden mountainous places

in those secreted fern hollows

her water running down
like laughing salmon.

In 1969, the brave amongst us
leapt from the train bridge
into her icy depths

emerged vivified youthful goddesses

our pebble-eyes
bright with river water

rivulets cascaded through our hair
down sleek backs browned by sun-filled days
over breasts, buttocks as firm as cantaloupes, dimpled knees

through muscled toes.

* * *

And Ambleside's tall mango-blooming rhododendrons
that we sat under at dusk
knees pulled to chins

the sweet tang of tall grasses
plucked and chewed
lingering on our lips

water lapping the shore
like a cougar's kittens.

We were Kozmic then
in pink and purple paisley

transmogrified by John Lennon shades—
two darkened brass-wire-rimmed-quarter-sized lenses

Janis Joplin hats—
Navaho-beaded, softly-felted-floppy luxuriousness
with fluted edges
like an oyster shell

and *Oh Mon!*
by Peace, Love, and Happiness.

* * *

Behind us, the ball field
where every year at May Day
maypoles festooned with vibrant ribbons
red, white, blue
burgeoned fertility

and the pubescent May Queen was crowned.

Our hearts swelled
our feet marched
to swirling crescendos
of bagpipes summoning

their pipers stood in circles
legs rooted in the Earth
like mossy tree trunks

their kilts swayed rhythmically

feathers in caps lifted softly
tickled by a kissing wind.

* * *

Just beyond, Joe Capilano's spirit house
small, green-hued with lichen
that I walked past every day
when I was thirteen.

I sensed him there
his skull, mandible, long leg bones
the ribs that held his heart
part of the Earth

and he sensed me.

Without eyes, ears, speech
we knew each other.

Ghosted then—

tiny whirlwinds

swirling bits of dry leaves

accompanied me to school
waited in the playground

walked me home at night.

I grieve for Joe
for his once magnificent
view of the Narrows

old-time village X̱wáý̱xway
Place of Masks

where he carved canoes
from whole trees

and Slahkayulsh
He is standing up!

which he protects in death
as in life.

And I grieve for my own great grandfather Stephen
whose memorial stone long ago lost in Stanley Park
lies buried under pungent duff in the cedar-spiced forest
by the roots of the towering hollow tree

and for the hollow tree
once a home to black bears, felled
after a West Coast storm, removed.

Who could have predicted the bridge?

its two resident lions *couchant*
heralds of Britain
one to each side of the causeway?

Who could have predicted Vancouver
in 1791?

* * *

Hollyburn—

her bones remain

her darkly firred slopes
precipitous ravines
secreted places high above
still ferned, still cool

but altered.

She is not herself.

Capilano—

her magical, laughing-salmon water?

Diminished,
a hundredfold.

I hold them in my heart—
the mountain and the river
as I knew them in the '60s

the refuge of memories.

* * *

I'm Going Up the Country...
where I've never been before

to sing madrigals in the mountains
frolic in salmon-radiant water
bathe in sun and swim all day

waltz away mourning
fly up and over green-firred slopes

drift through precipitous ravines
where no street lights intrude

but nine-starred Pleiades
smiles, a benefactress
in the night.

Oh mon!
I'm in search of headwaters.

I'm in search of Kozmic,
transmogrified.

Part III

Long Time Passing

To Change the World: London, 1972

Judith Barrington

No one understood my abrupt exit from life with Tony—and why should they since I offered no explanation? I'd summoned them so recently to the white lace and champagne all round. Now I was commuting south instead of north and making nobody's breakfast but my own. The grass on Clapham Common was muddy and its dogs dispirited, but inside my purple mini, the space was mine and mine alone; my energy filled it up and pressed outward against the windows as I sang along with John Lennon's "Imagine." I didn't know what kind of world I wanted to dream up, but I felt delirious listening to John's version.

I was staying with my friend Lydia and it was she who provided the clue. Before disappearing to visit her parents one Sunday, she left the *Times* strewn across her brown velvet couch. The clock plodded along as I read the paper with less than half my mind, picking up and throwing down sections. Then the headline "Women's Liberation Workshop" caught my eye—just a small paragraph about a new location where reading materials and information about women's groups could be found.

I'd never paid much attention to politics. Over time I'd fallen away from the assumptions of my staunch Tory family, though I'd failed to develop an alternative point of view. But now I'd begun to feel restless; the sound of "Women's Liberation Workshop" whispered like a titillating proposition in my ear as I plodded through another workweek.

Oxford Street in London was deserted the following Sunday when I cruised along with the *Times* clipping on the passenger seat. I glanced at it to check the name of the street off Piccadilly Circus. What was I doing? I briefly considered turning round and going back to Lydia's: I could find something to read; make phone calls; someone would be home for a long, desultory chat. But here came the statue of Eros, his wings spread above the splashing fountain, his one leg lifted in a joyful dance. Cheery-looking students were paddling in the water, dancing too; at this hour, nobody had yet passed out drunk.

Shaver's Place was only a narrow alley, the kind of dark passageway where a movie shootout might take place with bullets ricocheting off the dumpsters. I parked near one end and walked past unmarked doors. When I found the right one and pushed it open, a sign hand-drawn with a black felt pen declared "Women's Liberation: upstairs." In case the staircase itself was not clear enough, a wobbly arrow pointed the way. The small room I stepped into was made even more cramped by the metal bookshelves that covered three walls; in front of a sooty window, the desk held several Rolodexes and stacks of a mimeographed newsletter. A woman in jeans and a flannel shirt, laundered to a faint memory of its Black Watch tartan, swiveled to face the room. Three others sat on the floor, chatting and drinking Nescafé.

The woman at the desk probably thought I'd come to the wrong place.

"Yeah?" she said.

"Sorry," I said, unprepared to explain myself. "I just thought maybe I'd pick up some information..." I shrugged apologetically.

Softening a bit, the woman handed me a newsletter and flashed a quick grin that revealed a front tooth twisted sideways. I grinned back, but she clamped her lips down as if too much had been revealed, and gestured with her head to the shelves, where piles of papers were stacked.

The three women on the floor scooted closer together, stirring up discernible dust. Murmuring "sorry" again, I walked carefully around them.

"Lists are free," the desk woman said to my back, "and the articles are marked."

I thanked her and wandered about, picking up papers randomly while she sorted the newsletters into piles; the others stopped talking and watched me until I felt flustered. Embarrassed, I threw some money into the donation box and hurried down the stairs. Just before I opened the street door, I heard a burst of laughter from above. Were they laughing at me?

Back at the flat, I made myself a mug of tea and sat down to examine my haul. The title of the first article was printed in bold capitals: "The Myth of the Vaginal Orgasm." I quickly put it face down on the couch beside me, though there was no one home to catch me reading it. I'd heard the word *vaginal* used in a medical context, but nobody had ever said the O-word in my presence, even though I'd become familiar with the thing itself during sex with women—never in my marriage. Now, picking it up and reading on, I discovered that not only could one say it and think about it, one could write a treatise on the subject, which apparently had been neglected in "the male literature." Strange—I'd never thought of literature as male or female before. Reading my way through the pile of papers, I discovered that housework bloody well ought to be paid for, that women's clothes symbolize our oppression, and that if we told the truth about our lives the world would split open.

At the bottom of the stack I came across a single sheet headed "Consciousness Raising Groups—London." I had no idea what such a group did but I scanned the list for my part of town as if it were exactly what I'd been looking for. When I phoned the Holland Park group, I reached a woman named Miriam.

"Yup?" she answered in a nonchalant American accent. I

mumbled something about the group and she told me the next meeting was on Wednesday at someone's flat. I wrote down the address.

※

It is difficult to compare the British movement to the one in the States since each grew out of a very different history—many of the Americans coming from civil rights and anti-war activism, and the British formed more by trade-union and anti-nuclear struggles. Of course it was more complicated than that, but by most reckonings our organizing lagged a couple of years behind: it was November 1972 when I accompanied the members of my new CR group to the Second National Women's Liberation Conference held at Acton Town Hall.

At the plenary session, where we were to create policy statements for the UK movement as a whole, the hall grew dense with smoke and argument. Twenty minutes into the meeting, a woman sprinted from the second row onto the stage and grabbed the microphone from the hand of a beleaguered woman who was trying to explain the childcare arrangements. My stomach gave a lurch as the intruder began to shout out a series of slogans; this was clearly not going to be an orderly affair. After a while, though, I got used to it as woman after woman ran up to grab the mike and the audience loosened up enough to heckle.

"We'll never get anywhere if we're run by a bunch of fucking separatists," yelled a small, catlike woman who had managed to seize her moment on stage. To which Miriam and half a dozen others hurled a chorus of responses:

"We won't get anywhere under the thumb of the fucking male-dominated left either!"

"This is a women's movement, assholes!"

As the morning progressed, I realized that we were sitting in clumps of the ideologically like-minded: radical feminists on one side of the room and socialist-feminists opposite. Scattered around were a few others I would come to recognize—five or six disheveled Maoists, two rows of respectable equal-pay types, and several journalists whose philosophy was unclear. The divides were sharper and fiercer than I'd realized, although the various camps looked very much the same: six hundred pairs of blue jeans sat on six hundred metal folding chairs. The only skirt in the room belonged to a woman with a cloud of red hair, and she could get away with it because she'd been in jail. Anyway, as I saw when she prowled onto the stage and began to speak, it was a denim skirt.

As her eloquence rolled over the crowd, the vowels, as well as the skirt, revealed that she was one of the few non-American leaders. Her fingers were long and sexy. Her calves—the only ones visible the whole weekend—were firm and revolutionary. She quoted Marx frighteningly often and each time she did, her skirt whipped against her legs as she whirled around looking for detractors. She was utterly terrifying.

Miriam, however, dismissed all this Marxism as irrelevant. We were separatists, she said, her cornflower-blue eyes deceptively sweet. All that male theory was for the boys; we weren't going to bother with it anymore. The other members of our group, sitting in a line halfway back in the auditorium, looked relieved: their mothers didn't want Communist daughters either. As for me, I was relieved because I hadn't read Marx and didn't want anyone to find out.

When the session ended, there was a scraping of chairs and a burst of excited chatter as women wandered into the hallways to examine an array of smudgy position papers. I was threading a path through the throngs and heading for the door, ready to slip off and have a sandwich, when I noticed a small group of women sitting on a bench. One was wearing black jeans, something that I'd never seen before. Two had leather jackets. And two were kissing. Not a darling-how-lovely-to-see-you kiss on the cheek. And not a see-you-later-dear peck either. A real, low-down, tongues-involved smooch. I bolted out into the street.

Only four of my group showed up for the dance that evening. There were a thousand pairs of jeans gyrating, stretching, and bopping across the wooden floor to a female rock band. Beer splashed from paper cups and smoke piled up so thick you could barely see the door if you happened to be watching for someone. I was trying not to watch too obviously for the black jeans or the leather jackets. Most women danced in groups or alone, weaving through the crowd, hooking up with another dancer for a few minutes, and then melting away. In the corner, I thought I saw two couples holding each other, dancing close. I threw myself vigorously into our group effort. Miriam, who deplored the uptight dancing of the British, squatted low and tossed her long hair backward and forward.

Collapsing onto a rickety wooden chair by the wall, I lit a cigarette and watched women flinging off their flannel shirts and letting their bare breasts bounce. I felt oddly peaceful, as if I'd always known that one day I'd end up here.

"*Hal*-lo der." The faintly foreign vowels belonged to a stately woman with fine blonde hair that fell below her waist, and a soggy, hand-rolled cigarette stuck to her lip.

I stood and gave her the chair so she could prop up her leg, which was in a plaster cast to the knee. She turned out to be Monica Sjoo, a Swedish painter who was notorious since the women's art exhibition at the Swiss Cottage library had been closed down by the police on account of her six-foot-tall painting "God Giving Birth."

There was a stir at the door. Dancers started moving toward the table where we'd paid to get in. Monica beckoned to someone who had left the crowd and was strolling past us.

"What's up?"

The woman shrugged. "It's just some blokes in drag trying to get in." She looked impressively bored and wandered on.

"Faggots!" said Monica, heaving herself out of the chair. "Bloody men think they belong everywhere!"

As the rumor of an invasion of men scurried around the floor, more and more women stopped dancing and turned to watch the entrance. A few pulled on their discarded shirts, leaving them unbuttoned while they waited to see what would happen. The band played on, banging out a beat that rattled the beer kegs. The crowd by the door gradually moved back, parting as if to make way for royalty, while at the same time linking arms to create a barrier. Two figures appeared and stood motionless. When one of them raised a commanding hand, the band stopped, the drum petering out in a trickle of thumps.

Excessively tall and slender, the newcomers appeared to be young women from a Henry James novel. They both wore elaborate gowns that hugged their bodies, buttoned shoes, sweeping hats and elbow-length white gloves. One had dark curls that fell onto the shoulder straps of her pale green dress. The other wore yellow and a hat adorned with narcissi. Slowly, swinging their parasols, they moved forward into the room. Women started to whisper: "Don't let them in, they're men!" but the strangers just strolled on as if they were at a Buckingham Palace garden party. They paraded in a circle, stepping out with pointed toes, swiveling their upper torsos to the left and right.

Monica nudged me in the ribs. "I know them," she hissed. "It's Jackie and Pat. I know them."

"Jackie and Pat?" I repeated stupidly, thinking she meant the male versions of those names.

"They're women," Monica said firmly. "This is an *action*."

"Oh, I see," I said, not getting it in the least.

Pretty soon the two men—or whatever they were—arrived back at the doorway. They turned one last time to face the wall of women and threw out handfuls of business cards. I walked out on to the dance floor and picked one up. "Sistershow" it said. "Feminist political theatre by Jackie Thrupp and Pat Van Twest." When I looked up, they'd already sashayed out the door and a buzz was going around the room. Women were starting to defend their right to dress the way they wanted, even if they did all look the same. "What the fuck was all that about?" someone demanded. "Did you see those terrible shoes?" someone else muttered.

Eventually, the band struck up again. Monica hobbled out on her cast, pulling me along, my arm firmly clasped in her large, paint-flecked hand. Miriam boogied around with the rest of our group, and the crowd began to dance, singing along—soon shouting—with the band: *Freedom's just another word for nothing left to lose…*

The room started to pulse; I stripped off my shirt, twirled it high, and tossed it away. I stamped my feet to the beat and melted into the rhythm of the crowd. How had I come to belong among these wild, smart women who danced and kissed and, I had no doubt, would surely change the world? I loved their bravado, their bluster, and their astonishing belief in themselves and each other. Even now, that female energy remains so seductive that I have to remind myself of the painful hostilities, the recklessness, and the pettiness that existed alongside the bravery.

Getting It

Kate Farrell

"He'll be coming down soon," Landon whispered, gesturing to the staircase in the front hallway.

I nodded, looking up from my work in the dimly lit parlor library. "Thanks, Landon," I almost mouthed rather than said aloud. It was the second warning he'd given me.

I rose from the antique leather chair, wondering where I should stand or what appropriate pose to take. Deciding to stand by the library shelves along the front wall, I fingered the books already catalogued there, a pointless task, but one that would afford me an instant glimpse of Werner Erhard when he did descend the stairs from the upper floors.

I wondered if Werner would sense I was a spy in his private residence.

Reluctant to change my position, I glanced around the opulent front rooms lit only by floor lamps strategically placed to provide pools of light for reading or conversing in the high-ceilinged Victorian mansion. The library enveloped the parlor with built-in shelves of dark wood on all its walls, except for the deep, cushioned window seat that curved against the rounded bay windows, the base of a turret that extended to the third floor. Sumptuous leather armchairs held matching cushions arranged just so in the parlor library and the adjacent dining room.

I peered through the shadows of the front hallway, its Persian rug runner padding footsteps, listening. Then, suddenly, Werner was there, striding quickly across from the stairs to me, tall, lean, handsome, in a black leather jacket and his trademark loose slacks, smiling broadly. Landon, his ever-faithful valet, hurried behind him.

Embracing me like a lover, Werner said with a perfectly culti-vated urbanity, "Thank you for working on my library. I love you." He kissed me on the cheek in his typical, intimate style. He did not meet my eyes, though I gazed directly into his. Then with a turn and an exit out the front door with Landon, he was gone. I heard Landon lock the door, securing it.

Of course, I'd seen Werner before and spoken to him, but only in public settings during trainings or at a seminar. One of the first Erhard Seminars Training (est) graduates back in early 1973, I loved the four-day training, which brought me in touch with my wounded little girl self, my childhood pain and neglect, the basis of my life-long anxieties. Along with my friend, Mary, I was one of the first "assistants," making cold calls in a phone room above Finocchio's off Broadway, up the alley steps on Kearny Street, around the corner from the famous late-night café, Enrico's. We worked in cubicles with index cards in boxes, noting date, time, and responses, enroll-ing people for trainings to the drumbeat of Finocchio's drag queen musical review.

My volunteer work with est reminded me of the political activ-ism of the '60s, promoting a cause. But this time we were making the world a better place by releasing the human potential. Though many '60s activists had become bitter or disengaged by the '70s, I was drawn to new possibilities, the inner journey, and personal transformation. In the San Francisco Bay Area, I was not alone. The disciplines of Zen, yoga, and Tai Chi, along with new psychologies, created a frontier for self-development, one that could ripple out into our communities—a heightened consciousness without drugs. We could inform our lives and those of others through inner prac-tice. In a way, this strategy was a full circle back to some tenets of the

Beats in the '50s and early '60s: to infiltrate the establishment from the inside and create enlightened social change.

With its rapid success, est soon leased an entire building, and I followed. Bright, young, and energetic, the staffers and volunteers were a lively crew, welcoming and enthusiastic. To me, participating became an adventure in yet another great San Francisco movement. Young and recently divorced, I pursued many paths, ever curious.

In the basement of the new three-story office on posh Union Street, a veritable beehive of efficiency, our team prepared for an evening on the phones. We'd all come from our day jobs to put in our volunteer shift.

We began with a brief, focused training on communication skills. After a team meditation, we set our intentions for 100 percent results, touched hands in a circle like a football team, set up a cheer, and literally ran up the stairs to the phone cubicles. The results were remarkable. Coaches would wander around checking our tone and delivery, encouraging us, giving us tips as we signed up graduates for advanced seminars. One night I had better than 100 percent results: I signed up everyone on my list, plus a roommate, using my newfound skills.

The coaches acknowledged me for my ongoing productivity in their nightly reports. Since I was a professional librarian and tested assistant, Werner, through staff, eventually requested that I work on his personal library at Franklin House, his private office and residence.

❧

Gaining access to this exclusive house intrigued me. It was an opportunity to go behind the scenes and read the very books that Werner read. Little did I anticipate how different the Franklin House environment would be from the excitement and fun of the seminars and the animated office.

Confused, I reported to an address on Washington Street around the corner from Werner's mini-mansion on Franklin Street and entered a modest rented flat for my interview. A mousy-looking staffer directed me to a barren table so we could chat. She seemed timid, yet pointedly determined to convey the rules to me.

Maybe she thought I didn't look like a proper librarian. Polyester pantsuits with a flared hem and colorful print shirts were a staple in my '70s wardrobe. I was thin, tall—even taller on my platform espadrilles—and stylish with a shiny Sassoon pageboy cut.

"There are standards for working in Franklin House," she said, showing me a packet of papers. "The most critical is discretion."

"I understand. It's quite an honor to be an assistant here," I said, looking my sincere best.

"Werner would not have asked you to assist in his library if he did not trust you," she said with an earnestness that bordered on anxiety. "Please read over these documents first and sign them."

Scanning, I quickly signed the protocols and accepted copies in the packet that I was to review and practice. Though this was a new procedure, it seemed reasonable enough for a private residence.

"You are to enter and exit Franklin House through this flat. Never go to the front door. Follow me to the sign-in log," she said, directing me to a table by the back door.

We took a newly paved path from the back door, through a fence gate and along a wire enclosure with a growling watchdog inside. She instructed me not to speak to the dog or engage him in any way. We continued to the back door of Franklin House and into its Victorian kitchen. Silently touring the well-appointed rooms on the first floor, we descended well-worn steps to the basement and my work area.

Here I received the tools of the trade for cataloging Werner's books: an electric stylus, library reference books, and shelves of books with blank spines ready for their Dewey decimal numbers. My job was to read through the enormous backlog of books, catalog them on slips of paper, assign their Dewey numbers, etch the numbers on the spines of the books with the electric stylus, and shelve each book in the library.

My hours were flexible, to come and go as my free time allowed, until the job was done. Though a silent and austere place in spite of its lavish furnishings, I found the Franklin House inner circle's discipline and high expectations exhilarating. I enjoyed working at a level of excellence, quickly and efficiently, reading through the many esoteric books with record speed, organizing them by number on the shelves. In my outside work experiences, I was often perceived as intimidating or competitive. It was a relief and delight to simply do my best and be expected to do so.

However, as time went on, I began to sense increasing tension. House alarms went off at random times, for "testing" they said. I noticed a tented room along the side of the house that I heard was painted all black and was taboo: the meditation room. I was never to ask about it, much less enter it. I was told that all the library books must now be shelved exactly one-quarter inch from the shelf's edge and to measure the distance. Over the holidays, three elegantly decorated fir trees were removed and replaced because they were dropping needles. What was at first admirable and disciplined was, to me, becoming obsessive or perhaps paranoid.

Coupled with those observations, I was dismayed at the type of books in the library—so many on mind control techniques. After months alone, reading and cataloging books, taking books home and studying them, having but not sharing my rising suspicions, I began to conclude that the lofty est training was simply a repackaged mix of scientology, Dianetics, mind control, brainwashing, psycho-cybernetics, with Zen discipline thrown in for a refined veneer.

While working in the library on a sunny afternoon, I was surprised to see an older man approach me with some printed pamphlets.

"These are precious to Werner," he said in a kindly voice. "Please preserve them in the library."

"Certainly," I said and suggested a Princeton pamphlet file.

The gracious gentleman left and agreed to procure Princeton files.

When I read the printed material he gave me, I was stunned: it contained simple Dale Carnegie techniques. To me such pop culture was hardly worth the paper. But when I realized how much these superficial tips fit Werner's actual behavior, I had to admit these tools were a clear contrivance of his and of the trainers. I felt disheartened and disappointed.

One day Landon gave me permission to locate and catalog books on the second and third floors. I was curious to see what books might be in the upper, even more private, levels of this house.

When I reached the attic room that was Werner's personal office, I became uneasy. Just entering such a sacrosanct place by myself was unnerving. It was all white: the shag carpet, the painted walls and attic beams, the furniture. The highest turret bay windows were hung with white curtains. On shelves in that room were videotapes of Werner's public speeches for his viewing and refining—narcissistic enough. But it was the collection of specialized dictionaries that caught my attention. In a white bookcase on a sidewall were dictionaries of all types: military, medical, law, rhetoric, science, philosophy, psychology, shelves of them.

Werner's fixation with the exact meaning of words and the precise delivery of his own speeches showed me the mechanics of a mastermind. I saw the emperor revealed, and he had no clothes. Werner Erhard was a fabricated illusion.

Later that week I entered a side gate of a Victorian house on Steiner near Sacramento Street and went around to the back door. John Weir Perry, the illustrious Jungian psychiatrist, greeted me with a warm bear hug. John had helped me in the early '70s, and I had returned to therapy to work on yet another destructive relationship, a pattern I hoped to break. We sat cross-legged on a Persian carpet. John was tall, distinguished, gray haired and mustached, with piercing blue eyes that seemed to glance off mine like lasers. Ever elegant yet hip, he refused to sit in chairs, certainly not on a couch.

"I've been working in Werner's library..." I began.

John almost covered his ears; they certainly turned red. The mere mention of Werner Erhard was enough to make his blood boil.

"That man! The things he says might be true, but in his mouth they ring false."

"He seems to be helping a lot of people."

"I doubt it," John said.

"You may be right. I have to tell you what I've found and my suspicions…"

"Well, in that case, please proceed."

As I poured out my concerns about the oddities at Franklin House, I felt fortunate to be talking to a Jungian who understood the qualities of mind control, the interplay between inner and outer worlds, the subtleties of synchronicity. John did not dismiss my concerns about brainwashing. In fact, he warned me to be aware, to connect to my shadow, to ask for a dream.

I soon returned to Franklin House, knowing full well that I dare not speak against Werner, who demanded loyalty of volunteers and staff alike. Also, I'd been told that Werner knew it was my expert efficient work that was responsible for organizing his library. So, I suppose I wanted to complete the job, almost done. Or perhaps in the dim reach of lamplight I was putting the pieces of the puzzle together, mentally reviewing the books. That was when Landon entered to say that Werner would be coming down.

As Werner strode into the front room that night with his easy, practiced, TV-emcee style and casual embrace, I wanted him to meet my gaze. When he did not, I felt a victory of sorts. I had nothing to hide, but I supposed he did. It was also my wake-up call: it was time for me to leave. As difficult as it was to talk my way out of my volunteer job with the staff, I found the words, the carefully reasoned arguments, to break free.

᠅

When I next saw John Perry, I was pleased to report an important dream. Settling on the plush rug, I eagerly shared it.

"It was so vivid and yet surprising, John," I said. "It was a night-time scene outside Franklin House, lit with a translucent, soft-blue light, like a Chagall painting. I was floating above, watching. There was a large dump truck on the street, all white. Paper trash was pouring out of the windows of Franklin House, mostly from the top floor, out the attic windows. I thought, *How could there be so much trash?* Yet it kept coming, piles and piles of trash, crumpled papers, folded papers, spilling out in slow motion, massive amounts, hanging in the air and then falling into the truck.

"Then I saw some specially folded papers and I took them, simply reached out and they were mine. As I slowly, carefully unfolded the blank papers, I saw jewels: ruby, sapphire, a diamond."

John was silent, then quietly said, "You found the truth among all that trash, the pearl. That you will keep."

Pondering on what that might be, I finally whispered, "My worth. My value. My skill. That I will always keep."

Prose Third Place Winner

Bugged

Judy Gumbo Albert

Attempts have been made to interview SUBJECT, however, during these attempts SUBJECT, inside her apartment, was able to avoid facing the interviewing agents and made the statement, "See my attorney" through the door. Another attempt will be made to interview SUBJECT at New York. This attempt will take place while SUBJECT is on the street or getting in to a car. A face to face confrontation is deemed worthwhile. (FBI BuFile #100-451-802)

I remember a time when all my friends suspected they were under surveillance. It may have been true. It may have been the myth of being watched revived our sense of self-importance at a time when our power to change the world was ending. My boyfriend Stew and I had once been Yippies. Yippies used the media to create myths that were bigger than reality: We ran a pig for president, brought the New York Stock Exchange to a halt by throwing money at stockbrokers, and levitated the Pentagon. By 1973, we might as well have crumbled what remained of our Yippie magic tricks into a pot pipe and smoked it. But the FBI neither forgave nor forgot. Agents would come knocking on the black metal door of Stew's and my New York City apartment with monotonous regularity. I'd grab the four-foot-long steel rod that braced the deadbolt into my floor and verbally abuse them from behind my closed door. Fed up with such a vigilant life, Stew and

I decided on an impulse to quit New York City, to leave behind both our public lives and the FBI.

In early summer of 1973, Stew and I rented a tiny cabin in the Catskill Mountains off Highway 28A, two and a half hours north of New York City, a half hour drive from Woodstock, up a hill behind a trailer occupied by two lanky, elderly alcoholics who I'd hear argue with each other when I'd ride by. The exterior of our cabin was white, chipped, and worn. Its oblong porch led into a living room wallpapered in the 1930s with beige florets and never updated. On one side was a sunporch, on the other a kitchen. The cabin's heat came from a six-inch firebox in a wood-burning stove in the living room, its cold running water from a stream. The front lawn outside the cabin was a cushion of aromatic brown pine needles where I could sit, roll a peaceful joint and listen to Senator Sam Ervin, a hoot owl on the radio, say, "Ah'm just a simple country lawyer," as he took the Nixon Administration apart. A balmy October seduced me with its warmth and downpour of red, yellow, and gold leaves.

"Let's not leave," I said to Stew. "Let's buy this place." By then I'd landed my first real job teaching sociology at Newark Community College. Around the time Vice President Spiro Agnew resigned, Stew and I bought the cabin for $10,000, considerably less than the $100,000 in bribes Agnew was accused of taking. Our mortgage cost $80 a month. I panicked after we signed the papers, questioning whether owning property meant I had become my parents. Had I, like my mother, given up living according to my values and, no matter how decrepit and run down my property, joined the ranks of the middle class? Then I remembered that, for all my Communist father's schemes to make a buck, he remained committed to the socialist utopia Russia never became. My Yippie ideal of turning the White House into a crash pad would simply take longer than I expected.

I took pleasure in the challenge of living in a green pine forest on a gentle Catskill mountain draped in mist. Still, neither Stew nor I were what I'd call prepared for winter. I had grown up in urban

Toronto, not the frozen north. Stew grew up in Brooklyn. When I first saw frost outline the edges of fallen leaves in silver, I took it as a sign to do as we'd been advised. I filled the four slim metal tanks outside our cabin with natural gas and bought eight cords of seasoned firewood from a local cop and general fix-it man with uncared for, twisted teeth by name of Johnny Hasenflu. Stew's beard grew bushy; he became a mountain man in a gray striped cap and puffy green down jacket. My brown hair turned scraggly from infrequent washings; layer upon layer of clothing made me a rotund forest gnome.

I marked the change of seasons: dead deer slung over hoods and roofs of cars meant fall; the slaughter of the Christmas trees announced the coming winter. First, our outdoor TV antenna froze in locked position. Our set could bring in only fuzzy PBS from Albany. Next our water pipes—and shortly afterward, the stream itself—froze. Our lack of hot water became moot; all the cabin's faucets went dry. I'd melt snow in a pot while Stew split firewood, swinging his red axe high above his blond curly head as if he were a professional lumberjack. The challenge of cold weather did not deter me. Stew and I moved our mattress from the sunporch into the living room and made love sandwiched between two electric blankets. One night a Catskill storm crept in with catlike tread. I woke to find a million crystals coating every pine needle and refracting sunlight into rainbows, accompanied by a carillon of tiny bells.

I had determined to continue to live a Yippie life: provocative, oppositional, and, as much as Stew and I could make it, neither paranoid nor serious. Still, both moods dribbled into our mountain refuge. One friend, terrified by the war on black people and the counterculture disguised as the war on drugs, escaped New York City during a drug scare instigated by that same Governor Rockefeller who ordered the massacre of prisoners at Attica. My friend deposited with us a green plastic garbage bag filled halfway up with low-grade marijuana. I buried her stash under a fence of flat gray stones that some forgotten pioneer had piled one on another to mark our property line. Rip Van Winkle, or so the story goes, had inhabited these very mountains. I told myself I hid the pot in case Rip woke up looking for a toke. Still, after that visit, I revived my city habit of listening for clicks on the phone.

One morning I watched a line of hunters in red plaid jackets and green caps emerge out of the mist outside my cabin. Shotguns at the ready, they marched in military formation over leaves the color of mahogany. I did not admit to myself that these men could be anything more than what they appeared. Instead, I yelled, "This is private property! No hunting allowed!"

"Pardon us, ma'am," the trespassers replied and tromped on down my hill.

I did begin to wonder why our local cop and handyman knocked more often on the cabin door inside our screened-in porch. "Need more wood?" he'd mumble through yellowed teeth. Still, I had no proof. Until one day, when a James Dean wannabe in a black leather jacket roared up to our cabin on his Harley to rat out his mother. She worked in the Old Guard House, a gray stone building from the 1700s that functioned as our town's post office. The son told us his mother was close friends with two local FBI agents. Decades later I obtained an FBI file (BuFile #174-1901) that confirmed his story. The young man's mother did not simply monitor our mail. She had willingly supplied the agents with *"more information about the subjects than that which would be requested under a mail cover."* After the visit, I'd glare at young man's mother each time I'd pick up our mail at PO Box 36. I also found myself empathizing with a British spy by name of David Taylor whose October 18, 1777, death by hanging from an apple tree outside that very post office had been immortalized with a blue-and-gold metal sign.

In early winter of 1975, Stew and I decided to visit the urbanity of New York City, to inhale its excitement while taking the opportunity to drop in on Bill and Margie, friends who happened to be lawyers. I hoped that such a visit would help dispel the paranoia that now threatened to despoil our isolation.

In the city, I parked our ancient yellow Volvo close by Bill and

Margie's Gay Street home in Greenwich Village. I could not put my finger on it exactly, but the air around me felt charged with suspicious ions. I spotted (or so I thought) a man in a beige trench coat and fedora lurking in the dark shadows of a nearby stairwell. I ignored him.

"This is New York." I told myself. "Everybody lurks in New York."

Early in the morning of December 13, Stew and I returned to our car. Again, I saw a man. This time his trench coat was black. I watched him scurry down the sidewalk, a rat exposed to daylight. I worried I'd succumbed to New York City paranoia. Then, in one of those moments for which I am forever grateful, I decided to walk around my car's perimeter. Looking for I knew not what. Which is exactly when I saw it. A smear in the middle of the rear bumper, as if some employee at a carwash had tried to wipe away the dirt I had accumulated on the trip down. In the center of the spot, a black wire hung down, six inches long. I squatted in the gutter, avoiding a stream of gray ice water as best I could and contemplated the wire. The curiosity I've had my entire life trumped any foreboding. I called Stew over.

"Whaddaya think this is?" I asked.

Stew looked at the wire, stroked his beard, shook his head, but made no comment. Stew knew nothing about cars. I'd tried to teach him to drive once on an empty Catskill road but cut my lesson short after he'd growled his way through two stop signs without stopping. Still, I needed his reassurance. Three weeks earlier, in a fit of know-it-all feminist machismo, I'd installed a new battery in my Volvo by myself, poles reversed, and sent the car's electrical system up in smoke.

I understand now that fear can breed recklessness in addition to passivity. At the time, I told myself that if the wire came from a bomb placed underneath my car by the FBI or some God knows who right-winger, going out in a flaming blaze of glory would be a quintessential Yippie act. Such a death might at least attract the media.

"You wait on the sidewalk." I commanded. "I'm going to turn the engine on and see if it starts."

Stew refused. He sat down heavily in the passenger seat. He told me later he did not want to see a headline that read: "Sexist Survives."

I turned the key. No expectant silence. No click. No explosion. The Volvo's engine kicked in. My breath rushed out of my lungs as if escaping jail. I returned to the rear of the car and knelt once more in the freezing slush. I reached my arm up behind my No Nukes bumper sticker. My fingers brushed an object I knew did not belong. I tugged. My hand emerged clutching a size C battery attached to a piece of three-quarter-inch black electrical tape. Stew and I spoke in one voice: "Let's get the fuck outta here."

The more I navigated Seventy-Ninth Street's curves through Central Park, the more four navy-blue, late-model American cars followed me. I turned left up Madison Avenue past Upper East Side shops decked in holly and sophisticated white Christmas lights, then back across Eighty-Sixth to the West Side, driving for what felt like days. All this time my new best friends stayed close, a car chase in slow motion, never out of range, making no attempt at concealment. As I turned down Broadway, I spotted a "Comidas/Chinois" sign blinking in neon red and gold. Across from it was an empty parking spot.

"Time to go for Chinese," I managed to get the words out. Stew agreed instantly. Chinese food is comfort food for Jews of my generation. I parked, leaving my car to its fate. I was shaking so hard I dropped my quarter for the meter into a pile of slush and lost it. Stew headed toward the farthest end of the restaurant, his face ashen under his blond curls. An indifferent waiter plopped down two bowls in which barbequed pork and white tofu shards floated like creatures in an oil slick. The soup's steam smelled like fear would, if fear came coated in tamarind and chili oil.

"Back to Bill and Margie's," Stew said after soup had freed his brain to strategize. I agreed. If you think you're in trouble with the law, the best place to be is with your lawyers. No cars followed us to Gay Street. With longer arms and stronger fingers than I could ever dream of, Bill pulled an object from under the Volvo's bumper. It was a box. Made of black metal. It was six inches long by four inches wide. An antenna hung off one corner, attached by a putty-like substance. Four size C batteries were secured to top and bottom with electrical tape. All four batteries were intact.

"I believe this might be the first time in my experience that one of these was actually found by someone," Bill opined.

Over the years, I've asked myself which of us—me or the FBI— was the bigger schmuck. I was foolish enough to abandon my car in front of that Chinese restaurant. The FBI agents had replaced the tracking device I'd disabled with a second, fully functional one. Had they not done so, all I'd have had to demonstrate surveillance would have been a single size C battery and a piece of crumpled black tape.

The *New York Post* helped promote our Yippie myth by publishing a photo of Bill, Stew, and me. Bill stood behind the Volvo, resignation in his eyes. Stew and I, in our favorite striped Guatemalan vests, cradled the tracking device in our hands. I had a frown on my face. But inside I felt elated. I'd been awarded the grand prize: proof positive that Stew and I were under surveillance. I'd discover decades later that the FBI had vented their frustration with an observation to their superiors worthy of Franz Kafka: "*SUBJECTS are difficult to surveil because they are paranoid about being surveilled.*" They had also blacked out the FBI BuFile number on this report.

The Assertive Woman

Darlene Frank

The beauty of Santa Barbara captivated me from the start, and I settled happily into this coastal California paradise, where a college friend had guided me after four blustery winters in Buffalo. A hangloose attitude prevailed at the methadone clinic where I worked as a mental health assistant, and I adored the cottage my partner, Ted, and I shared in a quiet canyon. I baked bread and made yogurt, filled our sunny kitchen with plants, and enjoyed our comfortable hippie lifestyle. I felt a satisfaction in my life, a warmth and ease I had never known.

Yet I also felt socially awkward and uncertain about my career. Conflict with co-workers sometimes kept me awake at night, and junkies were not the most promising population to work with. What was next?

It was then, in the mid-1970s, that I discovered assertiveness training for women.

Curious, I enrolled in a class on this subject at a local college, where week after week my classmates returned with stories of how they'd broken long-held habits, talked back to ex-husbands, and stood up for themselves on the job and at home. I wanted on board.

This topic would never have blossomed in the 1950s. But the Vietnam War, student protests, and the civil rights movement of the 1960s had broken barriers, raked the cultural soil with a vengeance, and fertilized any dormant seeds of rebellion. The 1970s saw the flowering of the feminist movement; women were feeling the strokes of their power and the restlessness it stirred inside them when it wasn't expressed.

Just three years earlier, in 1972, fresh out of college and stranded at a two-week temp job in St. Louis on my cross-country trip to California, I'd witnessed a historical moment. On my last day of work at Zinsco Electrical Products, word came down from on high that women employees would henceforth be permitted to wear pants to the office.

Women would no longer listen in silence as others dictated their lives, or their wardrobes.

Before I took the assertiveness class, I had not thought much about what it meant to be feminine or a woman. My heroes were men, I preferred male over female friends, and I believed that art and literature were far more worthy than women's traditional domestic pursuits. I believed this despite the fact that my weekends were consumed with just the kind of cooking and decorating projects that Martha Stewart would refine in the 1990s, and in the '70s were hallmarks of a countercultural lifestyle: I sewed patchwork pillow covers and a dress, baked my own bread, even crocheted an entire lace curtain, an interminable feat I will never repeat.

Discovering assertiveness training gave me the motivation and means to remake myself, and I set about it in earnest. I would distance myself further from the Mennonite women I grew up with who complied so readily with the church and their husbands. I would sound as confident as others in staff meetings or when I made a request of my boss. I soon cut off the waist-length, flower-child hair I'd worn since college and sported a shoulder-length style that needed a blow dryer every morning. There was no turning back—an underused and long-silenced part of myself was about to step into expression.

To my surprise, and against my initial objections, I was soon teaching others what I had learned. I taught assertiveness skills to the clinic staff (at their request), to the junkies (at my boss's request), and eventually (at yet another's request) to inmates at the Atascadero State Hospital for the criminally insane (it was as bizarre as it sounds). I didn't teach anything original, just parroted what my teacher had taught to our class, in hopes I'd absorb the techniques through the drill of repetition to others. I, who had trouble delivering the rent check to the landlord for fear I might have to engage in a few words of conversation, was teaching assertiveness training.

I even managed to get hired to teach in a local adult education program, where the usual pattern was for a throng of students (99 percent of them female) to show up on the first night of class expecting, I'm sure, a strong, savvy, confident teacher, only to find timid, ill-at-ease me. Attendance on night two always dropped dramatically and, by the end of the training, what remained was a small group of people somewhat like myself, grateful, I imagined, to have found the instructor was not the loudmouthed pack leader of their imagination, but barely more assertive than they. None of us needed to learn how to curb our verbal aggression, rather how to give ourselves some small voice at all. I think they felt safe with me, though that in no way claims I was an adequate teacher.

The process of remaking yourself, however, is neither straightforward nor simple, and the following story reveals my stumbling foray into this promising venture. Early on in my learning, before I was teaching others and when I'd only begun trying out these new behaviors, I signed up for a weekend workshop with Stanlee Phelps, coauthor of *The Assertive Woman,* a popular book that helped launch the women's assertiveness movement.

Just gazing at Phelps's lovely picture on the back of the book, I knew I wanted to be like her, have what she had—that indisputable bone of confidence that would give me a beautiful bearing and let me weave my way seamlessly through the world and my life.

The workshop was held in an elegant historic house in Santa Barbara rented out for such occasions; the front door opened onto a spacious lobby with a wide curving staircase that swept to the second floor. A crowd of women as eager as I to take charge of their lives assembled there on a Saturday morning. To the right of the entrance was a large room filled with chairs—our classroom. I slipped into a seat near the back, not wanting to be too visible to the teacher in case a close view revealed some deep flaw in my ability to ever be as assertive as she. Several women milled around the table at the front of the room, talking casually with a woman who was laying out books and papers on the table, who, I assumed, was Stanlee Phelps's assistant.

In the book jacket photo of Phelps, her hair was full and smooth and set in a neat pageboy, her lipstick carefully applied to accent her mouth. Her eyes were large and bright. To me, her picture seemed not only that of an assertive woman, but the perfect woman, and I wanted to meet (and become) such a woman.

The assistant called the group to order and began her opening remarks. I imagined Phelps had been upstairs getting ready for the class and by now she was standing on the sweeping staircase, just around the corner and out of our view, waiting for her assistant to introduce her. "Now let me present Stanlee Phelps, the Assertive Woman we all aspire to be," she'd say, and Phelps would step off the staircase and into the room wearing an elegant formal dress, to our applause.

We were probably ten minutes into the workshop when I awoke, very slowly, to the truth: The woman speaking *was* Phelps, and the women milling around the table before class started had been talking informally with the Assertive Woman herself.

I was shaken by this revelation, and spent a few stunned moments readjusting my mental construct. First of all, Phelps did not look like her picture. This might have been the first live author I'd seen compared to her photo, which I later realized was one of those PR shots that shows a person as they look for the picture-taking only, an image that can bear little resemblance to how they look in everyday life or even at public appearances. The Phelps I saw in person wore her hair in a more casual, less-combed style, and wore less makeup. The shape of her face even looked different, likely due to the hairstyle.

But what shook me even more was facing up to the mental image I had created of the Assertive Woman. I realized that Phelps's photographed face had reminded me of the small dolls I had seen in the homes of Mennonite women when I was a girl. The dolls were a fad for a while, used as decorations in the bathroom. They were the size of a Barbie doll, and each one wore a large crocheted or taffeta skirt that fit over and concealed a spare roll of toilet paper on top of the toilet tank. It seemed wherever we went on our Sunday afternoon visits, there was another doll with a different colored skirt sitting on top of the toilet. What had struck me about the dolls was that they looked so unlike the women who owned them. Their faces were painted with red lips and rouged cheeks; they were fancy dolls with bouffant blonde or auburn hair, and their dresses were unlike anything a Mennonite woman wore or owned. It struck me as odd that women who wore long hair, head coverings, and no makeup would have these alien creatures in their bathrooms. It also struck me as odd that grown women liked dolls.

Never having owned a formal dress myself, but believing, I suppose, that "normal" women wore them, I had put the photo of Phelps's face on top of such a dress and imagined her wearing it to make her grand entrance. I saw her coming down the stairs and into the room in a similarly wide taffeta skirt, a kind of a ball-gown dress, elegantly formal, with elbow-length white gloves, her porcelain, picture-pretty face atop it all, as decked out as a doll.

Did I actually believe a teacher might show up in a gown? Among all of us in our '70s pantsuits and bell-bottom jeans? Apparently so. What I thought she might do after being introduced is another question—I hadn't gone beyond her magnificent entrance.

The doll of course was the image I held not only of Phelps, but of the Assertive Woman as well, an image so far removed in style or substance from any woman I knew or could hope to become that it was ludicrous. A woman so unreal and fairylike she would stop the proceedings in any room by stepping inside the door.

In the moments during which my fantasy image unraveled, I

learned the only lesson I recall from the entire weekend: The original Assertive Woman was ordinary in looks and manner, approachable and unintimidating, unassuming in style. She was any one of us who would simply become herself.

Collage

Ana Manwaring

Swirling patterns, brilliant colors
expanded days—
in thought, in image—
and music and music and music.
We connected through hair
and poetry.

Innocent in middy blouse and tie,
Turned on to yoghurt
in Vina del Mar Park,
my mother watching—
terrified.

I stomped and drummed and twirled.
Come on, light my fire,
I want to live.
To wake up and know,
tune into ecstatic freedom,
the world my lotus unfolding.

Boarding school, the door clanged
behind me.
I pierced my ears.

I wrote poems.
I guided the girls who
tasted the universe,
who rode the electric acid
conduits, who dropped-out
and met God.

After the acid, after the abortion,
turned-on, tuned-in, flying Air Leary
at the Human Be-in; smoking Bidis,
biding my time.

Wore woven Guatemala cloth skirts
and Venetian glass beads,
hair down to here.
But not when kickin' down
the Deb ball aisle,
straight cousin on one arm.
long-haired hippie lover on the other—
society's bride in seed-beaded white,
my mind opiate dreaming
ever further from my rearing.

One pill made you larger,
Orange Sunshine freed your mind—

Yet the clipping of days
and the folding of ways,
and the piecing together
of a psychedelic world—
ephemeral, an old collage
on fading newsprint.

How can you catch a sparrow?

Tripping on High

Venus Ann Maher

It's a special occasion and Mama says I'm old enough now. Everyone in our commune is dressing up for the procession. Our free school, Hearthshire, has three communes in San Francisco, and tonight we're going to walk between them to celebrate winter solstice, 1971.

"Here, honey, I have a gift for you," Mama says from her seat at the kitchen table. "You can have a quarter tab of this mescaline. Since you're eleven, and it's your first time, that should be about right."

I watch as she cuts a tiny square in half, and then in half again.

"Will this make me crazy like Johnny?" I ask.

Mom laughs. "No, not at all. He's just wild."

She hands me the quarter tab and my first trip begins. At first, I don't feel any different. Then I remember Stevie told me it takes a little while to come on, so I wait, curious. Twenty minutes later I can't stop grinning. I see pretty patterns everywhere. I feel like dancing, so I do. Weaving in and out of the throng in the living room on butterfly wings, I smile at them, and they grin back at me. I live in a very friendly world.

Now we're getting candles, and Mama's lighting them as we go out the door. How bright my little flame is! I'm holding the heart of warmth in my hands. I walk slowly. I can't let the precious flame go out.

"Come on slowpoke," Debbie yells from the front of the crowd. I shield my candle and move faster to catch up. She's a year younger so her Mom said no mescaline yet. Walking next to Deb, I smile at her blond hair shining in the candlelight.

Somebody starts a song and we sing "All you need is love." The song leads to more Beatles tunes— "Yellow Submarine" and "Strawberry Fields Forever." Then we're at Capp Street. There are so many of us, we jam up at the door. The chilly city wind swirls my courage away. Moments before, I was sweating, singing, a part of something larger than myself. Now I just feel small, cold, and a little shaky.

I make it inside. Someone hands me hot apple cider and points to the couch. I huddle up in a rainbow afghan on the back of the sofa, cradling my hot drink in trembling hands. I feel like a baby rabbit in her den. The world is big and scary.

"Where's my Mom?" I whisper to Debbie, who flopped down on the sofa next to me. She darts through the crowd and comes back with my mother. Thank God!

"I'm scared, Mama."

"I'm here. Everything's all right. Just snuggle up and this will pass." She makes a lap for me and I fit my whole self into it. We sit like that for a long time. Finally it's time to stretch. I kiss her cheek and get up, smiling again.

"Feel better?" she asks.

"Yep, I feel great!" It's true. I could do anything with the energy coursing through me.

We're on the move again. The songs are rowdier now as we walk to Valencia Street. We take up the whole sidewalk and overflow into the street, our songs echoing off the Victorian houses as we march between them.

At the next commune we make candles. I dip the doubled wick into the big cans of warm purple wax until my pair of candles is thick enough. Then I switch with Debbie and dip blue ends onto my pretty light-makers. I love my candles. It's as if I have created a place for light to be born.

I start to feel tired, but then someone turns the music up, and we're dancing. Everyone's swirling and gyrating to the Grateful

Dead and Santana. Later, the voice of Janis Joplin comes blasting out of the speakers and we all start to wail along. It's the most wonderful winter solstice ever.

Finally, I drop onto the pile of pillows in the corner, out of breath and out of energy. I don't want the night to end, but I'm more exhausted than I've ever been. My bed seems so far away. Mom dances nearer.

"Mama, do we have to walk home?" I yell over the music.

"No sweetie, you can stay here in the kids' room." She continues to dance in place as she asks, "How do you feel?"

"Tired but happy," I say.

"Was your first trip a good one, then?" Mom asks.

"Yeah, it was fun, except for being a baby bunny."

"I'm glad. Goodnight, Ann." She stops dancing long enough to hug me.

"'Night, Mama," I say, as I head for the bunk room.

※

It's spring now, and Mama says I'm ready for acid. It's called *sunshine* and we're going to take it tonight. Jenny's in. So is Debbie, 'cause her Mama finally said it's all right.

We drop the acid after dinner. The nausea passes quickly, but there are too many people. I wander away from the others and curl up in my bed. The walls are transparent. I can feel the frantic heartbeats and busy minds of everyone in the neighborhood. My skin feels the pressure; my pulse is racing. I can feel the entire city breathing, living, fighting, moving. The hills and valleys are filled with houses, all filled with people. It's too much! Anger, passion, sorrow, excitement course through me in waves. There are no barriers. I am battered by this raw power. I could explode, and they would never find all my pieces. Vibrating with energy, I surge out of my bed, out of my room, out of the house. In the backyard I beat the ground and wail, hoping the earth can save me. I crawl through the grass, seeking release from the unbearable pressure of humanity crushing me down. I am wailing.

Someone finds me. Someone is talking. Mama? No, it's Debbie. My friend takes my hands in hers and croons something familiar. I sit, looking up with her, into a sky mercifully free of the usual fog. The strains of "Twinkle, Twinkle Little Star" float on the air, as Debbie quietly hums to me. Suddenly I can breathe again. I find my body between the tiny points of light above, and the damp earth below. The stars, the hard ground, and that silly little song save me from dissolving into the chaos of the city night.

❧

It's summer and we're in the country! We get to stay on forty acres of wilderness in Northern California, which the grownups just call "The Land." It's our playground.

Jenny brings the tabs of acid down to the kids' house after breakfast. "Mom says it's a little strong, but really pure, so we should cut them in half, and only the big kids are allowed to take any." She puts the tiny squares down on the counter. As we crowd around, Debbie gets out her pocketknife and carefully cuts each tab in two.

"I don't think I want any. You guys go ahead," I say, remembering my last acid trip.

"Oh, come on, it won't the same without you," Jenny begs.

"I'll be here, just like before," Debbie promises.

I swallow past the lump of fear. "All right, I'm in."

"Happy tripping," Debbie intones, and places the minuscule rectangle on her tongue like the holiest of hippie sacraments. I take my share, as do Jenny, Marisa, and Carrie. Then we sit in the sun and wait for the trip to begin.

My stomach is a little queasy, and my body has that tingly chemical feeling that tells me the LSD is beginning to work.

Debbie giggles. "Look at those clouds," she says, pointing upward.

I peer into heaven. Lying back in the tender new grass, I give myself to that sky. I see women as graceful as ocean winds, and white horses running on blue fields. Eagles made of white mist dive across my vision, weaving the very air into miracles. I sit up, straining to understand. The eagles are pointing at the green hills below them, which roll out in wave after wave of glory. A thousand shades of green proclaim the land alive. Now the eagles are flying closer, pointing at my heart, showing me I am part of their grand weaving sky dance. I relax and lie down again under that blue arc of treasure. I am the eagle, the air, and the green land. We are made out of the same thing. Humans try to create little boxes out of the whole, but nothing can separate us. I feel connected to it all, but I'm my own self too.

Nothing is hammering at me like my last trip in the city. This feels great! I laugh out loud. Debbie echoes my laughter, then Carrie, Jenny, and Marisa begin. Whenever one of us stops, another starts. It is happily contagious, this sound of joy that tickles our hearts into beating louder and faster. The energy of it gets us up off the meadow's soft grass and dancing. I am Isadora Duncan, and my friends are goddesses and fairies, flapping and flittering about me in the wildflowers of this perfect world. Our laughter laces the air, drawing us down the path towards the dry streambed.

Suddenly, the world darkens, and joy turns to fear. Debbie cries out and cowers down. My dance stops midstep, arrested by the loss of light as the radiance drains from our breath. I kneel down and hug Debbie. Looking up, Jenny mouths the word *clouds*. The heart hasn't gone out of the world; it's the heavens crying. We weep with the rain for a time, but sorrow doesn't suit us. Soon water becomes our world—we become happy again. This time it is the below, not the above, that delights us. The rocks of the streambed become jewel-like when touched by the sky's tears. We wander along, picking up green jade, white lacy granite, and sparkly mica. I sit on the bank and sing. Marisa and Debbie sit down beside me.

Jenny is on top of the nearest hill, her arms upraised as she yells, "Come on you motherfucking clouds, give it up! Bring back the sunshine. Let's see some blue sky!"

Debbie begins intoning, "Sunshine, sunshine," and then Marisa starts the perfect song.

"Here comes the Sun, La, La, La, La..." And we all join in.

As the sun breaks free of her tired, gray handmaidens and strikes color into the world again, we all cheer, get up, and begin walking. We find Carrie over the next rise, staring raptly into the heart of a California poppy. We sweep her up in our march toward food and company.

Soon we arrive at the outdoor kitchen. Rainsong smiles at us and asks, "How's the trip going, girls?"

We hum and clap and sing our responses. Then we demand food.

"I've got just the thing," she says. Rustling around she brings each of us half an orange. Mine's beautiful! It holds a sweet message that enlivens my tongue. I want it to go on forever. With that taste on my palate, I can interpret any language. Its magic removes all barriers to communication. The orange lasts a long time. When it is finally gone, I feel sad and a little lonely. Then Debbie's mom brings me a bowl of rice with the cutest little raisins in it, and I eat it all up. I know I am coming down now, because the rice doesn't hold any secret meaning. The thousand shades of green have settled down into six or seven tones, and the sky is just the sky again. Besides, my body has that chemical all-used-up feeling, as though I've gone through three days of energy in one. My friends look tired too, as we sit around the outdoor kitchen telling stories. I can still hear the whisper of complete union, though I can no longer speak the language of the infinite. I do like dropping acid, but I don't like how it drops me down into exhaustion afterwards.

I look up at the sky, searching for eagles. There's one gliding behind that bank of trees. "Please help me remember I am one with everything—without the acid," I plead silently. A warm wind blows past, like the touch of feathers on my skin. I smile. I will remember.

The Day I Met the Suffragette

Lynn Sunday

I still remember what she looked like all these years later—a petite woman with a quiet demeanor and a look of determination in her clear green eyes. Her silvery hair, parted in the middle, came halfway to her shoulders. She wore no makeup I could see, except a little lipstick, and was simply dressed in lightweight cotton clothing and serviceable sandals; no being hobbled by high heels for her. And she was old enough to be my grandmother, in her early seventies, maybe, but straight backed and fast moving. I liked her immediately.

We met on August 26, 1970, fellow marchers in the Women's Strike for Equality—a national event celebrating the fiftieth anniversary of the Nineteenth Amendment granting women the right to vote. The strike called for women across the country to stop work that day to spotlight inequities in the workforce, in politics, and in social institutions such as marriage. That afternoon in New York City, tens of thousands of women gathered on the sweltering streets of Manhattan and marched down Fifth Avenue to the lawns behind the New York Public Library to demand equal rights under the law.

I was a twenty-six-year-old housewife, and leaving my husband home with our two sons to join the march was a personal declaration of independence. I'd been married for eight years to a man who espoused equal rights and justice for all—but at home, as the assumed head of our household, he felt entitled to be in charge.

He was okay with watching the kids three evenings a week while I took college classes—as long as I did the shopping, cooking, cleaning, laundry, and the balance of child care, in addition to my schoolwork. But he wasn't pleased when I joined the National Organization for Women. Or when I read *The Second Sex* by Simone De Beauvoir and began questioning the male/female status quo. Or when I told him he'd be feeding the kids dinner that evening, because *I* was striking for equality.

My husband shook his head at that. "If you women had to deal with the serious issues men do, you'd stop complaining fast. Well, be home before dark. The streets aren't safe."

I sighed. His comments irked me, but I kept silent, not wanting to argue. I kissed my family good-bye and left the apartment, promising to return before dark.

How can we be equal, I wondered, if half of us can't go out alone at night?

Filled with excitement and sense of resolve, I rode the subway downtown, exiting at Fifty-Seventh Street and heading east toward Fifth Avenue. The strike began in the late afternoon and would continue into the evening, to allow as many women as possible to participate. I was stunned by how many of us there were. Approaching Fifth Avenue, I looked out at a sea of female faces: women of all shapes and sizes, all colors, all ages, married and single, gay and straight. Some held signs bearing messages: *Women Unite! Equality Under The Law! We Are The Fifty-one Percent Minority, I Am Not A Barbie Doll!* And the slogan of the day—*Don't Iron While The Strike Is Hot.*

"THE TIME IS NOW!" someone yelled, and the mass of women began moving forward. This is it, I thought and thrilled by my own daring, merged with the crowd. When the march monitors on our block passed along that we would be taking the entire width of the street—not the *half* we'd been allotted by the city—we surged forward, arms linked. With cheers of victory we took Fifth Avenue from curb to curb, unchallenged by the police.

"WHAT DO WE WANT?"

"EQUALITY!"

"WHEN DO WE WANT IT?"

"NOW!"

Observers lined the streets: women with baby carriages, office workers, shopkeepers, tourists. The majority of people I saw were women, with a sprinkling of men. We were cheered and given the thumbs-up sign from the office windows of a liberal, congressional candidate. There were boos, jeers, and loud shouts of "GET BACK IN THE KITCHEN, YOU BRALESS BIMBOS!" from a crew of construction workers we passed.

Among the leading marchers were women of achievement: Betty Friedan, strike organizer, first president of NOW, and author of *The Feminine Mystique*; Gloria Steinem, political activist and founder of *New York Magazine*; Kate Millet, author of *Sexual Politics*; and straight-talking, peppery, Congresswoman Bella Abzug, tireless champion of women's rights. I felt honored to be among them.

But the highlight of the experience was my encounter with the silver-haired woman. Somewhere along the way we fell into step together. I smiled at her, impressed that a woman of her age would be marching. Linking arms, we walked side by side.

"This is my first march. I felt I had to come." I confided. "And you?"

The woman told me that a half century ago when she was twenty, she had marched with Susan B. Anthony to win women the vote.

"I was scared to death by my own daring. The world didn't take kindly to uppity women back then." She laughed, her eyes crinkling at the corners, and shook her head at the ways of the world. "My family was scandalized and my gentleman friend left me over it. But I marched anyway," she said.

And in that moment, I realized I was in the presence of a living, breathing, direct link with history—and that this courageous woman and others like her had put themselves on the line for something they believed was simple justice for everyone. Now I was part of the link.

I felt overwhelmed by emotion. "Thank you for my right to vote," I whispered. "I won't ever take it for granted—or any other right."

Our eyes met. An understanding passed between us. We hugged good-bye when the march ended at Bryant Park. Intending to head straight for the subway, I began weaving my way through the throngs of women who stood listening to the speakers. But I also felt compelled to stop and listen. The sky was darkening as I walked away from the crowd on my way home. My husband would have to understand.

The Trip

Lucille Lang Day

At the kitchen table in my apartment, I was reading a stack of research papers for my physicochemical biology class at University of California, Berkeley. Thinking about microtubules, I looked up at the huge hanging sculpture of a sperm penetrating an egg that I'd created with copper wire, glass fishing floats, and my Campfire Girl honor beads. At that moment Gil knocked. We saw each other a lot, and I guess you could say he was my boyfriend.

"I've got something good, Lucy," he said excitedly when I opened the door. "Orange Phoenix!"

"What's Orange Phoenix?" We headed toward my mattress in the living room, a more comfortable place to sit. I owned a bed, but it was stored at my mother's house because it was more fashionable to sleep on a mattress on the floor. My daughter, Liana, who was seven years old, slept in the bedroom. At the moment she was playing with her friends in the eucalyptus grove across the street.

"Orange Phoenix is the finest mescaline anywhere," Gil proclaimed, taking two orange capsules out of a foil wrapper and showing them to me in his palm. "Truly great stuff. Wanna drop it on Saturday?"

I'd met him the previous fall, 1970, when I enrolled in Introduction to Dramatic Literature. For my first project I'd selected a scene from *Oedipus Rex*. I'd be Jocasta. I scanned my classmates, looking for someone into whose arms I would like to throw myself, saying, "Oh, Oedipus, Oedipus…" I settled on a soft-featured young man with curly auburn hair that brushed his shoulders. I sat beside him and asked, "Would you be Oedipus for me?" Gil said yes.

He was a dramatic art major and an archetypal flower child who believed in peace, love, and smoking pot as often as possible. I looked like I belonged with him. My hair cascaded past my waist. I wore moccasins, bell-bottoms, and a peasant blouse.

Yet I had never taken a psychedelic drug. I'd had plenty of opportunities, but in those days everyone knew someone who'd had a bad trip, and the newspapers carried stories about people who'd been killed by jumping out of a window or off a roof during an acid trip. I didn't want to test my wings.

"I don't want a bad trip." I didn't want to miss out altogether on the psychedelic experience, but I was wary.

"People don't have bad trips on mescaline. This stuff is really pure."

I was a good student, majoring in biological sciences with specialization in cell and molecular biology, and I didn't want to mess up now. It was my senior year, and I had applications out to several universities for graduate school. Although I hadn't yet received my official acceptance letter, I hoped and expected to stay at Berkeley and join Wilbur Quay's research group to study age-dependent changes in the levels of brain enzymes and neurotransmitters in mice.

Except for smoking marijuana at parties and rock concerts, I'd pretty much avoided the Berkeley drug scene. My approach to drugs had taken shape at the beginning of my freshman year, when shopping for textbooks for my first quarter classes, I ran into one of my old boyfriends on Telegraph Avenue. He was very excited and showed me a wad of bills, explaining he'd just made a big deal in Los Angeles. I hoped he meant a movie deal but feared he meant a drug deal. I didn't ask. I just congratulated him and hurried on my way.

"Are you sure no one ever has a bad trip on mescaline?" I asked Gil.

"Well, maybe if it's contaminated with PCP or something, but you won't have a bad trip on this stuff."

"Have you tried it?"

"Yes."

"Okay, let's do it on Saturday. Liana will be with my mom." I was twenty-three years old and had been a single parent for most of the last eight years. My mom did what she could to help, which included babysitting Liana on weekends so that I could study and date.

Gil came back to my place Friday night. I poured two glasses of red wine and put Jim Morrison on the stereo. Gil wanted to make out, but I begged off, saying, "Not now. I've got a lot of stuff on my mind." My attraction to him was waning.

On Saturday morning we woke to the sound of neighbor children playing outdoors. I got up, put on my bell-bottom jeans and a lavender blouse, tied my macramé belt around my waist, and made chocolate Instant Breakfast and toast for both of us.

Gil took the Orange Phoenix out of the refrigerator and said, "Are you ready?"

I said yes, but I was both excited and scared. I thought any illegal drug might turn out to be something different from what it was supposed to be, and that one or both of us might have a bad trip despite Gil's reassurances. Still, I put one of the orange capsules on my tongue and washed it down with the last of my Instant Breakfast.

It was a warm morning for late winter, and we decided to take our trip in Golden Gate Park in San Francisco. As we drove across the Bay Bridge, the mescaline found its way to my brain. The beams and supports of the cantilever section formed intricate geometric patterns, a lattice of thousands of Xs shot through with multicolored beams of light. The great cables between the towers of the suspension span were upside-down rainbows; the towers themselves, reaching up to the throbbing clouds, were dazzling monuments with diamond-shaped windows through which poured the glittering sky. Everything was in motion, as though all matter were alive. Marveling at things I'd always taken for granted, I was glad that Gil was behind the wheel. I was in no shape to drive.

"How are you feeling?" Gil's question seemed silly and clinical.

I laughed. "Great! Do I look sick?"

"No, you look gorgeous." He reached out and took my hand. It was like an electric shock, and I pulled my hand away. I wasn't in love with him, and in my altered state of consciousness, I couldn't bear his touch.

We parked near the Conservatory of Flowers. The building was white and gleaming, with a central dome that made me think of the Taj Mahal. It was a radiant palace, its milky glass panes iridescent and, like everything else, pulsing as though breathing. The surrounding grounds were studded with palm trees and adorned with beds of shimmering red and yellow flowers.

"We can go inside later if you want," Gil said. "First, I want to show you something." He led me down a path lined with tree ferns that formed a magical forest. I was on a different planet. Nothing was static. It was as though I could see the molecular structure of everything, the airiness of atoms, the vibrations of electrons and photons whizzing about.

Again Gil reached for my hand, and again I pulled it away. I wanted to be left alone to enjoy the fantastical images around me. I could have spent hours just looking at a tree.

We passed a young woman with a baby in a carrier on her back, and great waves of love washed over me as I thought of my own little girl. I loved her more, I knew, than I'd ever loved anyone.

The preceding Christmas, Gil and I had gotten parts in a play at the Montclair Community Church, where his parents were members. My part was to recite a few lines from Lewis Caroll's "Jabberwocky." At rehearsals Liana took part in the children's group scenes, which included a game of ring-around-the-rosy, and she wanted very much to be in the Christmas Eve performance. However, my ex-husband's father and stepmother had invited her to spend Christmas with them, and they wanted to pick her up the afternoon of Christmas Eve. If Liana took part in the play, I'd have to drive her to San Mateo (a two-hour round-trip) on Christmas day. Gil begged me to let her be in the play. He even had the minister talk to me about it, but still I said no.

As we came out of the fern forest into a meadow, Gil asked, "What are you thinking?'

The grass was deeply layered, forming vibrating patterns. "Liana should have been in the play." I felt guilty, but at the same time, the world was so beautiful that I thought no mistake could be irredeemable. I would be a better mother, I decided, from now on.

Gil and I walked through groves and gardens, stopping periodically to examine a flower beating like a heart, a vibrating pinecone, or a lake in which spectacular murals appeared and disappeared. The world was rich and vibrant, an ever-changing tapestry. I felt lucky to be alive and part of it.

I stood in a meadow, looking at panorama of trees: redwoods, oaks, cypresses, pines, and eucalyptuses of many shades, not only green. The eucalyptuses had yellow and gray bark, as though painted, and silvery leaves. All of the trees were dappled with swirling bits of red and blue. Above them, clouds formed whirling patterns. The colors, textures, and motions of the trees and clouds enthralled me. It was like being inside a van Gogh painting, and I wondered if this was how the world had always looked to him.

I was ecstatic. Previously, the closest I'd ever come to this feeling was when I was walking across the Berkeley campus—so beautiful, with its groves and rolling lawns, its pink and white rhododendrons, its majestic buildings, and Strawberry Creek running through the middle. I was thrilled to be there after having been a dropout, teen mother, and phone girl at Chicken Delight.

Gil kept trying to hold hands and have us look at each other, but I wasn't interested in the textures of his skin or the colors of his eyes. I didn't want to say, "Don't touch me," but I hoped he would figure it out.

"What do you think?" he asked as we walked past a stand of redwoods.

"About what?"

"About the mescaline."

I looked at the trees. The needles were various shades of green, lighter at the tips of branches. Sunlight played on them, forming glittery designs and erupting in little showers of light, as though each branch was tipped with a sparkler. The trunks rippled like multicolored water—red, purple, brown, blue, green. Knots on the trunks turned into roses that bloomed as I watched. I knew that Gil was hoping that sharing all of this would bring us closer together and maybe even change my outlook on life. Instead it was having the exact opposite effect. I felt more estranged from him and more certain of who I was. "I think it's marvelous, but I wouldn't want to be in this state all the time."

"Why not?"

"The world couldn't function if everyone were in this state all the time."

"Why not?" he persisted.

Despite the great beauty around me and the pleasure of seeing everything in a new way, I hadn't lost sight of the fact that I also deeply enjoyed solving differential equations, conjugating French verbs, and analyzing poems. I knew I would never be able to do these things on a psychedelic drug. "You couldn't get any work done," I said. "For example, I couldn't write a paper or solve a chemistry problem." I looked at the clouds. They were sparkling and undulating. I'd never realized how truly gorgeous clouds are. I loved seeing this, but at the same time I realized that I loved my normal state of consciousness more.

"What difference does it make?" His skin was a mass of amoeboid red and purple blotches, his nose large, bulbous, and throbbing.

"The real world is important to some people."

"This is the real world."

I turned away from him to enjoy the trees, then stopped to

examine a leaf. It was large as an elephant ear and scaly as the skin of a lizard, with exquisite, multi-colored diamond designs on a green background. It reminded me of Indian beadwork, and I wanted to remember it. I might not ever take mescaline again, and I wouldn't get to see this leaf again even if I did.

Gil said, "Look at that," pointing to a red car parked by the side of the road. I suppose he saw something magnificent there, but I didn't want to be interrupted.

We reached the buffalo herd just beyond Spreckels Lake. They were stunning horned and bearded creatures with elegant brown-orange coats on their backs and darker fur on their bellies. As I watched, their coats changed to red and yellow, and they grew to the size of dinosaurs, then shrunk to the size of cows. I could have watched them forever, but it was getting late and we were hungry, so we headed back to the car.

❧

As I drove to my mother's house the following day to pick up Liana, I was back inside my everyday mind, but things were different. I had broken up with Gil.

When I entered my mom and dad's house, Liana rushed into my arms and hugged me as though I'd been in New York for six months. The feelings of intense love I'd felt the previous day when I saw the woman and baby washed over me again, and I held Liana closer.

My mom came into the room, and when I let go of Liana, she opened her arms and hugged me, saying, "I love you too, Lucy. You're my best friend." More waves of love broke over me. I remembered how as a teenager I'd resented her so strongly that I lived to defy her and was obsessed by all the ways she'd hurt me when I was a child. I couldn't even succeed in high school until I moved out of her home.

Somewhere along the line, I now realized, it had stopped mattering that she'd snuck out of the house leaving me with babysitters and yelled at me when I skinned my knees. I had forgiven everything: the yelling, the spankings, and the lies. I accepted that she wasn't perfect. Why should she be? Nobody else was. She did my laundry, babysat Liana for free, and listened intently to blow-by-blow accounts of my failed romances. Maybe she was my best friend too. The thought made me laugh.

Editors' Note: This essay was adapted for this anthology from a chapter of Lucille Lang Day's memoir, Married at Fourteen: A True Story *(Heyday, 2012).*

Peyote Sunrise

Helen Ohlson

We, of the bell-bottoms
met them in the desert
good people who will
let you crash.
Peace, Love, and Understanding
in the sands of New Mexico.

The spark that was there
was bigger than all of us
but we were no less a part;
what was there
was bigger than the desert.

and I envied the girl who
called herself Stardust,

her thinking she could live like that.
Flowering in gauze dresses
with a sunburst of blonde hair
a man to build her night fire
peyote to help the sun rise
so free,

she moved back East
and wanted to be like me.

Woman's Work

Katie Glauber Bush

"You'll want something to fall back on," my mother warned.

The phrase "if you don't get married" was left unspoken.

I chose home economics as my major at the University of Louisville. It was a logical choice for a girl who, since the age of ten, devoured every issue of *Family Circle* and *Woman's Day*. I minored in biology. My college classes were a jumble of mastering bound buttonholes, memorizing the twelve cranial nerves, dissecting rats, and reading books like *Let's Set the Table*. I learned how to make paella, could slice tissue samples thin enough to mount on a microscope slide, and acquiesced to my mother's warning and earned my teaching certification. I filled my after-class time with anti-war demonstrations, Earth Days, and grape boycotts for Caesar Chavez, graduating in 1972.

The women in my family were teachers; I discovered that I was not. One year after graduation, I had just finished my first—and last—year of teaching. It was an honorable profession but one for which an insecure young woman, who needed plenty of pats on the back and "atta-girls," was ill suited. Much to my father's dismay, I did not sign up to return to teaching the following fall.

In an effort to help steer me on the path to a career he felt I could handle, he came home from work late one afternoon brimming with good news. He had seen what he thought might be my next career move. On his way home from work, he had stopped at our local A&P to pick up an item Mother had requested. There, an attractive young woman held a black plastic tray and handed out Purnell's Old Folks sausage samples. My dad came home and announced that I should make the move from teacher to sampling savant. I still believe he wasn't sure I was attractive enough.

It was a turning point in my life. My parents were loving and not the least bit abusive, but their efforts created a household of four meek, obedient children who were trained to fear failure and the risks that preceded it. Though my confidence was Dead On Arrival, I knew I could do more than hand out sausage samples.

Late one afternoon, I came home and heard my mother on the phone. She was talking to her childhood friend, my godmother Marie. Marie contacted Mom every decade—or death in the family—whichever came first. My grandfather had recently passed away. Marie had been the only bohemian in her small town in Idaho in the late 1930s. In an effort to find a place in this world where she could be a bit more anonymous, Marie moved to New York City. She studied piano at the Julliard School of Music, but ended up with a career in advertising, writing jingles for television commercials.

"No, Marie, she's finished her year of teaching and doesn't want to go back," Mom was explaining. "I'm not sure what to suggest to her."

Marie quickly replied with an invitation to New York. She offered to set up some meetings with people who might have use of or advice for someone who had taught seventh graders how to make A-line skirts and peanut butter cookies. One week later, I flew from Louisville to New York. I took my first cab ride from LaGuardia to the Upper West Side of Manhattan. Marie and her longtime lover, Bill, lived in a one-bedroom flat near Columbus Circle. Their apartment was filled with Bill's paintings.

That first night, Marie arrived home from work with a baguette in her grocery bag. I thought you could only buy them in Paris, as I had only seen them in subtitled foreign movies. She tossed a salad with lettuces I'd never seen and a dressing she whipped up herself. Bill pulled the rest of dinner from the oven. The apartment smelled of lemons, olive oil, roasted chicken, and the linseed oil from Bill's painting-in-progress.

Once we sat down to dinner, Marie explained to me that each evening she and Bill spoke to one another in French just to keep up their skills. Little did she anticipate that her godchild had aced Mademoiselle Schuler's third and fourth year high school French class. As I joined in the conversation, my mind reeled with thoughts of living in a world this exciting.

Marie had set up an appointment with a test kitchen home economist who created recipes for Blue Bonnet Margarine, Planters Peanuts, and Fleischmann's Yeast. The next day I visited a photography studio and met with a food stylist who made Pepperidge Farm foods camera ready. My final day in New York, Marie had set up a meeting with her former employer at the J. Walter Thompson advertising agency.

I wasn't sure what I was doing there and neither was the gentleman who was meeting with me. But he sent me upstairs to the eleventh floor to meet with B. J. McCabe, who headed up a group of people who wrote marketing, publicity, and educational materials for a long list of grocery store food products. I spoke with B. J. and presumed I was simply there to find out what I would have to study in school next in order to have a job like that. I had no idea she was considering the conversation an interview.

I believed I had no experience or education to back up a career with the agency and, adopting my parents' thinking, I shared that sad fact right up front. After our conversation, we met my godmother and her Mad Men friend for drinks in the executive dining room at the agency—which became a bar after four o'clock each afternoon. My godmother read the situation immediately and shocked me when she whispered that this had been an actual interview.

B. J.'s final statement to me was a suggestion that if I were really interested in this type of work, I might attend the AHEA convention held in Atlantic City in July. She and her clients, Roy Fischman and Frank Goeckel of Standard Brands, had a booth in the conference exhibit hall and would be hosting a special event later that week. That piece of info just breezed over my head as I sat there sipping a bourbon and Coke while everyone else sucked down martinis.

Later, Marie pushed and prodded me, explaining that if I really wanted the job and wanted to move to New York City, I needed to go home and make arrangements to head to Atlantic City in July. Up to that moment it had never occurred to me that getting a job and moving to New York was an option in my life. I watched my friends, one by one, marry nice young men and set up housekeeping. I lived with my parents, unhappy in my first job and scared to pick up the phone and make my own dental appointments. What did I have to lose? I was afraid anyway. If I was afraid to make a move across the street, then I might as well move across the country. I flew back home and made my airplane reservation to fly to Atlantic City.

I worked up my resume and sent it to B. J., adding a note thanking her for her time. I completed the writing sample she requested and, despite an overwhelming wave of self-doubt, sent it to her. Two weeks later, I boarded the plane to Newark, New Jersey. Waiting for the connecting flight to Atlantic City, I noticed a number of women sitting around me waiting for the plane. They were a kaleidoscope of shirtwaist dresses, pop beads, and silk scarves. When the announcement came over the loudspeakers that they were beginning to board my row, I eagerly made my way to the gate, handed my boarding pass to the attendant, and walked out onto the tarmac. Ahead of me was the smallest plane I had ever seen. It accommodated about a dozen people, and the other eleven were women dressed to kill. I was wearing clean blue jeans and a pink oxford cloth shirt.

Once seated, the woman next to me asked, "Are you headed to Atlantic City for the American Home Economics Association convention?"

I confirmed that I was, delighted that I now knew what the letters AHEA stood for.

"Where are you staying?" she continued.

"Staying?" I stammered. It had never occurred to me to research hotels and make a reservation in Atlantic City. I might also add it never occurred to my parents or anyone else I knew. No one in my circle of family and friends was "in business" or had ever traveled "on business."

I had $300 in my purse and owned no credit cards. Very few people in my universe owned bankcards or would ever consider buying anything except a car or house on credit. I presumed that once I landed in Atlantic City I would simply look around the airport for hotel billboards, pick one and take a taxi over to check into a room. I had no notion that by the early 1970s Atlantic City had fallen into a disgraceful state of decline. Just four hotels and a few fudge and souvenir shops lined the boardwalk that formed a fragile line between the ocean and a ghetto of gutted houses, dark streets, and despair.

Once the plane hit its flying altitude for the twenty-minute flight, the turbulence created a whirlwind in my stomach. I retched from Newark to Atlantic City. As we were landing, my seatmate, who was a good three decades older, took pity on me.

"Why don't you share a cab over to the Haddon Hall hotel with me," she offered. "If they don't have a room for you, you can sleep on a cot in mine."

Without any hesitation, I simply got in the taxi and went with this stranger to Haddon Hall. There was one small room left on an airless vent shaft in the center of the building, and I grabbed it. It was a palace to me. I unpacked my clothes, washed up, and headed down the boardwalk to the Atlantic City Convention Center.

The place was filled with women queuing up to enter the exhibition hall. At the door, someone asked to see my registration badge. "Badge?" I asked. In horror, I discovered that I needed to officially register for the conference and pay an attendee fee of $95. I only had enough money for three nights in the hotel, three light meals a day, and a taxi ride to the airport for my return flight.

Was this to be the end of my dream to create a future without sausage samples?

With a calm I had no notion I possessed, I marched from the attendee sign-in desk up to the exhibitor registration desk and said I was there to pick up my exhibitor's badge.

"Who are you with?" a young woman with bright red lips asked.

"Standard Brands," I lied.

"I don't see a badge for you here," she responded.

"B. J. McCabe made the arrangements for me." Lying was getting easier by the minute. "In fact, she asked me to meet her, Frank Goeckel, and Roy Fischman here." Dropping these key sponsor names had the desired effect, and I walked away with an exhibitor's badge and free entry into the conference.

B. J. was surprised to see me, and it took her a minute to realize who I was. "Right, you're the kid who came by the agency a few weeks ago," she said. She never thought she would see me again. "Join us Thursday for the clam bake and otherwise, just enjoy the conference," she said.

Holy smoke, I've just been blown off, I thought. Had I traveled all the way to New Jersey just to find out that I had been right all along and she had never even considered hiring me?

After the initial panic subsided, the remaining panic showed up. Pulling myself together, I decided to stop by the Standard Brands booth every day but otherwise make the best of the conference and network like crazy with other companies exhibiting there.

Despite my ease in telling my first big string of lies, I was shame-filled. I took great pains to take off my badge and hide it in my purse every time I stopped by the Standard Brands booth. It clearly said *Exhibitor* on it, and I knew that if B. J. saw the badge, she would never hire an unscrupulous liar.

The final day of the conference, I walked by the booth one more time and thanked B. J. for meeting with me. She did a double take, then wished me luck in my job search. As I left the booth, I realized I had forgotten to take off my badge. I returned home convinced that I would never be hired. Three weeks later I got the call from the agency rep offering me the job for $10,000 a year.

In 1979, on my last day of work at J. Walter Thompson, B. J. hosted my going-away party. I was heading off to Chicago for a good position with another great agency.

"Here you go, kid," she said and presented me with the resume I mailed to her when first applying for the job. There, on the top of the page, B. J. had scrawled in red the directive to her secretary: *Tell her thanks but no thanks.*

I asked her about the comment.

"Oh that?" B. J. laughed. "After your visit to New York and our interview session, I knew I couldn't take on the responsibility of hiring a naive young kid. I worried myself sick that you'd be eaten alive up here," she explained. "It wasn't until I saw you wearing the Standard Brands exhibitor badge that I realized you either had no clue you needed to register or didn't have the money to pay for the conference. Either way, I was impressed that you bluffed your way in. I decided you would survive on your own."

B. J. believed in me, almost from the beginning. I knew it and didn't want to let her or myself down. I worked in the JWT flagship New York office for close to seven years. It was a transformative time and place where a shy, junior high school home economics teacher from Kentucky morphed into an agency veteran.

I moved five more times in my career and worked thirty-eight years in the industry. I appeared as a client spokesperson on network television, wrote copy for consumer products that are household names, mentored a few young women along the way—and rarely ate sausage again.

Marching with Kay Boyle

Marianne Goldsmith

On a warm Saturday morning, we are gathering near Market Street in San Francisco, waiting for the demonstration to begin. The chatter around me is mostly in English, but I can't help catching bits of rapid-fire Spanish, and lamenting my limited translation skills.

I have arrived with the writer Kay Boyle. We will be protesting the arrest of thousands of political prisoners in Chile, victims of the military coup in September 1973, eight months ago. We will demand our government stop supporting the junta, whose regime cultivates a climate of fear, through brutal suppression of human rights.

Taking part in protests has become a ritual for me, as familiar as observing Jewish holidays or the fourth of July. I've marched to end war in Vietnam, to free Soviet Jewry, to preserve abortion rights and fair employment for women.

We are a few hundred, mostly young, standing in groups in the sunlight. We are Anglo, Latino, and a few African-Americans, wearing sunglasses, pullovers, and jeans. I wrap a scarf around my hair to keep it from flipping across my face in the wind.

I'm flattered that Kay asked me to march with her. She is my teacher in the graduate writing program at San Francisco State, and my landlady. I rent a room in her Victorian home in Haight-Ashbury. Kay looks immaculate, as always. Now in her seventies, she has the voice and carriage of an aristocrat dressed in a black silk suit. She goes to the salon every week, her hair carefully styled in short silver-gray waves. She's wearing her "war paint," as she calls it, to smooth lines of age: pancake makeup over her pale skin, dark eyebrows penciled in above her blue eyes, coral on her lips, rouge on the high cheekbones.

We mingle with the growing crowd, greeting friends from our Amnesty International group. Kay takes care to introduce me to each person who approaches her, and there are many writers, reporters, local celebrities, along with former students and faculty who used to walk the picket lines with her during the '68 strike at San Francisco State.

I am curious to learn more about Kay, from the stories she tells and from exploring her many novels and short story collections shelved in the dining room. She started out among the expatriate writers in Paris of the 1920s, publishing in leading avant-garde literary journals. Her circle included James Joyce and family, and Marcel Duchamp (she keeps his bed in the downstairs guest room). What intrigue me most are the political stories, portraits of life in Europe as fascism took hold and the Nazi party rose to power. Her novels were popular through the '30s and '40s. Her stories appeared in the *New Yorker, Harper's,* and *Vanity Fair.* She won two O. Henry awards. So, why have I never heard of her before? I will not find the answer to that question until later, when her biographers reveal details of investigations during the McCarthy era. It took years before she could clear her name and her husband's, and she found herself essentially blacklisted by American publishers.

I am grappling with writing as a way of getting at my own truth, of interpreting what is happening around me. I am hoping that when I grow older, I will have elegant, silver hair like Kay, that I will understand what's going on and be strong enough to stand up for what matters—human rights, freedom, justice. At twenty-six, I'm both confident and wildly insecure that I will make something meaningful of myself. When I look in the mirror at the young woman with long, dark hair, I don't see pretty. I see not pretty enough, thin or hip or chic enough. The freckle on my nose bothers me; ditto the number of books I haven't read, or written. By my watch, I'm way behind. How will I figure out this mystery? What have I got but a bit of wit, charm, talent to work with to be able to publish and have a voice, pay the bills, plough through the long list of plans I've made? All this anxious dreaming is curbed by my awareness of other worlds, realities beyond my control. In Chile, I have learned that women activists are likely to end up arrested and raped. At least I can rest assured that the only party interested in my doings is my mother in Texas, who writes, "I worry about you in that kooky city."

❧

"Chile, sí, junta no! Chile, sí, junta no!"

Organizers in a jeep wave their arms, chanting through bull-horns, as we move south of Market, some holding banners or waving signs: "Chile Vencerá! Chile will Triumph!" "Respect Human Rights in Chile!" "Free All Political Prisoners!" Organizers wearing arm-bands urge us to walk faster, stay in line. Policemen follow them and us on motorcycles, or stand at intersections, ushering us across, while they hold back traffic. From the windows of stalled cars, drivers lean out to read our slogans; passengers on buses and streetcars stare as we parade along like a massive, multicolored centipede. We pass a few drunks sitting on the sidewalk. Outside a bar, a man invites us in: "We need the business," says he.

A group of protesters around us begin their own chant: "*Death to the junta! Workers of the world, unite!*"

"I believe we're in the wrong crowd," Kay tells me, and we escape quickly, joining the others in front of the *San Francisco Chronicle* office: "*Print the truth about Chile! Print the truth about Chile!*" We want the atrocities of the Pinochet regime exposed, reports of kidnapped civilians, detention, torture, disappearances. "*El pueblo unido jamás será vencido.*"

No one sings, "*We shall overcome,*" cries "*Peace Now,*" or "*Hell no, we won't go!"* Kay tells me that in '67, demonstrations against the war in Vietnam were so massive, she could see crowds stretching from Golden Gate Park all the way down Fulton Street—20,000 people. Her new novel, *The Underground Woman*, is about to be published. The story is based, in part, on Kay's experiences in 1967. Together with a group that included Joan Baez and her mother, she was arrested for blocking the entrance to the Oakland Induction center. The women became friends while serving ten days in Santa Rita jail. It's "Mama" Baez who helped Kay launch our Amnesty International group. At our bimonthly meetings, I draft polite letters, requesting the release of our adopted political prisoner, citing the Universal Declaration of Human Rights. I know how slim my chances are that the letters will ever be read. Still, I carefully retype the draft in my room, and I know Kay is doing the same in her upstairs apartment.

No way does she fit the mythical image of the 1920s "Lost Generation." Standing tall, shoulders squared, Kay is fearless, resolute, waving her placard, chanting with the others. It's a major annoyance to her, the media's romanticizing about the writers and artists she knew in Paris. "We didn't sit around all day in cafés," she says. "Whenever we did see each other, we didn't talk about what we were writing. We talked about politics." She speaks with a slight British inflection, punctuating the narrative with a raised eyebrow, a toss of a hand, or a pause between a long, descriptive subject and its predicate.

She tells me about traveling from France to Spain in the late 1930s, smuggling diaries back across the Spanish border. Her American passport allowed her to clear customs undetected, carrying reports of torture and massacre of those who fought against Franco. I know her stories are true, even if she does have a tendency to dramatize them.

Now, it seems, our wars are labeled "conflicts." Most of us have never been to Chile; some may not even know where it lies on a map—a long, narrow strip between the Andes and the Pacific.

I spot a policeman singling out one of the marchers, a young woman in tight pants. "Have you ever thought about being in one of those beauty contests?" he asks her.

We cover five more blocks and cross Market Street again, passing a swarm of tourists at the cable car turnaround. From there, it's an uphill climb past souvenir shops, chanting for freedom in Chile. Onward to Union Square, with its gigantic palm trees, shining, elegant storefronts and erratic, congested traffic. We weave our way between slow and fast walkers toward the central plaza above the street. Stylish women we pass don't seem to notice us, as they enter and exit luxury department stores, wearing delicate leather shoes and carrying bright shopping bags. Watching these women pursue their pleasures, I realize how tired I am. My feet ache. My voice is hoarse from chanting. I long for coffee, a cushioned chair.

We are forced to break ranks to get through the crowd and climb the long stairway leading up to the plaza, where the final rally is about to begin. I try not to lose sight of Kay's silver hair and black jacket. A few marchers are being interviewed on camera, while others have found seats on benches, stretching their legs in the sun. At their feet, clusters of pigeons peck around for crumbs. At the far end of the plaza, a stage has been set up, and the sound crew is working on a mic check.

The Powell Street cable car passes by, heavy whizzing metal, clanging up Powell Street. My head hurts from squinting in the sunlight. I look around, but now all the benches are full. I'm embarrassed; how quickly I'm disintegrating.

Before I can think of an exit strategy, Kay appears at my side, without her sign. "I've heard quite enough speeches," she says in a low voice. "Shall we go?"

On our way out, we are greeted by a group of black musicians, drumming and whistling. A young street mime performs in white face for tourists, who applaud wildly as he leaps in the air, executes a perfect split, and then cartwheels across the pavement.

The sky is an opaque, California blue. Behind the neat, green hedges bordering the plaza, rhododendrons have burst into full bloom—pale pink, lavender rose, magenta. They say rhododendrons fare well around here, adapting to the soil and hospitable environment.

I pray juntas never grow in this climate.

White Sugar

Kathryn Wilder

I was still in high school when my friend Sylvie's boyfriend got busted for draft evasion. His crime of not filing a change of address with the United States Postal Service in Berkeley, California, had nothing to do with his acquaintance with people like Angela Davis or members of the Black Panthers or the American Communist Party, but the judge wouldn't listen to him about moving and getting behind on his mail, so he accepted the position of political prisoner and went to the federal pen outside Texarkana.

Which is what led me to Chicago in a roundabout way. His two-year sentence was too long, so Sylvie went to visit him, with her sister and me going along for support. It was the first time I'd been east of California, and it seemed I got South, Midwest, and East all rolled into one when the trip climaxed in Chicago a year later.

After the flight from San Francisco and the long bus ride across Texas, we got a small room with two lumpy beds in a dumpy little motel, showering before taxiing out to the prison for visiting hours. Sylvie spent a long time with her boyfriend in the visiting room alongside the wives and children and babies and the inmates trying to get some without anybody seeing, the armed guards hovering over them all like God. Afterward, her sister and I stole hugs with the boyfriend when the guards weren't looking, not wanting him to get punished for having contact in that part of the country, in that decade, with three white girls.

One was bad enough. Could be it's the same today. I don't know, as I've never been back to Texarkana.

The light danced off his dark eyes and pretty grin as he held me tight, and I couldn't say a word for the wrongness of it all that stuck in my throat. I couldn't talk about it later, either, because Sylvie had her important feelings. When we got on the empty bus to Dallas we sat in separate rows. That piece of land between Texarkana and Dallas lies as flat on the horizon as it does on the map, yet it didn't feel that way after the perfect teeth and dimples and glittery eyes, his body barely taller than mine, us fitting together like a plug and an outlet in that quick prison hug. I rode the Greyhound across Texas as if it were a ship in torrential seas, my emotions such a mess inside me that throwing them up would have been a relief.

As we headed back toward our California lives, Sylvie's boyfriend was conspiring with his comrades, who had lined up along a row of windows across the compound and watched us through the bars. Kon, the tallest, picked me, and we started writing long censored letters about politics and The People and Capitalist Imperialism, and I quickly learned to spell Amerika with a "k" and "muthahfuckah." Soon we started writing about love, too, or what we imagined we wanted to do to each other's bodies.

Black Power and *Black Is Beautiful* were what people in the Bay Area chanted in 1973, and I agreed to meet this man in Chicago when he got paroled even though he'd sent me his picture and I did not see power or beauty, just prison written all over his face. But I made the arrangements and there I stood, eighteen years old, at the Chi-town bus station with Kon's uncle and aunt and their two young daughters as Kon stretched his long legs off the bus on which he'd traveled all the way from Leavenworth, where he'd been transferred earlier in our correspondence.

Our comrades weren't with us in the backseat of the Oldsmobile. We sat alone back there on the long drive to the uncle's house, the girls giggling up front, Kon wearing a too-big prison-issue jacket and funky brown prison pants, his skin yellowed by the years indoors, and he touched my arm. His uncle talked loudly as he drove, but what do you say to a man who's been locked up for forever, who's sitting next to a woman as if for the first time, and she's in a dress, her hair full of California sunshine and her legs all tan from summer, and she smells like something he hasn't known for so long he can't remember what it is. Woman and earth and—there, Kon put his finger on it right there at the inside of my elbow—she smells like woman and earth and *freedom*. I could see then what was forming in Kon's too-big prison pants and knew he didn't notice the girls with their round dark eyes and faces and long ringletted hair, or hear a word his uncle uttered, and I didn't hear much either, afraid of what was ahead. But I did see the girls, and I smiled at them and tried to play peek-a-boo as Kon grabbed my hand.

After two weeks in Chicago I got on the train to Seattle, Kon's face on the other side of the dirty Amtrak glass, him mouthing *Come on, baby, give me some sugah,* his lips kissing the air in the smelly downtown Chicago train station. I shook my head no, not wanting to give him anymore anything, and the train pulled slowly away, Kon beside it, the brown jacket draped over his thin frame, covering but not hiding the man beneath who was not the radical Communist Angela Davis–style black man who'd written me all those letters, but a twenty-eight-year-old boy who knew only jail cells and poolrooms—well enough to call home. He walked beside the train in the over-large shoes given him by the US government until the Amtrak pulled away—those shoes, the ugly brown coat, and two pairs of pants and two shirts I bought with my Macy's credit card were all he owned in the world.

I remember the crying, raw voice of pain when he came inside a woman for the first time after four years of hard time for an $800 bank robbery gone bad. That voice sliced me open as I tried to hold the whole story inside me—Kon, eighteen when he went to the joint the first time, then twice more; the man of the prison hug inside another Berkeley girl, not me; Angela Davis all big hair and beautiful and *real*—and we spent too much time in the uncle's basement bedroom, me staring at the fading afternoon light seeping through the curtained ground-level windows and listening to the little girls' voices floating down from upstairs and Kon's coming screams, and I snuck into the shower as soon as I could but it was too late. Something had settled on me and collected in my pores, like the filth I felt at Texarkana, the guards leering at us, the motel night manager offering a big discount as he rubbed on himself behind the counter, reminding me of childhood things I didn't want to remember: the neighbor's husband. My mother's boyfriend.

After the shower Kon wanted more—four times he screamed that way until finally it turned to a whimper—and I don't know if it was the sounds or the time down there that got us kicked out in the middle of the night to wander the streets at 1 a.m., but I remember the yelling, the uncle repeating *my daughters*, and Kon and me standing outside at one in the morning with no ride, no friends, no place to go.

We walked to the L, which was as empty inside as me, the stories having slipped out on the way to the station, and rode to the Southside where we went in and out of tall skinny hotels that touched each other in the dark night—there were no trees in that part of town, just the ugly gray buildings—and in and out we went through revolving doors to dirty looks and nasty words, and finally a Persian man rented us a room I paid for, saying he didn't want us getting killed wandering interracially through the streets in the middle of the night: mugged, beaten, raped, lynched by either black or white in Chicago, which was a lot more like Texas than Berkeley in those days. And maybe still is—I don't know, as I've never been back there, either.

After we fucked again and slept a few hours, we went deeper into the Southside on the L, passing rows of tenement houses with broken windows all boarded up and people still living inside, then walked past dead dogs rotting in the street, ending up in an apartment with big windows. I saw green outside but it was so hot and muggy you couldn't go out to be in it, and if you did, you had to wear something over your dress if you were a white girl in that neighborhood.

Just green through the windows and Kon playing the title song to Marvin Gaye's latest album *Let's Get It On* over and over on someone else's stereo—*I ain't gonna hurry, nah I ain't gonna push...come on darlin' / stop beatin' round the bu-ush.*

We'd forgotten the communication skills we had mastered in our letters, and I still wasn't used to fucking men I wasn't attracted to, and when I'd seen the prison photo of this tall, hollowed-out, yellow-skinned, prison-clad black man I knew he was nothing like the one I fit so well with in that prison hug. Sylvie and her sister had helped me think I could do it—they even helped me pick out the dress I wore when I met Kon at the bus station, short and tight and sky-blue with white daisies on it—and I tried to look beyond the man who had left his youth behind, carried his mistakes forward, and grew up in a yard unlike any I had ever seen, but ten years in the joint is a long time and the politics we wrote about, spelling Amerika with a "k" and "muthahfuckah," and even the love we pretended we felt for each other, didn't have any place in the middle of the night in the middle of Chi-town in the middle of 1973.

The last time I heard from Kon he was running from trouble he'd found in a poolroom bar, him still on parole, me back in Berkeley. He needed money and a safe place to hide, and I thought about it for maybe twenty seconds, the politics I said I stood for and the dazzling eyes of Sylvie's boyfriend and Angela Davis all echoing inside my head. I knew his uncle would not help him again—could only see Kon through the lenses of his daughters, and the wrongness of the way Kon and I misspelled words together, and maybe something else I couldn't see, like what all that time in the basement bedroom really meant—and I said no anyway.

Kon had followed the train that day begging for sugar, and I guess that's the other time I said no, as I just couldn't bring myself to kiss the glass between us or even the air, though I did put my palm to the window when he put his on the other side, and he smiled in that too-big coat, and I saw dimples I hadn't noticed before.

A young black woman and her kids sat across the aisle from me. They'd boarded in the South and were already dirty and tired from train-time. I sat crying quietly at what had or hadn't happened as green pastures and white dairy barns floated by, and I heard the little ten-year-old girl whisper to her mama that I was the white girl hugging on that nigra back at the station and could she come sit by me. Her mama never spoke to me, which I thought I understood after watching black men in Texarkana cross streets to get away from us white girls when we smiled and said hi, but I didn't really, never would. At night the little girl and I slept side by side under the thin Amtrak blankets, trying to stay warm crossing the Rockies. Going through Glacier, we stood in that space between the railcars where we could lean out and feel the snow-air on our cheeks and smell the pines. She had never felt anything like that before. It was almost like a shower. We hugged at the Seattle train station after those three days and two nights on Amtrak, and even her mother got teary-eyed when we said good-bye.

Somehow I got from Amtrak to Greyhound and ended up on a bench outside the bus station in Medford, Oregon, waiting for my sister at 1 a.m. It was so different from Chicago at that hour or even 1 a.m. on the train, me and the little girl snuggled up together, that I had no words to offer my sister when she pulled up in her VW Bug and long skirt and long hair, Oregon all shiny around her, because she had never seen the grime and crimes of a city so big and ugly and mean that it closed the hearts of young men long before they had the wisdom to do anything about it, and when they got the wisdom they knew that nothing could be done. And she'd never felt anything like scared to death being the wrong color in the wrong country, or he is, and either way it could get you killed. She lived with lots of pine trees, buildings set far apart, and views of the mountains, and she must have smelled like woman and earth and freedom, but I didn't want her smell or hug, just the longest shower of my life.

The funny thing is that when Kon and I were kicked out into the streets of Chicago by his uncle that night, we walked past all these lounging young black men leaning back against the steps of their mamas' houses, talking shit and watching us go by.

"In a couple of years," Kon whispered, "half these boys will be junkies or in prison or dead."

I snuck peeks, wanting to see what an almost-junky, almost-convict looked like, never dreaming that all I had to do was look at Kon and me in a mirror, my hair stringy and skin gone pasty with the dirty heat of late Chicago summer; Kon gaunt with hunger for something he wanted much more than he wanted me but would never have.

Nobody in Chicago gave a shit how he spelled Amerika, and Kon went back to what he did best: making mistakes. My mistake was that when I saw his picture long before I got to Chicago, I knew Kon wasn't what I wanted him to be, and I did everything I did anyway. Which didn't bring me any closer to what I thought I wanted, just closer to someplace else I had to go.

A Clean Glass Ceiling

Osha Belle Hayden

Okay, I'll admit that washing windows on skyscrapers isn't rocket science. That's not the point. The point is that women were not allowed to do it in the seventies when women were staging protests in the struggle to gain equal rights. It was time to change the status quo.

In order to save enough money to finance a year of mime school in Paris, I knew I would need a good income. As I scanned the classifieds for a job that paid well, one ad caught my attention: "Wanted: Window Washer for commercial high rise building, downtown Boston…" The combination of good pay and physical exercise packaged in a nontraditional job appealed to me.

When I walked into the manager's office, he looked up from my application straight at my breasts, slid his gaze down my body and slowly back up again, finally meeting my eyes with a cocky grin. He looked to be in his midthirties; he was wearing a brown blazer, a white shirt, and an air of superiority.

"You're applying for *Window* Washer?" he asked incredulously.

"Yes, sir, I am," I replied, ignoring the leer.

"I don't have a window washing job for you but there's an opening for a maid," he said in a patronizing tone.

"I'm not interested in being a maid. I'm here for the window washer position." I insisted, careful to keep my tone even.

"Well, that's not—" The phone on his desk rang, interrupting us.

"Hold on," he said as he picked up the phone. "Yes?...I hear you. Let me call you right back."

The manager looked up at me with a bemused expression. "Why don't you hang around for a minute. Take a seat in the lobby. I may have something for you."

Although he seemed set against hiring a woman for this job, I decided to wait five minutes before leaving. After a couple of minutes, he called me back in.

"Okay, we'll give you a try. You've got the window washer job if you're *sure* you want it. You know this building has eighteen floors, so you'll be high up."

Surprised by his turnaround, I was about to thank him when he added in a mocking tone, "I hope you're not planning to wear a skirt and heels to work. People could see up your dress from below."

I sighed inwardly, thinking, *You jerk. This is one big joke to you. Someone superior has forced you to give me a chance.*

"These are my interview clothes, and I'm not afraid of heights," I declared flatly, unwilling to dignify his sarcasm.

"Then be here at eight a.m. Monday morning."

"I'll be here." Despite his rudeness, I looked him straight in the eye and added, "Thanks for the opportunity."

Outside on the pavement, I exclaimed, "Yes!" and did a joyful little dance.

Monday morning, I showed up early in jeans and braids, ready to work. Situated right on the waterfront, the building was a tall silhouette punctuating an expansive vista of sea and sky. There were parking lots on the sides, and the back of the building went straight down to the water.

Eddie, an experienced union man was the leader of the crew. I learned that he'd been washing windows professionally for decades, and knew all the tricks of the trade. Jimmy, the other crew member, was closer to my age, in his twenties. A patient teacher, Eddie demonstrated his techniques and made sure I knew how to do the work safely. He didn't balk at the fact that I was a woman and treated me with respect—I loved him for that.

Since there was no scaffolding on this building, you had to take one window out to make room to balance on the windowsill. Then you had to lean outside the building to wash the outer windows, hanging on with one hand, working the squeegee with the other. There were no safety harnesses or ropes, just one hand between you and a perilous plunge.

By the end of my first week, I was encouraged to learn that a second woman had been hired to join the crew. *Impressive— we're making progress.* Instead of attending the local bra-burning events, I was taking direct action. Burning a bra didn't get you a job in a man's world, or equal pay or equal rights. I was determined to break through the glass ceiling and prove that a woman could do the job just as well as a man. Like so many women, I was tired of the lecherous leers and assumptions that I was just eye candy.

Eighteen floors up, I enjoyed the freedom of sitting outside on a sill high over the water.

The mime in me was entertained by imagining comedy routines á la *I Love Lucy* episodes. *Here she is, one leg stuck in a bucket, leaning out the window, dodging poop bombs from the seagulls.*

The physical work and the bracing salt air invigorated me. I relished the smooth back and forth motion of the squeegee on glass, stretching from the waist, feeling my muscles work. It beat sitting in an office all day.

A man in one of the offices was horrified when I came in and announced, "I'm here to clean the windows."

He took one look at me with my squeegee and sat straight up, "Oh no! We're on the seventeenth floor. It's much too dangerous. Can they send someone else?" He seemed shocked at the idea of a woman cleaning the windows.

"It's okay. It won't take me long. I'll be perfectly safe."

"Please, no!" he begged, his eyes wide with panic. "I can't bear to watch you risk your life like this. Just skip my office; the windows are clean enough."

"Look, it's no more dangerous for me just because I'm a woman. Why don't you go wait in the lobby—take a coffee break? I'll be done in ten minutes," I said, ushering him out of the office so he wouldn't have to watch. It seemed funny, but sad too, that he was not concerned about having a man "risk his life" to clean the windows.

On another day, I began to climb out onto the windowsill when I saw a photographer leaning out of a window from the next office with his camera aimed straight at me. Quickly, I pulled back inside. I might have been the first woman window washer in Boston, but I didn't want to be famous for that. When I have my picture in the paper, I thought, it's going to be for something more meaningful than window washing. Mine was just a small step on the path for women's rights; it was not the prize.

When I showed up to work a month later and learned that management had fired Eddie and Jimmy, I was heartbroken. Sure, I wanted to prove that I, as a woman, could do the job, but I never intended to put the men out of work. It made no sense for management to let go the most experienced workers on the crew unless they had decided to get cheaper labor by hiring women. Now the crew consisted solely of us two women. We were responsible for cleaning the windows, inside and out, on the entire building.

A few weeks later, the manager decided to change the payment method so that instead of being paid by the hour, we would be paid by the number of windows we cleaned—which amounted to a pay cut. We were both already working as hard and as fast as we could. Disheartened by this announcement, I thought, *We're working so hard—why are they cutting our pay? Is there any limit to this greed?*

The bright note was that by then I'd accomplished my mission: I had broken the glass ceiling by being the first female professional window washer in Boston. My choice now was whether to continue to work and accept being exploited because I was a woman—or quit.

It was obvious now that the plan had been to fire the union men and hire women to replace them, and have us work for less pay. What had appeared to be an opportunity was in reality a ploy to extract more work for less pay from a minority workforce.

Why was I surprised? This seemed to be the path every group that longed for equality had to trod. Was exploitation the price of freedom?

The path to women's rights and equal pay would be a long one, paved with many stones. I had just laid one of them.

Stranger to Myself

Rhonda Rae Baker

I was born in 1962, near the Columbia River, in Umatilla, Oregon. My birth mother sailed into the impenetrable shadows of memory after abandoning me with a babysitter. When it became clear my mother was not returning, the babysitter, in turn, gave me to someone else. And so I came into the world, a stranger on the shore of life.

My adoptive parents accepted me into their family as a special gift and blessed addition. Raised in their sheltered home, I grew compliant with their instruction. "God blesses good girls," my mother would say, "Keep yourself pure or no man will want you." And, "All women need a man," as if we were the weaker sex.

Inside my heart, I felt like a slave required to fulfill my parents' wishes or become a castaway once again. I imagined any transgression would cause me to be sent away. This fear of abandonment loomed over me, like a tornado about to drop at any moment.

The storm I feared became a self-fulfilled prophecy when I found myself at an impasse.

❧

It's November 1978 in Yakima Valley, Washington. I'm a sixteen-year-old sophomore in high school who's sick every morning, so my boyfriend takes me to an older friend's home. She doesn't flinch when I explain my scenario. She recommends Planned Parenthood and gives me the address. I admit to my brain what my gut has already told me: I'm pregnant. I feel stupid and irresponsible, but I need to be an adult now. I promise to go.

Planned Parenthood is on Main Street, so I circle the block and park inconspicuously, forcing myself to leave the safety of my yellow Falcon. When there's no one around, I dart through the door and scale the stairs two at a time.

I step to the receptionist window, and she asks why I'm here. "I'm pregnant," I say in stifled breath, then squeak out my name. She nods in understanding and gestures toward a row of chairs under a large bank of windows for me to have a seat. I look across the open area and choose to cower against the back wall, hoping no one will recognize me. A radio in the corner croons "Hold the Line." The beat and lyrics soothe me, "Love isn't always on time."

When a nurse calls my name, I follow as a puppet on strings to an exam room. She says, "Have a seat," poises pen over clipboard, and begins her interrogation. "What brings you to our office?"

I tell her my period is late and confess, "I've not known about birth control." I look away, embarrassed by how reckless this sounds.

"We're here to help girls like you," she says. "How many sexual partners have you had and when were you with them?"

"I had a boyfriend when I was fourteen…" The details burn my throat like dragon's breath. I almost throw up the memory.

The nurse waits for me to expound.

"There was also a man at my uncle's, during spring break last year, who came into my room uninvited." Suddenly, it's hot in here. I wrench at my cowl neck sweater for air. "A few months after that, I met my current boyfriend."

"Well"—she stands and reaches into a drawer—"take your clothes off from the waist down, and cover with this." She seems disappointed. "The doctor will take a swab to check for venereal disease." She exits and I hear the clipboard drop in the door's file pocket.

I remove my clogs and bell-bottoms, step up to the exam table, and hold tight to my cover. The desire to escape overtakes me, but I'm half-naked and can't move.

Another woman enters, introducing herself as the Physician's Assistant. She leans against the counter to read my chart. "When was your last period?"

"Late August." I lie—it was earlier, but I don't want her to know I waited so long.

She sets the clipboard down and turns a dial, "You're probably nine weeks." She gestures vertically. "Let's have a look."

I lay back on the exam table. She dons gloves and lifts my feet into stirrups, exposing me *down there*. I tense my muscles for protection.

She tells me to relax, presses something warm into my private area.

I feel a deep prick and she removes the expanded object.

She stands between my legs. "Hold still," she says and inserts her fingers. "I need to check the angle and size of your uterus." She presses my abdomen, then feels around inside.

I grimace and anchor my eyes to the bare ceiling.

"It appears you're about ten weeks." She steps back, removes the gloves, and discards them. "Have you thought about a plan?" She extends her hand to help me sit.

"No, I have no idea." Heartbeats echo in my ears as she takes more notes.

"You can dress now. I'll return to discuss your options," she says as she walks out.

"Thank you," I say to the door and dress quickly. I sit in the chair and remind myself, *You can handle this!* I hear a tap, and she enters without acknowledgment.

"I'm a Good Girl," I declare. "This wasn't supposed to happen."

She smiles. "The only difference between good girls and bad girls is that some get caught." She pats my folded hands, as if I'm a little girl. "You do have choices regarding your body. It's your responsibility to protect your health, especially when sexually active." She opens the cabinet and hands me a booklet. "This should help answer questions you have."

"Thank you." I read the cover. *Women Unite: Our Bodies Ourselves.*

"Are you ready to talk about your next step?"

My shoulders relax a bit as I look up and nod. "Yes."

"You have three options." She leans against the counter. "You tell your parents and maybe they'll help raise the baby—"

"I can't tell my parents," I interrupt. "My mother said if I get pregnant, she'll send me away." I lean forward, catch my breath, and sit up straight again. "She told me last spring, when I tried to talk about my friend."

The nurse's eyebrows rise, so I go on to explain how this friend had to leave town.

"You can carry the baby, like your friend, and have it adopted," she offers.

I close my eyes, shake my head no, and inhale. "I'm adopted!" I look into her eyes and exhale. "I could never write off a child."

"I see." She hesitates. "We have a clinic to help young women in trouble."

"That's what I need," I whisper.

She leans over and rests her hand on my knees. "The doctor doesn't ask personal information but requires cash up front. Do you have financial support?"

"My boyfriend will pay whatever the cost." *I'll force him.*

She writes down a number, hands it to me, and goes on. "If you choose abortion, it must be done right away." She advises me to return for follow-up and birth control in two weeks. "Good luck," she tells me as I leave.

My eyes won't focus on the Planned Parenthood booklet. I'm not united with any woman.

I lay awake in my canopy bed, a princess who deplores the kiss of life. I used to believe in fairy godmothers and dream of puppy love, but there's no shoulder to lean on. Turn, turn, turn, *Who am I...how did I end up alone?*

The song "Dream Weaver" haunts me. It was on the radio when my first boyfriend defiled me. I didn't consent; didn't even know what sex was. Yet I remained with him because I thought I had to, until I couldn't take being used anymore. *Why didn't I resist him sooner?*

Then, last summer, my current boyfriend took me to the drive-in to see *Grease*. I asked him if we were a couple. He sang, "You're the One that I Want." *I'm so gullible.* I gave myself to him, hopelessly devoted.

I'm not Sweet Sixteen, as my parents imagine. When I cut my long blonde hair, to look like Farrah, my father cried for his little girl. *What would he think of me now?*

I'll reverse this trouble before it's too late.

❧

Three days later, my boyfriend picks me up from school. The clinic requires an escort because they complete the procedure under sedation. We hide his red Mustang blocks away and walk. The entry feels like an abandoned cave, wrapped in dark paneling, with orange upholstered chairs. I step to the window and introduce myself while he sits with a magazine.

The receptionist verifies my ID, ensures I have a driver, and collects our money. I sign a medical release and accept this choice as mine.

A nurse calls me right away and leads me down a narrow hallway, into my own Twilight Zone. I smell antiseptic. The room we enter has bright lights and medical instruments all around.

The nurse gestures for me to sit. She checks my vitals and hands me a hospital gown. "Remove your clothes, ties go in back. When you're ready, open the door." She exits. "The doctor will be in soon."

I undress and slip on the gown. I crack the door and leap to the metal table. I want to bolt—hide in a field like a mouse and deny my own existence.

The doctor enters with the nurse in shadow. He asks me if I understand my choice.

I nod and respond, "I have no choice."

He briefs me on the procedure and recovery with bored detachment.

The nurse tells me to lie down. She sticks an IV in my arm and gives me the sedative. I taste cold metal and my backbone shivers.

The doctor moves a cabinet on wheels, tells me to scoot closer, and lifts my feet into stirrups. He reaches inside with one hand and presses my stomach with the other. He sits on a stool, preps my body, and a local. "To numb your cervix," he explains.

I feel the needle poke.

He continues, "If you're uncomfortable, let us know."

I can't see what he does, but feel something enter me, and hear a vacuum.

The nurse says, "Breathe deep; you'll feel heavy menstrual cramps."

I hear a baby, desperate screams muffled through the walls.

The doctor struggles with the loud machine's hose, then grumbles, "You're into twelve weeks."

I defend myself. "The other doctor said I was ten weeks." My eyes fasten to the nurse, who watches me.

The doctor requests additional supplies. I'm not sure what, as he sounds like Charlie Brown's teacher, "Wah wah wah." He inserts another device. "To dilate your cervix," he says and then reminds me to keep my hands to the side.

I hear a baby scream, closer than before. My body cramps deeper with each tug and pull. I'm trapped in a whirlpool.

"Imagine the ocean and let waves wash your body clean," the nurse seems to say. Maybe it's only the voice in my head.

I drown in a sea of accusation. *You're a bad girl. You deserve to be punished.* Contractions immobilize my body, but don't stop the tsunami of this moment. I suffocate a little more with every wave of pain. I say in terror, "There's a knife inside."

The doctor turns the noise down and tells the nurse to increase my pain medication. She hands the doctor another utensil. He continues to vacuum, twists the instrument inside me, and adds another sharp object that yanks harder.

I smell fresh blood, not menstrual. I feel disemboweled.

The nurse steps close, takes a deep breath with me, and caresses my hand.

I hear cries again and squeeze her hand. My soul dies more with each heartbeat, as though I've lost the will to go on. Life and breath for me cease, as the procedure continues.

The doctor shuts down his device and administers another shot. "To slow hemorrhage." He stands, removes his gloves. "We're done," he says and leaves the room.

I release the nurse's hand when she moves and follow her with my eyes, as she cleans the room and sets a jar-like container to the side. I chide myself for being female. *Why do I always go to extremes?* Tears run down the sides of my face. *Will he still love me, even though I'm damaged goods? I must take better care of myself and learn to be a strong woman.*

The nurse pulls me out of my thoughts. "How do you feel?"

I'm speechless and turn my head away.

She prepares another shot and explains. "So your body won't think it delivered."

I respond, "Why would my body think that if I was only ten weeks?"

She pats my shoulder. "Breasts lactate after birth." She extracts the IV, gives me sanitary supplies, tells me to dress when I feel stable, and leaves me alone.

My legs wobble as I stand and dress. I glance towards the gallon jar hidden under cover. Curiosity beckons a closer look, a lure for truth. I step to the counter and listen for footsteps, a jury in the court of law. I peek under the blue cloth. Mixed in a thick, dark pool of red tissue I recognize an arm with a tiny hand…a leg with a foot and what appears to be a head, now crushed and deformed. I jump back and bend over so I won't puke. I realize the mass they sucked from my body was a baby. The procedure killed a live person. *I'm a murderer.*

I wander down a bright tunnel to the entry cave and stumble toward my boyfriend. As I stare up into his warm eyes and reach for his hand, I hear the baby cry again and grab his leather jacket instead. "Where'd the mother and baby go?"

"No one else is here," he says. "You're white as a ghost." *He has no clue.*

Afraid I'll sink into nothingness, I hide my face from his gaze.

He wraps his arm around my shoulders, and we stride tandem, back into reality.

I never told anyone I had an abortion that day. To save my life I took another, which shattered my heart and soul. I became even more a stranger to myself. My life felt obscured with no inner sextant to guide me, and I was lost in a fog of compliant naivety for years.

It took thirty-two years to reach out and find my original family, too late to tell my birth mother, "Thank you for giving me life." I respect her decision, even though my heart longed for her return.

It took another twelve years to break free of an abusive marriage and discover purpose in my life.

I've learned it's never too late to make a difference. I understand now that my choice was based on fear of another rejection, and I share this story so others can know they're not alone. I've learned to forgive my own humanity, and I hope you are encouraged to do the same.

Catch the Wind

Marielena Zuniga

The black-and-white photo of a young woman sits on the older woman's desk. The older woman wants to weep for the young woman. She wants to love her. She wants to tell the young woman she will be all right.

The young woman in the photo is nineteen, stands in a park somewhere on a summer's day wearing a Mary Quant minidress, bangs that meet her Twiggy-mascaraed lashes, her hair hanging like a dark veil around her shoulders. She has a shy smile on her pale, lipsticked mouth and an eager invitation to life in her eyes. She wears an expression only youth can pull off, one of innocence and fearlessness.

She stands in her opaque-lace stockings and Mary Janes in the midst of change, straddling two generations—her mother's and her own. She doesn't know what's ahead and if she did, she would run. She would flee to England in the hopes of meeting her beloved Paul McCartney or fly to Haight-Ashbury to wear flowers in her hair.

But she has no idea of what's to come, poor child—the struggles in the workplace for equality, the broken hearts, the loneliness, the searching for identity as a woman who was raised with the conventional principles of the 1950s and found herself thrust into a world tilting headlong into the drugs, sex, and rock 'n' roll of the 1960s. And so, the older woman wants to weep for the young woman. She wants to love the person she, the young woman, doesn't know yet she will become.

She begins, as most of her generation, by bucking the norm. She doesn't want to be a wife, tied to a husband and children in a cookie-cutter house in the suburbs. So, she doesn't marry, doesn't follow the traditional path of her mother. Later, she will look at her choice from "both sides now," as Joni Mitchell sang, and learn that "something's lost, but something's gained in living every day."

Instead, she works at a nine-to-five job. She wants to write and so she does, for a large daily newspaper. The Women's News Department is stuck in the corner of the newsroom, where she and three other women write about weddings and engagements. She wants to write about how women are changing the world, and her first article tells the story of a woman trekking from coast to coast, alone, protesting the Vietnam War.

No matter. The managing editor makes a point of telling the women they do not write as well as the male reporters. That they never will. Each day, on page six, the newspaper prints a photo of a woman in a bikini or other scant clothing. When the Women's News editor protests to the managing editor, he brushes her aside. *These photos sells newspapers*, he barks. *Chauvinist pig*, she whispers back at her desk.

The young woman listens. And learns. She is green in this newspaper business and she watches the changing world pass across her desk in the news. Nixon resigns, followed by Agnew. The Vietnam War rages on with men of her age slaughtered. Four dead in Ohio. Women are demanding rights. Burning bras. Others are speaking of the Age of Aquarius, of spiritual enlightenment, of meditation. The Beatles travel to India with their guru. She feels as if she is in one of their songs, watching the world through kaleidoscope eyes.

Sitting in the newsroom, daily deadlines pressing, she flashes back to the Fab Four. She adores them, and in her teenaged years, saw them four times in concert—twice in Philadelphia and twice in New York City. In memory, she is fourteen again, boarding the train in Trenton for Shea Stadium, the car pressed with screaming, pubescent girls. They are alive with a passion that only youth can flaunt, fraught with an excitement akin to orgasm.

She and friends devise schemes to meet the Beatles. That never happens. But one of her harebrained ideas à la Lucy Ricardo lands her in a hotel lobby at five o'clock in the morning getting the autographs of Herman's Hermits and the Who. At her desk now, she shakes her head.

An editor screams for copy. She begins typing on her IBM Selectric typewriter. Where did that time go, so quickly, she asks?

This is what she doesn't know yet. That time goes quickly. That what seems forever in youth becomes quickened, and even more so in later years, like evening light slipping through your fingers. The older woman wants to weep for all the lessons the young woman learns, for all the tears she sheds as she goes about "finding herself."

What she finds isn't always pretty. She has self-doubts. A man she loves introduces her to the songs of Judy Collins, of wildflowers and "Michael from the Mountains" and she wants to hide behind his smile. But he leaves her for someone else. She is still too young to know the meaning of love, so in hindsight, she is grateful.

But her heart is broken—and tender. She feels the injustice of the times, of discrimination, of rights denied minorities, of wars that never should be, of women who want their voices heard. She yearns to make a difference. She tries to catch the wind.

One day, she surprises the newsroom and says she is leaving. *Another newspaper?* they ask. After all, many of her colleagues have gone on to bigger city newspapers. Better paying jobs. No. She is going to southern Georgia. To work with the poor. As part of a mission program. They don't understand. They look at her like she's gone daft. Maybe she has. But she knows her life is not there, not in that newsroom.

In Georgia, she finds purpose and meaning. She works in the African-American community at a day care center and also for the weekly newspaper in a small Southern town. She finds that prejudice still exists, but when given a choice, people will love instead of hate. That sometimes a listening heart is needed, but that action is also needed at a grassroots level. That people need and want education, employment, a future—and hope. She sees that change happens slowly, although in youth, she wants it to happen like the crack of thunder and a cleansing storm.

Now, the older woman looks at another photo on her desk. The younger woman's hair is graying, although she still colors it and vows that soon she will stop that nonsense. She carries extra pounds and her eyes reflect a sadness earned only through life. She goes on to write for many publications and organizations, especially about women's issues, wins many writing awards, and in this way, she finds, as psychologist Carol Gilligan has written, "a different voice." Her own voice.

In a passing conversation, a friend calls her "a pioneer for other women." She blushes. She hadn't considered the idea. Hadn't even thought of herself in this way. But again, this had been part of her growing up before the 1960s, in that other world that told women and girls: *Be polite. Be good. Don't speak up. Don't claim your power.*

But now she realizes that in some miniscule way she has been a trailblazer, a part of a swell of women who were saying to other women: *Listen. You have options. You can do things your mother never did. Your choices will have consequences—but you do have them. Make the most of them. For yourselves and for the world.*

She knows she lived through pivotal times. She is thankful. She feels as if she and many other women planted seeds during those decades—seeds that are now bearing rich fruit. She begs the world to not let that fruit decay on fallow ground. There is still much work to be done.

And they, the women of the 1960s and 1970s, have the experience and tools to continue tilling that ground until they unearth the promised land of equality, the promised land of a world where no one goes hungry and the rights of all humans are respected. But they can only do it with the help of all their sisters, young and old, and yes, with men who are willing to take their hands and lead gently with their hearts.

In some ways, she wants to be that young woman again, filled with energy and innocence. In many ways, she doesn't. She knows life can be hard. She knows that many times hope can abandon her in a second and leave her breathless. But she also knows now how strong she is, and that her strength comes from decades of good and poor choices, of disappointments and fleeting dreams, of joys that sparkled like stars and her deep spiritual convictions in a power greater than herself and the belief that in the end we all are, as Anne Frank said, basically good.

The older woman looks at both photos now and takes a deep breath. Yes, she weeps for the young woman, and all that is ahead of her, but she smiles at and loves the woman who survived. It has indeed been all right. And in that difficult journey, she has learned to embrace herself with reverence. Even though she still has her bad days, she has learned to turn with the seasons and understands that "There is a time to every purpose under heaven." She knows, as Joni sang, "There'll be new dreams, maybe better dreams and plenty, before the last revolving year is through."

She has found her voice. And herself. And most of all, she has learned to love herself. Finally. Yes, she has.

Times Change

Jasmine Belén

Time has pushed me from my youthful nest
Once a tie-dyed nimble maiden
at Woodstock fest
swaying to '60s rock and roll
to aged and reflective.
My brown hair's now magically blonde
my girth a little fuller
my cleavage a bit lower.

With the adding of years,
my body creaks and groans in protest,
but hey, my mind is aging wisely.
It's a rich landscape of kaleidoscopic memories
fueled by an era that schooled me.

With the quietude of time
poetic songs gleaned from the rhythm of a full life
have settled in my bones,
a trove of riches, to spill on this thirsty page.

No longer that foolhardy girl of yesterday
I can slip unnoticed into polite society
leaving just a hint of those reckless years.

I've gone from randomly acting out
to activism for a worthy cause—
though sometimes, I admit
 they both feel the same.
I have become a master of disguises
a magician, a poet, a visionary,
a compassionate citizen of planet earth
A brilliant masterpiece...
If I do say so myself

This old heart of mine steeped in colorful history
battered by loss and tossed on the stormy seas
holds a compass of faith that carried me home
 through the hazy fog of unrelenting sorrow.
This heart grew wings

Dancing here now in my flat-soled shoes
I am still as frisky as my wildest dreams
I don't envy the supple young anymore,
I pay homage to my body,
feast on the harvest of my years
and toast the glorious autumn of freedom
I find myself twirling in.

Flexing my wings for future flights
I listen to the distant song of an ancestor crone
as she sings of shimmering kingdoms
I've yet to travel.

Acknowledgments

It takes a great deal of support to bring a book into the world; this fact is especially true of anthologies, which are a collective effort by definition. *Times They Were A-Changing* is no exception, and any list of people we thank will be inadequate.

That said, we offer our gratitude to all the women who wrote and submitted their stories and poems to the anthology contest—both those whose work is included in the final publication and those whose work is not. Special thanks go to the contributing authors for cheerfully participating in the editorial process.

We thank Sheila Bender for her beautiful and moving Foreword, as well as the anthology's endorsers: Susan Wittig Albert, Joanne S. Bodin, Matilda Butler, Gloria Feldt, Brenda Knight, Sharon Lippincott, and Jerry Waxler for taking time out of their busy schedules to read and provide their thoughts on this collection.

We thank those who supported and helped spread the word about the anthology: Susan Wittig Albert and the Story Circle Network; Pat Bean, author of the Story Circle Network interview; Matilda Butler of WomensMemoirs.com; Angela Macintosh of Women on Writing (WOW); Susan Bono of *Tiny Lights*; and the California Writers Club, particularly the Santa Rosa and Napa branches.

Our thanks also goes to Submittable.com for providing a promotional rate for the anthology, as well as a superb online submissions website.

We thank Bryan Collins, whose evocative painting defines the cover.

And finally, we thank Brooke Warner of She Writes Press for her unending patience and support.

Contributors

Judy Gumbo Albert, *Third Place Prose Winner*
"Bugged"
Judy Gumbo Albert, PhD, was an original member of a 1960s countercultural group called the Yippies. She wrote for the Berkeley Barb and helped found the Berkeley Tribe. Albert visited former North Vietnam during the war. She organized demonstrations at People's Park, the Women's April 10th March on the Pentagon, and Mayday. In 1975, Albert discovered a tracking device on her car and was part of a lawsuit that successfully challenged warrantless wiretapping. Albert has taught Sociology and Women's Studies at East and West Coast colleges, but spent most of her career as an award-winning fundraiser for Planned Parenthood. Visit her at: www.yippiegirl.com.

Dorothy Alexander
"Dispatches from the Heartland"
Dorothy Alexander is a poet, storyteller, and publisher from Cheyenne, Oklahoma. She is co-owner and editor/publisher of Village Books Press, a two-woman independent poetry press that focuses on publishing Oklahoma poets. Alexander finds material for her own poems most often in the ordinary life and history of rural western Oklahoma where she was born and raised. She takes inspiration from the agrarian literary tradition and the populist

political movements that began in the 1890s in the rural United States. She writes primarily in the narrative form, what she sometimes calls "narcissistic" narrative.

Joan Annsfire, *First Place Poetry Winner*
"Under Siege"

Joan Annsfire is a poet, writer, longtime political activist, and retired librarian who lives in Berkeley, California. Her poetry has appeared in various places online, such as: Counterpunch web sites, Poet's Basement, 99 Poems for the 99%, Lavender Review, OccuPoetry; and in print journals, such as: Harrington Lesbian Literary Quarterly, Sinister Wisdom (many issues), The 13th Moon, Bridges, The Evergreen Chronicles; and in anthologies such as: The Other Side of the Postcard, The Queer Collection 2007, The Cancer Poetry Project Anthology, The Venomed Kiss, and Milk and Honey. Her short stories and memoir pieces have appeared both online, in literary journals, as well as anthologies.

Rhonda Rae Baker
"Stranger to Myself"

Rhonda Rae Baker has been a technical editor and records manager for an environmental/engineering corporation in the Pacific Northwest since 2004. She's a voracious reader of memoir, literature, self-improvement, and fiction. After a career metamorphosis in 1995, she aspired to write fiction. When she met her soul mate in 2007, she began writing creative nonfiction to share the legacy of her life through lessons learned. She began developing skills in memoir writing with Jennifer Lauck's teachings in 2010, and is a member of National Association of Memoir Writers.

Della Barrett
"Hold Your Head High"

Della Barrett is a mother of two and a grandmother of two. She is a part-time massage therapist and currently lives in British Columbia.

Judith Barrington
"To Change the World: London 1972"
Judith Barrington was born in Brighton, England in 1944, and moved to the United States in 1976. Although she has made her home in Oregon since then, she gives readings and workshops each year in Europe. Judith's Lifesaving: A Memoir won the Lambda Book Award and was a finalist for the PEN/Martha Albrand Award; Writing the Memoir: From Truth to Art is a best seller. Other awards include the Andrés Berger Award for Creative Nonfiction and the Stewart H. Holbrook Award for outstanding contributions to Oregon's literary life. She has also published five poetry books. Visit her at: www.judithbarrington.com.

Jasmine Belén, *Poetry Second Honorable Mention*
"Time Changes" and "Woodstock or Bust"
Originally from a small town in New England, Jasmine Belén lived in Sonoma County for thirty-eight years. She started writing poems and stories at the age of seven. After the tragic losses of her three children her creativity seemed frozen in time. To melt her sorrow and to heal her heart she began to create again. She delved first into the healing waters of art before the magic of language lured her home. After joining Suzanne Sherman's writers' group she has published several pieces in local periodicals and finished a book-length memoir.

June Blumenson
"Story Without End"
June Blumenson's poetry and stories have appeared in Nimrod International Journal, Adanna Literary Review, The French Literary Review, Boston Literary Magazine, Edge Magazine, Women's Press, and Open to Interpretation: Intimate Landscape. She was a finalist for the 2012 Pablo Neruda Prize for Poetry. She works with women in transition and regularly performs with a women's tap dance group throughout the Minneapolis metro area.

Katie Glauber Bush
"Woman's Work"

Katie Glauber Bush worked in public relations and marketing communications for nearly four decades. She authored The Baker's Dozen, one of two publications for Nabisco Brands honored with the Family Circle/Food Council of America Gold Leaf Award. She also wrote a children's film for Kellogg's International that won second place in its category in a French film festival. More recently, Bush won the 2011 Harriett A. Rose Legacies award from the Carnegie Center in Lexington, Kentucky for an essay/memoir piece.

Cathleen Cordova
"Round Eye in a World of Hurt"

Cathleen Cordova was recruited by Army Special Services for work in Vietnam in 1968. She returned stateside in 1973, to earn a Master's in International Administration. Cordova worked in Japan, Korea, Europe, and New York, before returning to California to begin a second career as a Community Service Officer with the Pleasanton Police Department. She retired in 2008, and devotes her time to veterans' organizations and causes.

Mary Pacifico Curtis
"Rice-Jungle War"

Mary Pacifico Curtis received an MFA in Creative Writing from Goddard College. Her poetry and prose has been published by LOST Magazine, The Rumpus, Longstoryshort.net, Clutching at Straws, Los Positas College Literary Anthology, Boston Literary Magazine, Unheard Magazine, Pitkin Review, Naugatuck River Review, and The Crab Orchard Review. When she is not writing, Curtis runs Pacifico Inc., a leading Silicon Valley PR and branding firm.

Katie Daley
"The Other Side of the Chasm, 1975"

Since 1999, Katie Daley has been on the performance poetry circuit across the United States and Canada. She has won two fellowships from the Ohio Arts Council and has published her work in various journals, including: *Seneca Review, Slipstream,* and *After the Bell: Contemporary American Prose about School.* She produced *Full Blast Alive: Voices from the Ruby Side,* a CD of her one-woman show, and *Zaggin' Like a Vagabond,* a CD of "poemusic" by Drifters Inn, a band she formed with her husband. She is currently working on a memoir about the yearlong hitchhiking journey she took across the US when she was eighteen.

Lucille Lang Day, *Prose First Honorable Mention*
"The Trip"

Lucille Lang Day is the author of a memoir, Married at Fourteen: A True Story. She has also published a children's book, Chain Letter, and eight poetry collections and chapbooks, most recently The Curvature of Blue. Her poetry and prose have appeared widely in such magazines and anthologies as The Cincinnati Review, The Hudson Review, The Threepenny Review, and Mother Songs (Norton). She received her MA in English and MFA in creative writing at San Francisco State University, her MA in zoology and her PhD in science and mathematics education at the University of California, Berkeley. Visit her at: http://lucillelangday.com.

Carol Derfner
"In the Family Way"

Carol Derfner's writing career began with poetry in the mid-1970s, but was interrupted by life until she retired in 2006. Currently she is writing full-time, producing short fiction and personal essays, as well a long-form memoir related to her life in Alaska in the 1960s and 1970s. Recognition she has received for original work in poetry, short fiction, and creative nonfiction include many prizes and scholarships, among them: scholarships for Memoir Workshop, Summer Writing Retreat sponsored by A Room Of Her Own Foundation in Abiquiu, New Mexico), and for Poetry And Memoir Workshop, Santa Fe, New Mexico.

Sara Etgen-Baker, *First Place Prose Winner*
"September Wind"

Sara Etgen-Baker is a retired educator who enjoys writing personal narratives and memoirs—many of which have been published in anthologies, such as: "Journey with Mother," "Mirror, Mirror on the Wall," and "When Santa Claus Came to Town." She's appeared at the Starving Artist Café in Little Rock, Arkansas, where she's had an opportunity to share her stories before a live audience. Several manuscripts have also appeared in *Looking Back Magazine* and *Storyteller Magazine*. She's a regular contributor to *Tiny Lights*, and is currently working on her first novel entitled, *Dillehay Crossing*. Visit her at: www.saraetgenbaker.blogspot.com.

Darlene Frank
"The Assertive Woman"

Darlene Frank is a writer, editor, and creativity coach who guides nonfiction authors on their writing journey in a way that demystifies the writing process and helps them create their best work. She also works with writers who have undergone a radical life transformation and want to create art from that experience. Darlene has taught writing and written two business books. Her creative nonfiction has appeared in three issues of the literary anthology Fault Zone. Visit her at: www.DarleneFrankWriting.com.

Marcia Gaye
"Two Sisters"

Marcia Gaye writes various types of fiction and nonfiction. Her award-winning poetry and stories have found publication in anthologies. Gaye enjoys writing in different genres and styles, including memoir, western, romance, and mystery. Songwriting is her private pleasure. In addition to her own writing, she has judged writing contests and provides editing services. A highlight of 2012 was taking a residency at the Writers' Colony of Dairy Hollow, where she worked on an in-progress historical western novel. Gaye has lived in fourteen states, coast to coast, North to South. She is a follower of Christ and a wife and mother.

Marianne Goldsmith
"Marching with Kay Boyle"
Marianne Goldsmith currently lives in Oakland, California. Her work has appeared in *The Jewish Bulletin*, *The Jewish Writing Project*, and *Persimmon Tree Magazine*.

Osha Belle Hayden
"A Clean Glass Ceiling"
Osha Belle Hayden, MA, is passionate about empowering people to create positive change. Her experience in psychotherapy, mediation, and health education informs her work as a trainer, coach, and writer. Osha's work has been published in the 2011 and 2012 volumes of the *Vintage Voices Anthology*, and in *Poems of Joy*, a multimedia iBook. She has performed in multiple venues, most recently in *The Ticking Clock*, a play about women's reproductive choices, at Sixth Street Playhouse in Santa Rosa, California.

Patricia Kay Helmetag
"Fear and Loving"
Patricia Kay Helmetag is a writer and graphic designer. She lives in Annapolis, Maryland, with R. Garrett Mitchell and their two beagle mixes. Her two daughters and five grandchildren live in Weaverville, North Carolina, and Boulder, Colorado. She is fulfilling a lifelong dream by bicycling across America for two to three weeks every summer with her childhood pal and University of Wisconsin roommate, Sally Schmidt.

Elizabeth Kerlikowske
"The Novelty Wears Off"
Elizabeth Kerlikowske came of age under the threat of nuclear war. She grew up in a conservative city that made her wildly radical. Now a professor at a community college, Kerlikowske is a mother of three, author of several books of poetry, and president of a nonprofit.

Nancy Kilgore
"The Revolution and Egg Salad Sandwiches"
Nancy Kilgore is a writer and psychotherapist in Vermont and New Hampshire. She has published in online and print journals; her first novel, Sea Level, won a 2011 Book of the Year Award through ForeWord Reviews.

Margot Maddison-MacFadyen
"Going Up the Country"
Originally from the west coast of British Columbia, Margot Maddison-MacFadyen currently makes Prince Edward Island her home. A PhD candidate in Interdisciplinary Studies at the Memorial University of Newfoundland, she has published academic articles in The Bermuda Journal of Archaeology, Maritime History, Slavery & Abolition: A Journal of Slave and Post-Slave Studies, The Newfoundland Quarterly, and in The Times of the Islands. Poems are forthcoming in Stone Voices, and in Descant Magazine, which shortlisted her work for the 2013 Winston Collins/Descant Poetry Prize for Best Canadian Poem.

Frances Maher
"Speaking at the Last SDS Convention"
Frances Maher is Professor Emerita of Education and Women's Studies at Wheaton College, Norton, Massachusetts, and a Resident Scholar at the Brandeis Women's Studies Research Center. After ten years as a high school American History teacher, she spent the next three decades training high school teachers and teaching Women's Studies courses at Wheaton College and elsewhere. She has

coauthored and published several books, among them *The Feminist Classroom* (1994) and *Privilege and Diversity in the Academy* (2007). She has been a feminist teacher and scholar for over forty years.

Venus Ann Maher, *Prose Third Honorable Mention*
"Tripping on High"
Dr. Venus Ann Maher is a chiropractor, writer, artist, singer/songwriter, and photographer. Her purpose in life is to make a difference through creativity and kindness. An unusual childhood in the communes of California was both difficult and joyous. Maher tells stories of those years in this anthology and in her future book, The Wild Years: Coming of Age in the Communes. She is also working on a shape-shifter, time-traveler, fantasy novel that incorporates everything she has learned in her unique experiences.

Ana Manwaring
"Collage"
Ana Manwaring writes, edits, and teaches creative writing. She's branded cattle in Hollister, outrun gun-totin' maniacs on lonely highways, lived on houseboats, consulted *brujos*, visited every California mission, worked for a PI, swum with dolphins—and she writes about it all. She's finished her first thriller, set in Mexico, and is working on a sequel. Follow Ana's *Petaluma Post* columns at: www.petalumapost.com. Visit her at: www.anamanwaring.com.

Elise Frances Miller, *Second Place Prose Winner*
"My People's Park"
Elise Frances Miller's novel, A Time to Cast Away Stones (Sand Hill Review Press), is set in Berkeley and Paris in 1968. With degrees from UC Berkeley and UCLA, Elise began writing as an art critic for the Los Angeles Times, Art News, The Reader, and San Diego Magazine. She taught high school and college humanities; she has served as communications director at San Diego State University and Stanford. Her short stories have appeared in The Sand Hill

Review (fiction editor, 2008), Fault Zone: Stepping Up to the Edge, and online. Visit her at: www.elisefmiller.com.

Merimee Moffett, *Poetry First Honorable Mention*
"Before the Summer of Love"
Merimee left Portland in May of 1970 with two Vietnam vets, their pot dealer, a girlfriend with a dog, her own dog, and all she could carry under the seat or in a small bag. She fell in love with New Mexico and never left. A mother of four and grandmother of four, she is still married to her love-at-first-sight Prince Charming, the father of her two daughters. She has been a career teacher; now retired, she teaches private writing classes. Her poems appear in many reviews and journals, including Persimmon Tree, Santa Fe Literary Review, and Mas Tequila Review.

Linda J. Nordquist
"Fast Forwarding Evolution"
Linda J. Nordquist is a writer, photographer, lapsed psychotherapist, and the author of The Andes for Beginners, a memoir/guidebook available in Peru. Her published short stories are: "Puddles" in The Writing Disorder and "Promises" in The Write Place at the Write Time. She is the author of e-books: Molten Murder, Beyond the Tipping Point, and Say Goodbye, Say Hello.

Jeanne Northrup
"This Girl Who Is Me"
Jeanne Northrup is a writer and a writing instructor at a Community College in south Louisiana. She grew up in northwestern Pennsylvania but has been all over the country. She is now semi-retired and working on several novels and collections of short stories and essays. Jeanne is also a teaching consultant with the Southeast Louisiana Writing Project. Somewhere, she has an abandoned dissertation concerning the trickster in American Indian literature. Her work has been published in anthologies and journals.

Jeanette M. Nowak
"The Wild, Wild West"
Jeanette M. Nowak grew up in East LA, the youngest of seven children whose parents were drug addicts and alcoholics. She's writing a memoir about her childhood; her story in this anthology is an example of the life she lived. As a child, she endured physical, sexual, and emotional abuse. As an adult, she suffered from PTSD and struggled to make sense of it all. She's hoping her story helps others to heal and forgive.

Helen Ohlson
"Peyote Sunrise"
Helen Ohlson has been on the Delaware writing scene since she became one of the founders of the Delaware Literary Connection in 1995. In 2006 she was selected by Fleda Brown, Delaware's Poet Laureate, to attend a state funded Writers' Retreat. Ohlson has won awards from the Delaware Press Association for her writing, including poetry. Her poetry has appeared in both print and online publications and she enjoys reading her poetry at local venues. Her writing group, which can be found at transcanalwriters.com, will soon be publishing a chapbook of their work.

Kathleen A. O'Shea
"On Being a Marxist Nun From Kansas"
Kathleen A. O'Shea, a former nun, is a Pulitzer Prize nominee, as well as a teacher, an activist, a social worker, and an independent researcher and lecturer. Her current projects include a novel loosely based on her experiences in Chile during the Allende-Pinochet years and a memoir, Many Mansions, about the beginnings of her thirty-five years as a Catholic nun. O'Shea recently led a memoir writing workshop for the International Women's Writing Guild entitled "Writing From Your Religious Past."

Joyce Royce, *Prose Second Honorable Mention*
"Headed North on a Southern Highway"
Attorney Julie Royce just released her legal thriller, PILZ. Royce has written two travel books, Traveling Michigan's Thumb and Traveling Michigan's Sunset Coast (Thunder Bay Press), and currently writes a monthly travel column for www.wanderingeducators.com. She has written magazine articles and has been included in several anthologies. She is editing Ardent Spirit, a historical fiction novel that recounts the life of American Indian fur-trader, Magdelaine LaFramboise. Visit her at: www.jkroyce.com.

Julie Ann Schrader
"Earth's Children"
Julie Ann Schrader is a psychotherapist, writer, and teacher. She has been writing poems, songs, and stories since childhood. She performed original songs for many years. She describes herself as a lover of words. Schrader is currently writing a work of historical fiction, memoir pieces, and short stories. She believes that it is vital to share stories of the 1970s, as it was a very influential and magical time. She has chosen one of her favorites for this anthology. She lives in the lovely Valley of the Moon in Northern California. Visit her at: www.Angelics-Spirit.com.

Laura Singh
"The Magician"
For the past thirty years, Laura Singh has been the fabric designer and owner, along with her husband, of Laura & Kiran, a Berkeley-based, home furnishing fabric company known for its contemporary designs in natural fabrics that are hand-crafted in India. Visit her at: www.laurakiran.com

Lynn Sunday
"The Day I Met the Suffragette"

Lynn Sunday is an artist and writer who lives near San Francisco with her husband and dogs. Her work has appeared in various anthologies: Passing It On, Lay *Practitioners* Share Dharma Wisdom, Chicken Soup for the Soul: Think Positive, The Magic of Mothers and Daughters, and Think Positive for Great Health. Sunday has appeared in publications such as Common Ground Magazine and The Noe Valley Voice. Sunday has spoken out for social justice causes, from women's rights to animal rights, all her life.

Jill Taft-Kaufman
"A Berkeley Spring"

Jill Taft-Kaufman went to Mills College in East Oakland and transferred to Berkeley to complete her Bachelors, Masters, and PhD. She is a professor at Central Michigan University in the Department of Communication and Dramatic Arts where she still feels passionate about her teaching. She directs as part of University Theatre and specializes in the scripting and performance of literature not originally written for the stage. She has published in numerous communication and theater journals and is an associate editor of Text and Performance Quarterly.

Judith Terzi
"Berkeley Raga"

Judith Terzi is the author of Sharing Tabouli (Finishing Line, 2011). Her recent poetry has appeared or is forthcoming in numerous journals and anthologies, including American Society: What Poets See (FutureCycle), Poemeleon, Poetry Project Erotic Poem Anthology (Tupelo), The Prose-Poem Project, Qarrtsiluni, South85, and elsewhere. Her poetry has received nominations for Best of the Net and Web. Visit her at: http://home.earthlink.net.

Susan Tornga
"Mrs. Lieutenant"

Susan Tornga was raised in Tucson, an upbringing that fueled her love for the Arizona desert. Her first novel, Seashells in the Desert, is set in Winslow, Arizona, in 1895. She dedicates this mystery to the women who endured countless hardships and risked so much to open the West for others. Tornga is a frequent contributor to Chicken Soup for the Soul and various on-line travel sites. Her stories and articles have won awards from Women on Writing and Writers' Weekly. She is an active member of Women Writing the West and Arizona Mystery Writers. Visit her at: www.susantornga.com and http://susantornga.wordpress.com.

Dianalee Velie
"Who Wrote the Book of Love?"

Dianalee Velie lives and writes in Newbury, New Hampshire. She is a graduate of Sarah Lawrence College, and has a Master of Arts in Writing from Manhattanville College, where she has served as faculty advisor of Inkwell: A Literary Magazine. She has taught poetry, memoir, and short story at universities and colleges in New York, Connecticut, and New Hampshire and in private workshops throughout the United States, Canada, and Europe. Her award-winning poetry and short stories have been published in hundreds of literary journals and many have been translated into Italian. She is seeking a publisher for her fourth collection of poetry, The Alchemy of Desire.

Patricia A. Vestal
"Proud Spinster"

After a career in publishing and education, Patricia Vestal has returned to her mountain roots in the culturally and naturally rich Asheville, North Carolina area. Her educational, professional, and creative experience encompasses playwriting, film and game scripting, poetry, prose, and journalism. Vestal has taught all of these genres through nonprofit theater, arts groups, and at the college level. She holds an MA in Drama from NYU's Tisch School of the Arts and a BA in Media from SUNY. Her writing has been variously published and produced and she recently won first place in a fantasy fiction contest.

Kathryn Wilder
"White Sugar"

Kathryn Wilder, a former heroin addict, has spent her life in California, Hawaii, and the American Southwest, on horseback, paddling outrigger canoes, and running rivers. Today she operates a natural-horsemanship training facility in southwestern Colorado with renowned mustang trainer Ramón Castro, along with family and friends. Her work has appeared in *Midway Journal, River Teeth, Southern Indiana Review, Fourth Genre, Sierra,* many Hawaiian magazines, *What Wildness Is This,* the *American Nature Writing* series, the *Walking the Twilight* anthologies, and elsewhere. "White Sugar" is from her memoir-in-progress, *A Woman Chasing Water.*

Marielena Zuniga
"Catch the Wind"

Marielena Zuniga is an award-winning journalist of thirty-five years, writing in newspapers, magazines, and in the corporate and nonprofit environments. She has been published in The Christian Science Monitor and in 2010, won a prestigious national journalism award for reporting on women's issues. In 2012 she placed fifth among thousands of entries in the Inspirational Category of the annual Writer's Digest Magazine writing competition. It is the third year she has placed in this category. She has a master's degree in counseling/psychology. In her spare time, she enjoys the company of good friends and good books.

Editors

Kate Farrell
"Getting It"

Kate Farrell earned a MA from UC Berkeley; taught language arts in high schools, colleges, and universities; founded the Word Weaving storytelling project in collaboration with the California Department of Education with a grant from the Zellerbach Family Fund, and published numerous educational materials. She is founder of Wisdom Has a Voice memoir project and edited Wisdom Has a Voice: Every Daughter's Memories of Mother (2011). Farrell is president of the Women's National Book Association, San Francisco Chapter, a board member of Redwood Branch of the California Writers Club, and a member of Story Circle Network and the National Association of Memoir Writers.

Linda Joy Myers
"Baptist Girl"

Linda Joy Myers is president and founder of the National Association of Memoir Writers, and the author of four books: *Don't Call Me Mother—A Daughter's Journey from Abandonment to Forgiveness, The Power of Memoir—How to Write Your Healing Story*, and a workbook *The Journey of Memoir: The Three Stages of Memoir Writing*. Her book *Becoming Whole—Writing Your Healing Story* was a finalist in *ForeWord Magazine's* Book of the Year Award.

A speaker and award-winning author, she co-teaches the program Write Your Memoir in Six Months, and offers editing, coaching, and mentoring for memoir, nonfiction, and fiction. Visit her at: www.namw.org and http://memoriesandmemoirs.com.

Amber Lea Starfire
"Altamont"

Amber Lea Starfire, whose passion is helping others tell their stories, is the author of *Week by Week: A Year's Worth of Journaling Prompts & Meditations* (2012) and *Not the Mother I Remember*, due for release in the fall of 2013. A writing teacher and editor, she earned her MFA in Creative Writing from University of San Francisco and is a member of the California Writers Club in Napa and Santa Rosa, the Story Circle Network, the National Association of Memoir Writers, and the International Association for Journal Writing. In her spare time, she enjoys spending time outdoors. Visit her at: www.writingthroughlife.com.

CPSIA information can be obtained at www.ICGtesting.com
Printed in the USA
LVOW06s2236091013

356263LV00009B/191/P